THE ANTINOMIAN CONTROVERSY

by

Charles Francis Adams

from his *Three Episodes in Massachusetts History*

Edited and with an Introduction by

Emery Battis

DA CAPO PRESS • NEW YORK • 1976

Library of Congress Cataloging in Publication Data

Adams, Charles Francis, 1835-1915.
   The Antinomian controversy.

   Reprint of the 1892 ed. published by Houghton Mifflin, Boston.
   1. Massachusetts—Church history. 2. Hutchinson, Anne (Marbury)
1591-1643. 3. Antinomianism. I. Title.
   BR555.M4A3 1975   277.44   74-164507
   ISBN 0-306-70290-8

This edition of *The Antinomian Controversy* is an unabridged reproduc-
tion of part II of Charles Francis Adams' *Three Episodes in Massachusetts
History* published in Boston in 1892. It includes a new introduction
prepared by Emery Battis for this Da Capo edition.

Published by Da Capo Press, Inc.
A Subsidiary of Plenum Publishing Corporation
227 West 17th Street, New York, N.Y. 10011

CONTENTS

INTRODUCTION

Writing was an Adams' inheritance, an irresistible, congenital urge which covered pages and volumes to mount into a massive familial bibliography. Charles Francis Adams, Jr. recalled his grandfather, John Quincy Adams "as always . . . writing, writing—with a perpetual inkstain on the forefinger and thumb of his right hand."[1] The "perpetual inkstain" was the badge of the clan. The members of each successive brood were enjoined at a tender age to keep a diary and from that point the writing itch became progressively congenial and addictive. Nearly every literary form—novel, poem, historical narrative, biography, autobiography, philosophy, scientific essay—had at some time been endeavored by one or another Adams. But the form that remained common to them all was the diary with its private pages of self-exploration and self-revelation. Though the Adamses had quitely shed the orthodoxies of their Puritan forebears, the New England way demanded an arena for a drama of the self. The everlasting Puritan would not be denied a stage for self-examination, self-flagellation, self-justification, self-congratulation, and for this purpose the pages of the diary proved agreeably responsive. The younger Charles Francis succumbed to the diarial disease of his ancestors

[1] Charles Francis Adams, Jr., *Autobiography*, (Boston, 1916), p. 9.

with scarcely a murmur: a shelf of small black-bound volumes attested to an addiction which persisted to the week of his death. In these little volumes the space for each day's jottings is cramped, the entries often casual and inconsequential, but in sum they reveal the man as he saw himself.

The pages of the year 1881, when Adams was at once engaged as businessman, railway arbitrator and historian of the Antinomian controversy, are pertinently revealing:

"January 3—Evening at home and tried to read some metaphysics being immensely amused at my absolute inability to understand a single paragraph of what I read."

"January 20—Finished Frothingham's 'Rise of the Republic.' This is a book of a class of which I get small profit. There is a good statement of events and much research, but neither interest of narrative or philosophy of thought. What is the good of annals except for philosophers to work on. Urgent that my present book must be an interesting narrative."

"February 11—At office all day just keeping the miserable machine in motion."

"March 10—I am now doing so many things and so very diverse, that it stands to reason I can do nothing well. I never shall learn not to dissipate force."

"June 17—Wrote as usual from 6 to 10, and indeed this is the great pleasure of my life now—these few morning hours when I go out of the present world—which I can't manage, into the past where I am master."

"December 19—Wrote until 10 O'cl[ock] as usual, peg-
ging away at the old Hutchinson controversy."

"December 31—Wrote just 100 pages of my New England this month . . . this has been my
year of greatest comfort and success—
my occupation has been a pleasure to
me."[2]

Thus we are given the portrait of the successful
businessman who hated business, the philosopher-
historian who neither understood nor cared for
metaphysics, and the compulsive activist whose
multifarious endeavours threatened mutual can-
cellation.

Adams set great store by his literary effort of that
year. It was, however, only the second stage of a
literary travail that intermittently covered eighteen
years. It had begun six years before when he had
been invited to deliver an address on the occasion of
the two hundred and fiftieth anniversary of the
permanent settlement of Weymouth, Massachusetts, a community neighboring the Adam's
hometown of Quincy. His almost casual and unwit-
ting acceptance of this invitation proved to be an
"epochal incident" as he later described it; "I had
in fact come to a turning point in life."[3] He was by
that time no novice at historical writing, having already produced in "A Chapter of Erie" a work of
substantial quality. But in that and other historical
essays his attention has been fastened on the very
recent American past. The Weymouth address, with
its focus on earliest colonial times offered a new fas-

[2] Charles Francis Adams, Jr., *Diary*, 1881, Adams Papers, Massachusetts Historical Society.

[3] *Autobiography*, pp. 179, 181

cination and challenge. He was startled that he, an Adams, should know so little about the past of that region with which his family name had been so long and intimately associated. In the spring of 1874 he "pegged away on Weymouth," probing its colonial beginnings and dwelling with particular fondness on the picaresque adventures of the waifs, strays and birds of passage who had touched tentatively on its wooded shores.[4]

The address was delivered on July Fourth, the occasion being marked by all the pomp and circumstance which a small country town could afford the celebration of that hallowed day. At the stroke of noon the blare of brass bands launched the procession on its way to the ceremonial grounds: veterans of the Grand Army of the Republic, Knights Templar, Conqueror Engine Company #41, Amazon Engine Company #42, Catholic Total Abstinence and Literary Association and a host of school children preceded the honored guests and speakers of the day. Prayers, hymns, and toasts to local dignitaries and institutions regaled the hour.[5] The main address by Mr. Charles Francis Adams, Jr., was a long, laudatory and occasionally turgid account of Weymouth's career from its modest yet often melodramatic origins down through the War of the Revolution. Larded with pseudo-Biblical prose and sprinkled with flowery descriptions, it was nonetheless warmly received and served the purpose of the hour.

[4] *Diary,* June 14, 1874.

[5] Charles Francis Adams, *Proceedings on the Two Hundred and Fiftieth Anniversary of the Permanent Settlement of Weymouth, with an Historical Address by Charles Francis Adams, Jr., July 4th, 1874,* (Boston, 1874), p. 77.

It was, Adams later confessed, "a crude and prentice-like piece of work," but it had worked its way on the author.[6] "A call had come!" he had found his true vocation or, at least, the avocation that was to command his attention and devotion for years to come.[7] Not long after, he took up the subject again, delving further into the fragmented sources of the ten year period between the settlement of the Pilgrims in Plymouth and the arrival of the Puritans in the Massachusetts Bay Colony. Out of these materials he drafted the first substantial history of the little groups of men who had strayed—some to settle, but most to wander away— onto the southern shore of Boston Bay where now stand the busy communities of Neponset, Quincy, Braintree and Weymouth.

This done, he turned his attention to an episode that was central and crucial in the early years of the Massachusetts Bay Colony, the so—called Antinomian Controversy. For a projected history of Quincy, as this was turning out to be, the relationship between the town and the controversy was tenuous at best. Mistress Anne Hutchinson and her brother-in-law, the Reverend John Wheelwright, central figures in the controversy, though residents of Boston, like many of their neighbors and adherents, held property and had set up farms at Mount Wollaston, now part of Quincy, but at that time accounted a reserve for the land-hungry residents of Boston. But it was enough that the episode suited Adams' narrative skills and philosophic turn. It fitted nicely into his present scheme:

---

[6] *Autobiography*, p. 182.
[7] *Ibid.*, p. 179.

Quincy as a miniscule universe responding to natural laws of progress, its harrassed residents exemplifying the subjugation and the freeing of the human mind and spirit. It is this work, a classic of its kind, which occupies the main body of the present volume.

Having concluded his account of the Antinomian Controversy, Adams paused for a time, his attention diverted to more immediate and mundane concerns. The two essays thus completed were printed privately in an edition of only eleven copies under the title of "Episodes in New England History." That was in 1883; in the next year Charles Francis Adams, Jr. became president of the Union Pacific Railroad, a position that commanded the bulk of his energies until he resigned in 1890.

When at last he was relieved of the burdens of that office he turned back with relief to his unfinished history of Quincy. The earlier sections were refined or expanded slightly where he had new information or improved understanding; "putting in my philosophy as it trots along," he said.[8] With Mrs. Hutchinson safely dispatched, he turned to the history of Quincy (née Braintree) proper, offering a detailed study of its institutions and growth, its divisions and subdivisions, down to the very time of his own active involvement in the political and cultural life of the town. At last, on October 8, 1892, the completed work, in two volumes, was published under the amended title of "Three Episodes in Massachusetts History." Adams looked hopefully for an enthusiastic public response to his effort, eagerly tallying the publisher's returns as

---

[8] *Diary,* July 27, 1891.

they became available. He craved a literary success, partially, perhaps, to satisfy himself that he had fulfilled the expectations imposed upon one of the Adams clan, and partially to compensate for his recent disappointments in the world of business. The year before he had found cause for elation in the success of his biography of Richard Henry Dana. "Highly encouraging that to an author! *Le roi s'amuse!*"[9] But the response to "Three Episodes" was disappointing and he searched for explanation. "This was largely my own fault in letting it come out amid the tumult of a presidential election," he reasoned. "The poor thing had no show."[10] Nonetheless the starveling remained his favorite child. He had gained great satisfaction from working on it and was pleased to have put on record the history of the region. "That I did," he stated. "It may not be great, and certainly has not, nor will it obtain a recognized place in general literature, but locally it is a classic; and when you come to classics 'local' and 'world' are relative." Though the world may have rejected, or at least ignored it, he felt sure that in Quincy it would be "even two centuries hence referred to and quoted."[11]

Adams was equally sensitive to the more learned opinions of experts in the field and here he found more room for solace. Herbert L. Osgood, the foremost colonial historian of the day, reviewed the book with enthusiasm, designating it "the most original and suggestive town history ever written in this country . . . The volume will surely take high

[9] *Ibid.*, April 7, 1891.
[10] *Ibid.*, Memoranda, 1892.
[11] *Autobiography*, p. 197.

rank among the products of American historical scholarship."[12] Indeed the reviews were generally laudatory, though two of the critics, both clergymen, questioned whether Adams had fully grasped the theological implications of the Antinomian Controversy.[13] Given his own viewpoint, Adams may well have ascribed this demurrer to the institutional prejudice of his clerical critics. However a later generation of very secular-minded historians was prompted to raise the same question again. But that was long after Charles Francis Adams had departed the scene, and at a time when few historians were disposed to accept unqualifiedly his anti-clerical sentiments or the optimistic progressivism of his historical view.

- ii -

Adams let it be known almost apologetically that his birthplace was Boston. A distressing irregularity, he thought, for one to whom the granite slopes of Quincy were "race place."[14] Not even to have been born on Beacon Hill, the scion of national fame and local fortune, sufficed to compensate in after years for this parental lack of foresight. Nor could he ever bring himself to like or feel at home in Boston. He had, he said, "tried it drunk and tried it sober; and drunk or sober, there is nothing in it, save Boston."[15]

"My youth and education," he complained, striking the Henrican strain of his more famous younger brother, were "a skillfully arranged series of mis-

[12] *Political Science Quarterly*, Vol. 8, (June 1893), pp. 346-348.
[13] *The Yale Review*, Vol. I, (May, 1892-February, 1893), pp. 368-380. *The Nation*, Vol. LV (July, 1892-December, 1892), pp. 394-395.
[14] *Autobiography*, p. 202.
[15] *Ibid.*, p. 39.

takes."[16] From private school he trod the well-worn family path to the Boston Public Latin School and thence to Harvard. Though it seemed predetermined that an Adams must follow the law, Charles resented and resisted that traditional design. Five years of practice convinced him that nothing short of a miracle would make a lawyer of him and he seized on the outbreak of the Civil War as an avenue of escape. "I have completely failed in my profession and I long to cut myself clear from it," he wrote, seeking his father's assent. "This mortifies me and the army must cover my defeat. My future must be business and literature, and I do not see why the army should not educate me for both."[17]

Charles did not bear lightly the mantle of the Adams' heritage. it seemed to him that his forbears, for all their great achievements, had missed the best of life. John Quincy Adams he recalled as perpetually working: "He never seemed to relax, nor could I imagine him playful."[18] Nor was the senior Charles Francis greatly different in this respect. "They were both of them affected with an everlasting sense of work to be accomplished—'so much to do, so little done . . . ! They were, in a word, by inheritance ingrained Puritans, and no Puritan by nature probably ever was really companionable."[19]

For one so thoroughly Puritan himself—Puritan in his efforts and ambitions, his perpetual drive to judge and prove himself—the younger Charles

[16] *Ibid.*, p. 4.
[17] Worthington Chauncey Ford, ed. *A Cycle of Adams Letters, 1861-1865*, Vol. I, (Boston, 1920), Charles Francis Adams, Jr. to Charles Francis Adams, November 26, 1861.
[18] *Autobiography*, p. 9.
[19] *Ibid.*, p. 10.

Francis maintained throughout his life a remarkably dim view of the Puritan strain and devoted much of his career to a noisy exorcism of its ghost. This may have been prompted by the desire to free himself of the incubus of a great name and the expectations of comparable achievement. In a life marked by action, production and reward, Charles continuously sought to reassure himself that he was his own man and his attainments of his own doing. Throughout his life he labored no less arduously and compulsively than his forbears. In the end, however, he recognized that he had divided and dissipated his energies in such a way that the monuments of his labor must at best be minor by comparison with theirs. This, he conceded, was a fault, but it was a fault which lay in his nature. "I have, perhaps, accomplished nothing considerable compared with what my three immediate ancestors accomplished;" he concluded, "but on the other hand I have done some things better than they ever did, and what is more and most of all, I have had a much better time in life—got more enjoyment out of it. In this respect I would not change with any of them."[20] But the real Puritan was the devil under the skin and this Charles Francis Adams could never escape for all his hedonistic claims and iconoclastic fulminations.

Ever fond of striking a pose, Adams contended that it was the army which had rounded off his education. "I have the instinct of growth since I entered the army," he wrote to Henry. "I feel in myself that I am more of a man and a better man

[20] *Ibid.*, p. 210.

than I ever was before."[21] Starting as a lieutenant of cavalry he saw sharp action on several battlefields, served usefully at the headquarters of Generals Meade and Grant, knew the sublime pleasure of leading his Negro regiment into Richmond at the hour of its capture, and at war's end was brevetted brigadier general.

"Idleness is a misery to me," he wrote, "and my idleness is a misery to everyone about me."[22] On that score he allowed little room for complaint. The quarter century following his military discharge was filled with a dizzying and diversified round of activity. A series of critical articles which he penned on the railroad system led to the formation of the Massachusettes Railway Commission and to his own appointment as its most useful member. His performance in that post, being widely influential and productive, led him ultimately to the presidency and problems of the great Union Pacific Railroad.

Despite a professed distaste for gamblers, Adams progressively, and sometimes incautiously, enlarged his investments in the booming post-war economy. Manufactures, mines, railroads and, most importantly, real estate all found a place in his bulging portfolio. By 1887 he had built his fortune to the point where he could announce, "I have all I want—and I want a great deal."[23] With assets of from two to three million dollars he could well afford the boast.

[21] *Cycle of Adams Letters,* Charles Francis Adams, Jr. to Henry Adams, January 23, 1863, p. 237.
[22] *Diary,* August 21, 1887.
[23] *Ibid.,* August 21, 1887.

But it was not in the Adams manner to devote oneself solely to personal advancement and enrichment. The Adamses knew their worth and felt their responsibility to provide leadership. Foregoing the national political arena of his forbears, Charles struck his spade in the more intimate and congenial soil of Quincy. For twenty years he and his elder brother John "practically managed Quincy affairs. It was Quincy's golden age," he exulted.[24] An elitist-reformer in the Mugwump style, Adams greatly reordered and improved the management of the town. But he reckoned without the new wave of popular democracy. Irish immigrant laborers, unconcerned with the niceties of small town government, seized on the vote to fulfill their immediate and pressing needs. The reign of "reasonable men" came to an end with the passage of a law providing a nine hour work day for municipal laborers. Adams agonizingly abandoned Quincy for residence in a more secluded and exclusive suburb north of Boston. "That was awful," he reflected. "Quincy was bone of my bone—flesh of the Adams flesh. There I had lived vicariously or in person since 1640."[25]

Adams' seven year career as president of the Union Pacific Railroad—so challenging and promising of honors if successful—proved an altogether frustrating and humiliating climax to his business career. He had taken over from Jay Gould in an effort to resume the payment of dividends and to regularize the road's chaotic relations with the federal government. But old problems defied solu-

[24] *Autobiography*, p. 177.
[25] *Ibid.*, p. 202.

tion and new ones compounded the morass. He was, he confessed, "wholly demoralized . . . I have nothing to say in extenuation. I displayed indecision and weakness."[26] Gould and his cohorts closed in and in utter humiliation Adams was forced to resign.

But it was an humiliation mixed with profound relief for he had been expelled from a life for which he felt nothing but distaste. He had long bewailed his bondage to that "miserable machine," "the prison house" on State Street.[27] For the generality of his fellow entrepreneurs he entertained a lively contempt. "Moral cutthroats and robbers" he termed the Wall Street crowd in the privacy of his diary.[28] His public summation was more tactful but no less condemnatory. "A less interesting crowd I do not care to encounter. Not one that I have ever known would I care to meet again, either in this world or the next . . . A set of mere money-getters and traders, they were essentially unattractive and uninteresting."[29]

Free at last of civic and business responsibilities, Adams could have given himself over to a life of comfortable and well-earned leisure. But it was not in the Adams nature to relax while will and energy drove him to test his capacities and prove his worth, and always to judge the result with a critical eye. "Taken as a whole my life has not been the success it ought to have been. Where did the fault come in," he queried.[30]

[26] *Ibid.*, p. 194.
[27] *Diary*, February 11, 1881, October 15, 1887.
[28] *Ibid.*, August 21, 1887.
[29] *Autobiography*, p. 190.
[30] *Ibid.*, p. 190.

One Sunday afternoon in August, 1887, while the problems of Quincy town meeting and the Union Pacific still boiled around him, he found an hour of quiet reflection in the pages of his diary. He was then fifty two, a healthy, active man in the prime of life. Through his own efforts, as he perhaps too readily boasted, he had made an ample fortune and advanced far in his own calling. But railroading wearied him, "surfeit had super-induced disgust."[31] The Gould forces were closing in and he knew that he lacked the "desperate courage" to play the game out.[32] "It is clear," he penned in his small, neat hand,

that if I mean to enjoy life at all—doing what I want to do—I have no time to lose . . . With me it is now or never . . . What I want for the rest of my life is plain. It is simply this; I want to live and so use my time, that when I am lying on my deathbed and the doctor tells me the end is very near, I can sink back on the pillow, and , as I see the pale faces about me, I can give a feeble, happy smile and say 'Well, I have had a good time in my later life anyhow.' The great thing is to feel that you have lived your life—that you have got out of it much at least of what there was in it for you to get. Above all to know that your best powers have been freely exercised. . . . Looking back over the last twenty years my memory always dwells with deepest satisfaction on the days and hours devoted to literary work—I had a good time, and I would like to live it all over.

The result of it all is that my better judgement tells me to retire as soon as may be from active business life and to seek refuge and enjoyment here in my library.[33]

[31] *Ibid.,* p. 195.
[32] *Diary,* Memoranda, August 21, 1887.
[33] *Ibid.,* Memoranda, August 21, 1887.

When retirement was at last forced on him it seemed a good omen that on the very next day his biography of Richard Henry Dana was published. "A case of out of darkness and into the light—it could not have been better arranged."[34] With that venture the floodgates were opened. Two years later the "Three Episodes" made its public appearance, and in the two years thereafter he published "Massachusetts; Its Historians and Its History," an iconoclastic blast against his predecessors in the field of Puritan historirgraphy, and "Antinomianism in the Colony of Massachusetts Bay," a carefully edited selection of important documents in that celebrated controversy.

In consideration of these and other like contributions he was installed in the presidential chair of the Massachusetts Historical Society in 1896, and four years later he was designated president of the American Historical Association. Articles, lectures, after-dinner speeches and letters to the press flowed from his pen in unremitting profusion. "Charles makes a speech or writes a letter to the papers every day," brother Brooks querulously observed.[35] No invitation was ignored, no issue or instance of interest passed unremarked. So intensely did the past and passing scene interest him that Charles simply could not resist the temptation to speak his piece. When all was done the Charles Francis Adams, Jr. bibliography contained four hundred and fifty published items, not including hundreds

---

[34] *Autobiography*, p. 198.

[35] Lyman H. Butterfield, "Introductory Note to 'Three Views of Charles Francis Adams, II'", *Massachusetts Historical Society, Proceedings*, Vol. 72, (October, 1957 December, 1960) p. 239.

of newspaper articles and letters to editors on every topic which struck his ire or fancy.[36] It was, he ruefully admitted, an evidence of his intellectual restlessness." A record in which it is not possible for a man to take any considerable or real satisfaction, for it is a record of dissipation and quantity, rather than one of quality and concentration."[37]

- iii -

Delighting in the dramatic, Adams enumerated the crises and turning points in his own life with an exactitude which might well distress a careful psychologist. The "epochal" significance of the Weymouth address which aroused his interest in early American history has already been noted. That occasion, it may be fairly granted, opened his eyes to a subject of which he had no previous knowledge. But two earlier crises seemed to him equally determinative in shaping his career as a historian. The first occurred at the age of thirteen when a chance reading of Macaulay's "England" exposed him to the excitement of historical study. "I then and there quickened, my aptitude asserted itself," he recalled. At the time, however, it was "not an overpowering call," not yet "strong enough to dictate a line of action."[38] Nonetheless he was sure that it was at that moment, so vividly recalled many years later, that the historian in him was born.

The next such crisis, seventeen years later, seemed even more epoch making, for it not only of-

---

[36] *Ibid.*, p. 239.
[37] *Autobiography*, p. 196.
[38] *Ibid.*, p. 25.

fered a framework for his historical study, but con-
genially ordered his political and social attitudes as
well. "When in England, in November, 1865,
shortly after my marriage," he wrote,

I one day chanced upon a copy of John Stuart Mill's
essay on August Comte, at that time just published. My
intellectual faculties had then been lying fallow for nearly
four years, and I was in a most recipient condition; and
that essay of Mill's revolutionized in a single morning my
whole mental attitude. I emerged from the theological
stage in which I had been nurtured, and passed into the
scientific. I had up to that time never even heard of
Darwin, inter arma, etc. From reading that compact little
volume of Mill's at Brighton in November, 1865, I date a
changed intellectual and moral being.[39]

In his excitement at the thought of this awakening Adams neglected to weigh the full burden of his
previous experience as a factor in shaping his recep-
tivity to the new philosophy. The youthful distaste
for religion, the revolt from established family patterns, the climate of opinion in which he had matured and—by no means least—the essentially secularized Puritanism of the Adams household, all
counted for something in the making of the evolutionary positivist. To judge from his own account—
though like much else it is probably over-dra-
matized in retrospect—a dislike of church and
church-going seized him while still young. "Educa-
tional mistake number two," he counted his early
religious training. "All through my childhood how I
disliked Sunday . . . Lord! that going to church!"[40]
Secularism, anti-clericalism and a general revulsion

[39] *Ibid.*, p. 179.
[40] *Ibid.*, p. 13.

against theology permeate the writings of his mature years. "Superstition," "a rubbish of learning," "pestiferous stuff" are the best terms he can find to describe the theological viewpoint.[41] The writings of John Witherspoon and Jonathan Edwards he dismissed as "intellectual impossibilities . . . trying to work premises at once arbitrary and absurd into some sort of conformity with the fitness of things. Mankind has—Laus Deo!—at least emerged from beneath that shadow."[42] Comte himself would not have put it more pungently. "The simple fact is," he magisterially concluded, "that the Calvinistic tenets of the seventeenth and eighteenth centuries constitute nothing less than an outrage on human nature, productive in all probability of no beneficial results whatever."[43]

Looking back on his intellectual crisis of 1865, Adams seems to have forgotten that the name and work of Darwin were nowhere mentioned in Mill's essay. But the ideas he met there prepared him to take the great evolutionist in stride. The secularist and empirical outlook of Comte was presented as the culmination of an evolutionary progress from earlier theological and metaphysical stages. Comte's explanation of the slow unfolding of civilization proved comfortably consonant with the Social

[41] Charles Francis Adams, Jr., *Three Episodes of Massachusetts History*, (Boston, 1896), p. 387. Charles Francis Adams, Jr., ed., *Antinomianism in the Colony of Massachusetts Bay, 1636–1638*, (Boston, 1894), p. 38. Charles Francis Adams, Jr., "Some Phases of Sexual Morality and Church Discipline in Colonial New England," *Massachusetts Historical Society, Proceedings*, Second Series, Vol. VI, (Boston, 1891) p. 500.

[42] *Diary*, November 10, 1889.

[43] Charles Francis Adams, Jr., *Massachusetts: Its Historians and Its History, An Object Lesson*, (Boston, 1894), p. 84.

Darwinism which was currently in vogue. No matter that Darwin was concerned with pigeons rather
than people, for Adams the new doctrine had the
golden authority of absolute law and provided a
comprehensive explanation of the historical process.
"We of the new school," he pontificated, "regard
the dividing line between us and historians of the
old school, the first day of October, 1859—the date
of the publication of Darwin's 'Origin of Species.'"[44]
From that hour forth, Adams contended, the historian was obligated to view the past, not as a mere
succession of instructive, but disparate episodes,
but as integral phases of a consecutive process of
evolution, "a connected whole," and must give due
weight to "the great law of natural selection as applied also to man."[45] So were Comte and Darwin
conveniently wedded. The history of mankind was
now seen as "one great drama—the Emancipation
of Man from Superstition and Caste . . . a struggle
not yet closed against arbitrary rule, whether by a
priesthood or through divine right, or by the
members of a caste or of a privileged class, whether
enobled, aristocratic or industrial."[46]

That last word "industrial" was included by
design to bring the process down to date. For
Adams, the thrust of the great struggle was to free
the individual man to think, worship and act as he
chose so long as he did not infringe upon the
identical rights of other men. He was, it is true,

[44] Charles Francis Adams, Jr., "The Sifted Grain and the Grain
Sifters," *The American Historical Review*, Vol. VI, No. 2 (January, 1901),
p. 199.

[45] *Ibid.*, pp. 199 ff.

[46] *Massachusetts*, pp. 1 ff., *Sifted Grain*, p. 201.

concerned about the self-seeking and irresponsible deportment of corporate wealth. But far more threatening, to his mind, were the emergent socialist doctrines. Adams was very much a man of his time and his conception of evolution was essentially terminal in that it moved in the direction of results largely attained by a favored few, and presumed by them to be desirable for the remainder. In essence the design satisfied the vaguely Jeffersonian and nativistic sentiments with which the Mugwump generation confronted the emergence of mass industrial society and the antagonistic collectivities into which it was being organized. The autonomous man, it seemed to Adams, was most threatened, not by the dogmas of popes, presbytrs and divine right monarchs, but by "the teachings of those socialists who preach a doctrine of collectivism, or the complete suppression of the individual."[47] Against this threat to democratic individualism—the end of the evolutionary line—the surest defense lay in the scattered agricultural communities of the American Middle West. This region, he significantly noted, had been peopled by "three of the most thoroughly virile, and withal, moral and intellectual branched of the human family, I refer to the Anglo-Saxon of New England descent and to the Teutonic and Scandinavian families."[48]

Adams held that sentimental bias was the greatest threat to the integrity of the new "scientific" history. The worst of historiographical sins was to view the record of the past "through eyes jaundiced by faith or patriotism or filial affection or partisan zeal."[49] Adams' *beau ideal* among his-

---

[47] *Sifted Grain*, p. 201.
[48] *Sifted Grain*, p. 211.
[49] *Massachusetts*, p. 40.

torians was Gibbon, "an orb of the first order," precisely because he was "a scholar, an investigator and a thinker [who] chanced also to be nothing else, not even what is known in common parlance as a Christian!"[50] Gibbon's great misfortune, Adams thought, was to have been born and worked "before Darwin gave to history unity and a scheme."[51]
But even with Darwin's scheme clearly before their eyes American historians of the nineteenth century were in a sad plight: "it is greatly to be feared that we in the matter of historical work are yet in the filiopietistic and patriotic stage of development."[52] And most guilty of all were those Massachusetts historians who, wrapped in ancestor worship, distorted the plain truths of history in order to present their Puritan forbears in a favorable light. There was, Adams contended, "almost no form of sophistry to which the historians of Massachusetts have not had recourse . . . deceiving themselves in their attempts to deceive others."[53]
On this theme of filiopietism Adams rang endless changes. Neither the demand of scientific objectivity nor confidence in the ineluctable forces of natural selection sufficed to deter him from moralizing with bitter zeal on this failing of his predecessors. "The very Boanerges of iconoclasm," he seemed to those of the "old school," but his effort prevailed despite their disparagements.[54] "The Antinomian Controversy" and "Massachusetts: Its Historians and Its History" had been written to set

[50] *Sifted Grain*, p. 217. *Massachusetts*, p. 40.
[51] *Sifted Grain*, p. 217.
[52] *Massachusetts*, p. 41.
[53] *Ibid.*, p. 12.
[54] Robert C. Winthrop, Jr., "Remarks on 'Massachusetts, Its Historians and History'", *Massachusetts Historical Society, Proceedings*, Second Series, Vol. VIII (Boston, 1894), p. 381.

the record straight. And indeed they worked well to that end, but perhaps in a way that Adams could not have anticipated, for historiography, like evolution has no terminal point.

- iv -

Adams had correctly assessed the Antinomian Controversy as the most crucial episode of Massachusetts' formative period. It is interesting to note that in more recent years the dispute with Roger Williams has received greater attention and prominence. While Williams has become a figure of international reknown and esteem, Anne Hutchinson has been relegated to comparative obscurity. The reasons for this are not hard to find. To the Twentieth Century mind the principles for which Roger Williams fought seem at once simpler and more basic to the purposes of his time, as we understand them, and more pertinent to the needs of ours. Altogether he has seemed the more attractive and comprehensible figure of the two. Not until quite recently has it become evident that, although Williams' conclusions on the nature of religious liberty may be congenial to our needs, the premises from which he derived them are totally alien to our way of thought. Rather than being the pre-Jeffersonian liberal which progressive historians delighted to depict, he has been revealed as more Puritan than the Puritans, and curiously old-fashioned even to their way of thinking. In his own time his doctrines were so esoteric and unrealistic as to deny him any significant following and to enable his opponents to remove him with a minimum of confusion.

By contrast Mrs. Hutchinson and her faction were immediately recognized as a dangerous threat to the stability and continuity of the Puritan community. Her heterodoxies struck at the very heart of the intellectual and institutional order which Puritan ministers and magistrates were still laboriously constructing. Indeed, her ideas seemed the more dangerous because they were so intimately and logically derived from the tenets then propounded by the clergy. To many in the community it seemed that Mrs. Hutchinson had offered an altogether reasonable resolution to nagging theological dilemmas. As her following grew and came to include many men of political and economic influence the leaders of the colony became progressively alarmed. They feared that Mrs. Hutchinson's doctrines might well elevate the individual conscience above external authority—be it that of church or state—and exempt the believer from all moral restraints. So church and state joined forces to suppress the heresy and expel the Hutchinsonian faction from Massachusetts Bay.

Contemporaneous accounts of the controversy, penned by spokesmen of the victorious party, inevitably registered their partisan viewpoint. It was Mrs. Hutchinson's misfortune that her party held no polemecist of the stature and intellect of a Roger Williams, for example, to enter the lists in her defense. Governor John Winthrop, the most forceful of Mrs. Hutchinson's antagonists, lay down the text which Massachusetts historians were to uphold for over two centuries. At the outset of the controversy Winthrop had recorded his apprehensions in the pages of his private journal: "One Mrs. Hutchinson, a member of the church of Boston, a woman of ready wit and bold spirit, brought over with her two dangerous errors. . . . From these grew many branches."[55] When at last the struggle was over and Mrs. Hutchinson safely removed beyond the borders of Massachusetts, Winthrop drafted an account which undertook to justify the harsh measures taken against her faction. "She walked by such a rule as cannot stand with the peace of any state," he concluded, "for such bottomlesse revelations . . . being above Reason and Scripture, they are not subject to controll."[56]

Massachusetts historians of that and the following century were not prompted to modify this harshly partisan view. Reverend William Hubbard's "General History of New England" was indeed little more than a paraphrase of Winthrop's unpublished journal and inevitably reflected the opinions found there. The Hutchinsonians he dismissed as "men of corrupt minds and haughty spirits [who] secretly sowed seeds of division in the country and were ready to mutiny against the civil authority."[57] Nor was Captain Edward Johnson, a first hand observer of the conflict, more charitable in his estimate. "This master-piece of womens wit," he ironically dubbed poor Anne, who, with her "Sectaries had many pretty knacks to delude withall, and especially to please the Femall Sex. . . ."[58] At the close of the century Cotton

---

[55] John Winthrop, *Winthrop's Journal: "History of New England,"* ed. by James Kendall Hosmer, Vol. I, (New York, 1908), p. 195.

[56] Adams, *Antinomianism*, p. 177.

[57] William Hubbard, *A General History of New England from the Discovery to 1680,* (Cambridge, Mass., 1815), p. 282.

[58] Edward Johnson, *Wonder Working Providence of Sion's Saviour in New England,* (Andover, 1867), pp. 95, 100.

Mather, grand panjandrum of the Massachusetts clergy, surveyed the trials and achievements of the founding generation. The events of the intervening sixty years had not prompted him to modify the traditional view. A professedly tender concern for the feelings of her worthy descendents impelled him to conceal the identity of the "erroneous gentlewoman" who had caused all the trouble. But this sentiment did not deter him from depicting her as a "Virago" who threatened the community "with something like a Munster tragedy."[59]

Indeed so well ingrained was the conviction of Mrs. Hutchinson's turpitude that no less person than her own great-great-grandson accepted the Puritan party line. Governor (then Chief Justice) Thomas Hutchinson was author of the most carefully researched and judicious history of the colony written during the entire colonial period, and indeed, for many years thereafter. Though a full century and a quarter had passed since the controversy, he too was persuaded that the doctrines of his much maligned ancestress did "hardly consist with the rules of morality." Had her principles prevailed, he contended, they "had like to have produced ruin to both church and state."[60] Hutchinson's conclusions on this score were doubtless the product of his own conservative political philosophy. He was not one to be moved by the filiopietism which had controlled the minds of his predecessors.

[59] Cotton Mather, *Magnalia Christi Americana or the Ecclesiastical History of New England,* Vol. II, (Hartford, 1853), pp. 516, 518.

[60] Thomas Hutchinson, *The History of the Colony and Province of Massachusetts Bay,* ed. by Lawrence Shaw Mayo, (Cambridge, 1936), pp. 50, 62.

But filiopietism in Massachusetts had by no means seen its day. During the nineteenth century a stream of ponderous tomes emanated from the press exalting the Puritan Fathers of the Commonwealth as torchbearers of religious liberty, civil rights, political freedom and democracy. Every literary sinew was bent to the task of tracing a consistent cultural continuity in the history of Massachusetts. If the present generation were champions of freedom and democracy, then sentiment, if not reason, suggested that the roots of nineteenth century conviction must be found in seventeeth century conception. In the mid-nineteeth century there were pressing reasons for looking ever more longingly to the past. Massachusetts was passing the meridian of its greatness and most of its glory lay behind it.

From the outset the people of Massachusetts had been acutely conscious of the difference and distance which lay between them and the inhabitants of less favored communities. The colony had been founded as a Zion in the wilderness, a "city on a hill," where the elect of God might perform His will and make known His ways to the rest of mankind. Long after this original mission and its sustaining theology had passed into abeyance a tribalistic self-consciousness persisted, shaping alike self-image and images of the nether world beyond. During the pre-revolutionary era the widespread distrust of Yankee radicalism only served to reinforce a conviction of the superiority of their own institutions and the rectitude of their own opinions—a conviction which the ensuing tide of events seemed to confirm. The nineteenth century brought to Massachusetts political separatism, commercial ascendancy, leadership in the literary world and in the moral crusades of the day, all of which heightened the sense of regional identity and pride. When the issue of slavery precipitated sectional controversy and cleavage the Yankee was prompt to assume leadership in the anti-slavery cause and to submit himself as the anti-type of all that was corrupt and effete in Southern culture. But economic, aethetic and moral ascendancy were attended by the rumble of change and premonitions of declension. The rise of industry and the insurgence of immigrant laborers altered familiar social patterns and challenged comfortable assumptions. Political leadership and economic primacy were passing into the hands of younger, more energetic communities. The decline of influence and prestige reinforced a need to vaunt the extraordinary heritage and contribution of the Bay State. With the oldest historical society in the nation and dozens of learned antiquarians busily grubbing through the record of the past the instruments of self-justification and mythmaking were not wanting. There was much in the record of Massachusetts of which its people were not unreasonably proud. But there was also much which, by current standards, seemed to require extenuation—or at least an explanation which would relate the several ages of the past into forms consistent with each other, and with parochial pride. The Puritan age, remote and forbidding even by nineteeth century standards, had somehow to be reconciled with that spirit of democratic individualism which had precipitated the revolution of one century and aroused the moral fervor of the next.

The filiopietistic cause was partially served by the timely "rediscovery" of the Pilgrim fathers and the elaboration of a mythos surrounding that humble and courageous band. But his romantic novelty only begged the question. However sentimentally attractive the myth, the stubborn fact remained that the Pilgrims were never more than peripheral to the urgent dynamism which had made Massachusetts a potent force in American History. That power had been generated in the old Bay Colony. So the excesses of the Puritan culture had to be explained away; its intolerance, its persecution of dissenters, its crabbed way of life, and its stark and demanding theology, a theology light years away from the genteel Arminianism preached by Dr. Channing and his colleagues. Parochial pride, modernism—and the scornful reproaches of Quaker and Baptist historians—all cried for an explanation which would harmonize the dubious events of the seventeenth century with the heroic ages that had followed.

Most embarrassing for the filiopietists was the Puritan persecution of the otherwise minded in their midst. The imprisonment, mutilation, execution or expulsion of dissenters had commenced in the earliest months of the colony and continued until the exhaustion of the persecutors, the inexhaustibility of the persecuted and the stern pronouncement of royal authority brought it to an end. How to explain such behaviour on the part of the presumed progenitors of democracy and

freedom? Henry Martyn Dexter rang the battle cry
of the affray with his determination that the best
defense was a strong offensive. Referring to the
Quakers, but with words which might apply nearly
as well to all the dissenting groups, he contended
that it was they who had persecuted the Puritans.
The founders of the colony sought only to be left
alone to live in peace. Instead they found
themselves beleagured by troublesome bands of
otherwise minded whose riotous behaviour
threatened to subvert the peace and institutions of
the community.[61] Even before Dexter had submitted this bold thesis, its possibilities had been ex-
plored by John Gorham Palfrey. The original
charter of the colony, Palfrey asserted, bestowed on
the company the right to eject any persons whose
actions or purposes were injurious to the designs of
the grantees. The land had been conveyed to the
members of the Massachusetts Bay Company and
"their heires and assignes for ever, to their onlie
proper and absolute use and behoofe for ever-
more."[62] It seems improbable that King Charles anticipated that the document sealed under his hand
should be so illiberally interpreted and applied. But
knowingly or not, Palfrey contended, a right had
been conferred, for "no principle is better settled
than that a grant is to be interpreted favorably to
the grantees, inasmuch as the grantor, being able to
protect himself, is presumed to have done so to the
extent of his purpose."[63]

[61] Henry Martyn Dexter, *As To Roger Williams*, (Boston, 1876), *passim*.

[62] Nathaniel B. Shurtleff, ed., *Records of the Governor and Company of
the Massachusetts Bay*, Vol. I, (Boston, 1853), p. 6.

[63] John Gorham Palfrey, *A Compendious History of New England*, Vol.
I, (Boston, 1858), p. 306.

In the volumes of John Gorham Palfrey, Henry Martyn Dexter and George Ellis the subtle grays of the social spectrum underwent permutation to black and white. Inevitably Mrs. Hutchinson and her colleagues emerged as among the blackest specimens in the array. For Palfrey she was an inveterate troublemaker with "a propensity to fraction." The contagion of her ill temper," he noted, infected even the good men who sought to arrest her mischief making.[64] To George Ellis she was a "troublesome woman" armed with "censorious tongue."[65] Though he managed to find more sympathy for her than did Palfrey, Ellis agreed that her practices were disturbing to the community and that her expulsion was a matter of urgent need and justice. In general the filiopietistic attacks on Mrs. Hutchinson tended to stress the civil aspects of the case rather than the theological. The factionists were arraigned at the bar of history as political subversionists whose removal was essential to the security of the community. By this means the issue of religious liberty was conveniently circumvented and the Puritans, who had fled to America for religious freedom—according to the filiopietistic version— were spared the stigma of destroying that which they had presumably sought to establish.

These were the semi-official spokesmen of the community. Abetted by the stentorian commemorative addresses of countless orators and the adulatory local histories of dozens of antiquarians, they had succeeded in building a regional mythology

---

[64] *Ibid.*, I, pp. 207, 212.

[65] George E. Ellis, *The Puritan Age and Rule in the Colony of the Massachusetts Bay, 1629-1685*, (Boston, 1891), p. 336.

based largely on the Puritan self-appraisal. Indeed they had gone far toward making that mythology a pivotal part of the national mythos. At the very least a pre-Olympian pantheon of demi-gods had been delineated. But the task was not done without dissent. Through the centuries the Quaker and Baptist victims of persecution had found their defenders. Samuel Groome, Isaac Backus, James D. Knowles and other denominational champions had made sorties against the Puritan bastion and challenged its claims to suzerainty. The Antinomian Movement, for better or worse, had disintegrated almost as soon as organized, so for them there was no defender. But in 1858 a descendant of one of the faction—albeit his progenitor had proven a notorious hedger—produced a full scale blast against the whole Puritan system. Judge Peter Oliver, in his "Puritan Commonwealth", specifically attacked the intolerance and authoritarianism of the leaders of the colony. "The spirit of Puritanism," he charged, "was hostile to the principles of liberty [and] the Puritan Commonwealth was saved from absolute despotism only by the determined opposition of the freemen."[66] But even Oliver could not escape the established stereotype of Mrs. Hutchinson. He saw her as a woman whose "stern and masculine mind . . . triumphed over the tender affections of a wife and mother."[67] The "Jezebel" of John Winthrop, the "virago" of Cotton Mather persisted as an image even to those who hated her persecutors.[68]

[66] Peter Oliver, *The Puritan Commonwealth*, (Boston, 1856), p. 78.

[67] *Ibid.*, p. 181.

[68] Winthrop, *Journal*, Vol. I., p. 254.

These were, however, but small bore weapons aligned against the heavy artillery of the filiopietists. Neither in authority, prestige nor sheer volume of words could the denominational insurgents hope to dent the ranks of the establishment. To this uneven conflict Charles Francis Adams, Jr. brought an impressive weight of firepower. Armed with the national reputation of great name whose roots penetrated to the time and events of which he wrote, he promised to stand impartially above familial or parochial loyalties, to say what he saw and judge as he found. Guerdoned with the penons of the new science, he proposed to order objectively the events of the past within the framework of the grand evolutionary design—"the Emancipation of Man from Superstition and Caste." In "Three Episodes in Massachusetts History" he attacked with main force the Puritan culture which for a century and a half had shrouded Massachusetts in intellectual torpor and emotional morbidity. In "Massachusetts, Its Historians and Its History," he challenged the filiopietistic claim that Puritanism had in any way engendered religious liberty and political equality. The centerpiece of this ambitious design was the essay on the Antinomian Controversy. Adams singled out that episode as the fatal turning point in the history of Massachusetts liberties. It was then, he held, that the twig was bent and the tree inclined.

In brief the Adams thesis runs as follows. At the outset the Bay colony was an "active and intelligent community," openly receptive to new ideas.[69] But even thus early the church dominated the state and had communicated its superstition to the entire

[69] *Massachusetts*, p. 59.

population. Lacking the amenities and diversion of a settled society the only outlet for the emotional and intellectual needs of its people was to be found in religion. In this environment Mrs. Hutchinson's teachings inevitably aroused attention and controversy, despite the fact that the issues involved were so recondite that not even the clergy fully understood them. In actuality the controversy was not a religious dispute at all, but rather a diffuse and restless popular protest against the confining formulas imposed by the dominant oligarchy. Mrs. Hutchinson's tenets offered no improvement over the established beliefs of the community and the movement serve only to stiffen theocratic resistance to the more meritorious insurgencies which followed. It was "a premature agitation based on a false issue."[70] The Synod which condemned the Antinomian errors was a barren masquerade in which no one "had any distinct conception of what they were talking about."[71] The trial of Mrs. Hutchinson was "no trial at all, but a mockery of justice, rather, a bare-faced inquisitorial proceeding."[72] The struggle over, a once receptive and flexible community was frozen into attitude of conformism, intolerance and morbidity. The Synod of 1637 ushered Massachusetts into a "theologico-glacial period" which culminated in the "univeral insanity" of the Great Awakening.[73] But during that long period of time the sense of political independence remained alert, upheld even by the clergy. By 1761, with the agitation over the Writs of Assistance, the

---

[70] *Three Episodes*, p. 573.

[71] *Ibid.*, p. 473.

[72] *Ibid.*, p. 488.

[73] *Some Phases of Sexual Morality*, p. 499.

intellect of Massachusetts had worked itself out
from under "the incubus of superstition, prejudice
and narrow conformity imposed on it by the first
generation of magistrates and ministers."[74] In the
period of great political activity which followed—
from the Writs of Assistance to Shay's Rebellion—
"all religious and theological issues dropped out of
consideration."[75]

Although Adams had radically revised the traditional interpretation of the Antinomian Controversy, he genuinely sought a balanced assess-
ment of its dramatis personae. He had little sympathy for Mrs. Hutchinson, the chief victim of the
theocrats. "A female enthusiast, politican and
tease," obsessed with a craving for excitement and
notoriety, was his estimate.[76] Perhaps a trace of
anti-feminism can be detected in his suggestion that
Mrs. Hutchinson's deportment forcibly illustrated
the "malign influence" of women in political affairs.[77]

By contrast John Winthrop emerges as a
basically attractive figure, tolerant and generous by
nature. He was, however, Adams thought, childishly
superstitious and credulously submissive to the will
of the clergy. John Cotton, too, though a tolerant
and open minded individual, was seen as weakly
succumbing to the sway of his clerical brethren.
Deserting his own teachings under pressure "he
made haste to walk in a Covenant of Works—and
the walk was a very dirty one . . . the ignominious
page in an otherwise worthy life."[78]

[74] *Massachusetts*, p. 109.
[75] *Ibid.*, p. 95.
[76] *Three Episodes*, pp. 370, 538.
[77] *Ibid.*, p. 568.
[78] *Ibid.*, p. 514.

Adams recognized young Harry Vane as the foremost champion of religious liberty in his time, but even here he sought a balanced estimate. Though Vane was, in the abstract, more nearly right than Winthrop, at that time and place his presence was clearly inappropriate. Vane's "mind was destructive in it's temper."[79] This was a time for construction and growth, a time when "Massachusetts could far better spare Henry Vane from its councils than it could have spared John Winthrop."[80]

That there should be no misunderstanding of his intent, in "Massachusetts; Its Historians and its History" Adams spelled out in full his indictment of the filiopietists. He labelled as clearly preposterous their reasoning that intolerance and persecution were somehow justifiable in those who had themselves suffered persecution for their beliefs—that what was wrong in England was somehow made right in New England. "Why is it," he asked, "that acts of proscription and general banishment for opinion's sake are held up to execration when portrayed in one scene of a great drama, but in another scene of it are extenuated and made to conform to the precepts of wise statesmanship and lofty morality?"[81]

Nor would he accept his predecessors claim that through some mysterious chemistry Puritan intolerance and conformity had fostered the liberty and equality of a later era. "It is not easy, indeed, to see how the *post hoc propter* fallacy could be carried farther," he protested. "It is much like arguing, because a child of robust mind and active frame

[79] *Ibid.*, p. 465.
[80] *Ibid.*, p. 466.
[81] *Massachusetts*, p. 44.

survives stripes and starvation in infancy, and bad instruction and worse discipline in youth, struggling through to better things in manhood, that therefore the stripes and starvation, and bad instruction and worse discipline, in his case worked well and were the cause of his subsequent excellence."[82] Indeed, Adams argued, if credit for democratic growth were to be fairly allocated it must be bestowed on those dissenting "intruders" whom Puritan and filiopietist alike had so excoriated. "The Antinomian and Quaker and Baptist were the best friends the New England Puritan had, the acrid salt which saved him from corruption, this elementary truth never dawned on the mind of the filiopietistic investigator."[83]

With these two slender essays Adams signalled a shift in the perspectives of Puritan historiography. "The Antinomian Controversy" was the first detailed full-scale examination of that episode and for the first time its important role in the formative period of Massachusetts history was adequately noted. Adams' research into the factual detail of the subject was fresh and thorough. Errors of fact which had crept into earlier accounts were now rectified. The essay was penned in a trenchant and magisterial style befitting the judicial viewpoint of its author. It remains, nonetheless, a highly readable and colorful narrative, spiced with pungent observation and ironic asides. Most significantly Adams had once and for all demolished the mythology which had so long biassed New England historiography and thwarted a fuller understanding

[82] *Ibid.*, p. 110.
[83] *Ibid.*, p. 53.

of the Puritan culture. This was an achievement of considerably more than parochial concern. Because the ideas and attitudes that emanated from New England—and initially from Massachusetts—were so often vital in shaping the ends of the Republic, it was essential that the history of its early years be set aright.

This is not to suggest that Adams—nor indeed any of those who followed him—had the final word to say on the subject. Nor, as we can see from our present vantage point, was the work without significant flaws. Like his filiopietistic precursors in the field, Adams neglected the religious dimension of the controversy, which is to say that both failed to examine the Puritan culture in its own terms. The filiopietists had assessed the affray as essentially a civil disturbance, a tactic calculated to turn aside the accusation that the Puritans were guilty of religious intolerance. Adams, too, regarded the controversy as civil rather than religious in nature. He did so, being so thoroughly secularized he could not credit the Puritan theology as a sufficient ground for action. It was to him no more nor less than "superstition," so the real causes of action and counteraction must lie elsewhere. Adams' failure lay, not in his condemnation of the Puritan oligarchs, but in his disposition to judge their attitudes and behaviour by the standards of his own time. The historian cannot escape the responsibility of moral criticism, but such criticism becomes pointless when it fails to measure the cultural gap which separates the object from the viewer. When Adams attacked the Puritan magistrates and ministers for their intolerance he failed to consider the ground whereon they stood. It would no more have occurred to the Puritan leaders to allow a free establishment of religion in Massachusetts than it would have occurred to Charles Francis Adams to tolerate free love, or the nine hour day, in Quincy. Like John Winthrop, Adams feared not to attack the enormities of past ages, but remained a fairly steadfast champion of the essential orthodoxies of his own day. To view a society of the past exclusively in terms of the values of the present is to misunderstand that society altogether. And, in truth, Adams' attack on the Massachusetts "theocracy" sheds a good deal more light on the mind of the Mugwump than it does on the mind of the Puritan.

Adams also erred in his failure to sense the consistency and continuity of cultures. On this point the filiopietists had erred at the opposite extreme. So haplessly were they driven by parochial pride to find consistency and continuity in the record that they neglected to weight sufficiently the possibilities of internal variation and change. From beginning to end, it would appear from their account, the New Englander was libertarian and democrat. Conversely, Adams rendered an accounting that was rather too disjunctive and dualistic. History was conveniently periodized in terms of dramatic turning points as power shifted, often inexplicably, from one side to the other, from reform to reaction and back. Always, by assumption, moving ineluctably toward "the Emancipation of Man from Superstition and Caste."

The dualism of such a thesis was, of course, highly congenial and politically serviceable to liberal historians and readers of his own time and of the progressive age which followed. The forces of evil and the forces of good were aligned in clear opposition and the lessons of the past conveniently made to serve the purposes of the future. History thus used may be propaganda for good and beneficial purposes, but it remains, nonetheless, propaganda. As in the former case *The Antinomian Controversy* may serve to cast more light on the age of the Mugwump and Progressive than it does on the age of the Puritan.

Such, perhaps, is the fate of all historical writings in some degree, and of all but the very greatest in great degree. The function of the historian is to mediate the past to the present. He can never hope to leave the present wholly, nor can he fully enter the past. So his record of the past must very largely remain a record of the sentiments of his own time. But even under such limitations an historian can produce a classic work which frames a segment of the past in an entirely new perspective—a perspective peculiarly illuminating to the age and audience for which he writes. Such a classic was *The Antinomian Controversy.*

It should not be necessary to detail the views of those progressively minded historians who had occasion to deal with the Puritans during the thirty or forty years after Adams published his work. His interpretation of events served their purposes admirably and they digressed little from the pattern he had set down. Indeed, five years before "The Three Episodes" appeared, Charles' younger brother, Brooks, propounded ideas to much the same effect in "The Emancipation of Massa-

chusetts." It will be remembered that *The Antinomian Controversy* was privately printed some
years before its formal publications in 1892. It is
highly probable that Brooks had read one of the
eleven copies in his brother's possession. Although
Brooks professed larger purposes than an attack on
Puritanism, his book was so construed by critics
and public alike. The most significant difference in
the brothers' treatments of Puritan institutions and
leaders lay in the more strident censoriousness of
Brooks' pen. Typical is his reference to Mrs.
Hutchinson's "trial before that ghastliest den of
human iniquity, an ecclesiastical criminal court."[84]
Charles spoke deprecatingly of the volume, but he
had long known that restraint and balance were
never among Brooks' redeeming features.

During the nineteen-twenties James Truslow
Adams (no relation) and Vernon Parrington both
assessed the events or personages of the Hutchinson
affair with conclusions that often merely
paraphrase those of Charles Adams. Both historians
wrote from an ardently progressive perspective and
were doubtless more energetically liberal in most
things than Adams. But their treatment of the Antinomian Controversy—or indeed of the Puritan
regime—was not such as to make the degree of difference perceptible.

In 1930 the Massachusetts Tercentenary celebration was ushered in—not by a much needed, fresh
study of John Winthrop, the father of the Commonwealth—but by the almost simultaneous ap-

---

[84] Brooks Adams, *The Emancipation of Massachusetts: The Dream and
the Reality,* (Boston, 1887), p. 235.

pearance of three adulatory biographies of his chief victim, Anne Hutchinson. Written by women, all presented the martyred Anne as a prototype of the newly emancipated American female. Two of these biographies were romantic and novelistic in the extreme. The third, by Edith Curtis, offered a more concise and straightforward account. All regarded Mrs. Hutchinson with considerable sympathy, but in other respects the Adams' viewpoint remained strongly manifest. So three hundred years later the wheel had come the full turn. The American Jezebel had at last been sainted.

It is interesting, and perhaps significant, that those authors who jumped most enthusiastically on the Adams bandwagon were non-academic historians writing mainly for a lay audience. Or, as was the case with Parrington, a teacher of literature rather than of history. During this forty-year period the academic historians, most notably Herbert L. Osgood, Edward Channing and Charles McLean Andrews, followed a much more restrained course of analysis. Though not uncritical of Puritan leadership and institutions, they sought more cautiously than the progressives to assess events in terms of the needs and assumptions of the time in which they took place. In that respect the air was cleared for the extensive revisionism which Puritan historiography was to undergo in the nineteen-thirties and thereafter.

- v -

Perry Miller has doubtless been the major figure in the revision of Puritan historiography.

Throughout the decade of the 'Twenties Samuel
Eliot Morison and Kenneth Murdock labored effec-
tively but almost alone to soften the harsh contours
of the Puritan image. Since that time, thanks to
Miller's leadership and inspiration a small army of
younger historians has transformed the study of colonial New England into one of the liveliest seg-
ments of American historical study. Miller recalled
that when he commenced his exploration of the subject, a move discouraged by his mentors, the very
word Puritanism "served as a comprehensive sneer
against every tendency in American life which we
held reprehensible"[85] His labors for the next thirty
years were largely responsible for modifying that
lofty assumption. Searching for the mainspring of
Puritan thought and behaviour, Professor Miller
turned directly to that immense body of Puritan
literature that scholars had hitherto more often
cited than studied. What he found there significantly altered and enlarged our understanding of
the New England way. Largely because of his efforts historians have since been able to examine the
Puritan mind and to explore the political, social
and economic structures and processes of the Puritan community with balance and discernment and
without resort to the idolatry or iconoclasm which
characterized earlier works on the subject.

As a result of their studies we can now gain a
clearer picture of the lineaments of the Puritan
regime which condemned Anne Hutchinson. It was,
in these early years, clearly an oligarchy, but with a
strain of popular democracy which time and cir-

[85] Perry Miller, *Orthodoxy in Massachusetts, 1630–1650*, (Boston,
1959), p. viii.

cumstance would nurse to lively self-assertion and dominance. Though the Puritan autocrats contemned "meere democratie," with their own hands they had planted a seed which was to make New England seem a very hotbed of radicalism in the eyes of its colonial neighbors.

Theocracy was the term most commonly applied by liberal historians to the government of Massachusetts Bay. Whatever its shortcomings from the twentieth-century viewpoint, it now appears that this cognomen was a misnomer. The secular authorities recognized their duty to protect the one true religion and they generally welcomed and often sought the advice of the clergy. In this respect they differed no whit from the princes of other European communities in that day. But the Puritan magistrate, in law and in practice, insisted upon the independence of the civil government from the control of the church. Political powers were explicitly removed from the hands of the clergy. The civil officials, however, retained a comprehensive authority to direct the affairs of the church and to discipline any single congregation which strayed from orthodoxy. Indeed, Edmund Morgan concludes that prior to the foundation of Rhode Island "there was probably no place in the Western World where clergymen were as carefully cut off from political power as in Massachusetts."[86]

Although Perry Miller did not deal directly in detail with the Antinomian Controversy, he recognized the critical nature of the episode and provided the means of understanding the real and

[86] Edmund S. Morgan, *Roger Williams: The Church and the State*, (New York, 1967), p. 79.

essential quality of the issues involved. It was he who made the hitherto unnoticed point that the official reaction against the Hutchinson element was prompted in part by the "non-separatist" position the Puritan leaders had adopted for reasons of principle and practice.[87] Though conspicuously alienated from the Church of England they continued to profess their adherence to that institution and insisted that theirs was a reform movement from within the church. This gesture, they were confident, must enhance the legitimacy of their cause, improve their posture for an eventual takeover of the church, discourage separatism from within their own ranks, and mollify the crown authorities from whom they held their charter of government. When the Antinomian forces were scattered Puritan leaders were able to repart, with hope of approval at home, that they too had quelled a separatist revolt.

Miller also made it quite clear, despite the contrary claims of filiopietist and progressive historians, that religious considerations were of central and paramount concern in the Antinomian Controversy. The participants in that conflict had their own secular needs and interests and certain of these, as we shall see, bore forcibly on the course of the struggle. But it must be remembered that the Antinomian Controversy was, in the first instance, an intra-church debate between two groups whose members held their faith with great seriousness. Theology at this time was never far removed from life and the theology of the Puritan provided him with a detailed explanation and a rule for all

[87] Miller, op. cit., pp. 158–159.

aspects of his earthly existence. So intimate and organic was the defined relationship of secular and religious spheres that a duality was not conceded. The secular needs and interests of these people were, of course, no less real and pressing than our own, but they were viewed as aspects of a totality that was explicable only in theological terms.

The central issue at stake in the Antinomian Controversy—and indeed in the formation of Puritan theology and of the New England culture—was one which had troubled many religious systems over the centuries: whether the divine and its operations were to be comprehended in subjective, mystical terms or in objective, empirical terms. The problem was of more than academic interest for on its resolution might depend the interpretation of natural phenomena and even the structure of the social order, a consideration acutely felt in Puritan Massachusetts Bay.

In the early years of the colony its theologians and secular leaders were seeking a viable middle way between the threatening extremes of Antinomianism and Arminianism. The former view posited an indwelling of the divine in the elect which placed them above the law and exempted them from all considerations of conduct. God's grace was bestowed without respect to the virtues or failings of the recipients and thereafter unfailingly moved them in His way—a condition subjectively betokened by an inner stirring of the spirit and for which the objective evidence of external behaviour was in no way pertinent. The threat to Puritan orthodoxy and, it seemed, to the stability of the community was clear. If God's grace did all, then moral responsibility was an irrelevance, education and the exercise of reason became meaningless, God's scriptural pronouncement superfluous, and the church and its ministry unnecessary. Spiritual anarchy and an uncontrolled emotionalism seemed the inevitable consequence.

Conversely, Arminianism postulated an unencumbered freedom of the will and attributed salvation largely to man's consent and endeavor. This solution distinctly enlarged the boundaries of man's responsibility and provided objective grounds for the determination of his spiritual condition. But just as obviously it delimited God's freedom to bestow grace when and where He saw fit. For a century-and-a-half after its founding the history of New England was largely the history of its steady movement in the direction of Arminianism, a movement accelerated by the orthodox response to the Antinomian threat of 1636. But at the time this tendency was neither descried nor desired. The aim of the founders had been to define a middle way which would clearly declare God's authority and man's responsibility.

The root of the Puritan dilemma lay in Calvin's insistence that, though God was absolutely sovereign in His choice of the elect, man must act as though his effort counted for something in the choice. To resolve this dilemma the Puritan clergy had painstakingly set forth a theology in which human ethics might be logically deducible from divine grace. This, the covenant or federal theology, held that God's original covenant with man, broken by Adam's fall, had been replaced by a Covenant of Grace, wherein God proffered His grace to believers without respect to their efforts or virtues.[88] Under this new covenant God made His offer only to those who would consent to accept it. All that was expected of them was that they would try the powers God had given them. The way to gain assurance of grace was to give it a trial. Sanctification, they would find, readily and naturally followed justification and offered a handy proof that grace was indeed present.

But there remained a problem of priorities. An important school of Puritan thought contended that to gain grace, the believer must prepare himself, must recognize his helplessness, sorrow for his sinfulness and display the will to be saved.[89] This much, at least, seemed necessary to objectify the process of conversion and to impose some degree of responsibility upon the prospective Saint. But it was here that John Cotton—and in due course Anne Hutchinson—fell at odds with the clerical majority. It was the essence of Cotton's thought that he visualized a vast abyss between human nature and divine grace, a void that could be bridged only by God's will, not man's. The gift of God's grace, he contended, was absolute and gratuitous, bestowed without respect to either the virtues or apprehensions of man, and implanted by means of an intimate union with Christ which preceded any inclination of man to reach out in belief. From Cotton's

[88] Perry Miller, "The Marrow of Puritan Divinity" in *Errand Into the Wilderness* (Cambridge, Mass., 1956), Perry Miller, *The New England Mind: The Seventeenth Century,* (New York, 1939), passim.

[89] Perry Miller, "Preparation for Salvation in Seventeenth Century New England," in *Journal of the History of Ideas,* Vol. IV, No. 3 (June, 1943), pp. 253–286. Norman Pettit, *The Heart Prepared: Grace and Conversion in Puritan Spiritual Life,* (New Haven, 1966), passim.

point of view the doctrine of preparation smacked of the old Covenant of Works, a convenient device to whittle God's sovereignty down to a size where man might seize on its rewards. Belief, repentance, moral awareness and endeavor must be subsequent, not antecedent, to the gift of grace. The conversion experience, as Cotton understood it, was an illuministic awareness of union with the Holy Ghost. However, despite his emphasis on the free promise of God's grace, Cotton clearly stipulated that obedience to God's Law was thereafter a necessary condition of salvation. If good behavior did not follow, then the conversion experience had clearly been delusory.

Cotton's colleagues were much concerned about the irregularity of his doctrines. Their apprehensions seemed amply confirmed when Anne Hutchinson embraced these doctrines and in her ardor conveyed their implications well beyond Cotton's design. Not only did she minimize Cotton's firm enjoinders to moral effort, but she deduced from his words that the gift of grace implied the actual indwelling of the Lord, mystically uniting the elect to Himself and relieving them of the burden of their transgressions. Cotton had never failed to insist upon the linkage of the Spirit and the Law. Mrs. Hutchinson broke that link. But so subtle was the line of distinction between their beliefs that not until catastrophe was full upon them did Cotton sorrowfully grasp the difference.

Cotton's position after the trial of Mrs. Hutchinson was indeed an uncomfortable one, but not to the degree that he felt impelled to recant his beliefs. He had walked the razor's edge in his effort to balance grace and nature. He did not thereafter abandon the claims of grace, but took greater care than before to declare the requirements of nature.

The noisiest complaints of the progressive historians were levelled against the trial of the Hutchinsonians. Undeniably grave legal errors were committed, even according to the crude judicial standards of that day. But these are not precisely the errors ascribed by liberal commentators, who were too often prone to examine the proceedings from the perspective of twentieth century justice. The government had charged Mrs. Hutchinson and certain of her adherents with subscribing to a seditious libel. This was an offense well established in English law of the sixteenth and seventeenth centuries and then regarded as constituting a dangerous threat to the security of the state. A seditious libel at that time was, in effect, any statement that the government saw fit to regard as critical of its purposes or operations or of its personnel even in their most unofficial capacities. During this period British laws of sedition were evolving in response to the enhanced needs of an insecure dynasty and an emergent nation-state in a hostile world. Given the prevailing conception of church-state uniformity, sedition laws necessarily bore some concern for the security of the state church. Not until after 1704 was this rigorous legal interpretation of national security significantly liberalized.

It is hardly surprising, therefore, that the General Court of Massachusetts Bay felt the right and obligation to prevent a schism in the established, state-supported church. At this time very few nations were prepared to disavow that obligation. It appeared to the Court, with some justification in view of the dissidents' behavior, that the words of the defendants were of such a nature to promote a schism. Furthermore, Mrs. Hutchinson, by divulging her revelations in the course of the trial, had created so conclusive a presumption of guilt that the admission of further evidence against her was deemed unnecessary. The content of her locutions, voluntarily proclaimed before the Court, did in themselves constitute a seditious libel wherein she did impugn and threaten the whole state.

To the modern mind the conduct of these trials is shocking. But it must be remembered that in most respects the procedures employed were no different than those which currently obtained in English courts. At all times procedure was regulated to favor the interest and security of the state. The defendant was left ignorant of the details of the case against him and was denied the right of counsel during the trial. Judge and prosecutor alike questioned and harrassed both defendant and witnesses who enjoyed no immunity against self-incrimination. Nor was the absence of a jury in the Hutchinson case without respectable precedent in English law, under which sedition cases had largely gone by default to prerogative courts. However, in English courts, though the functions of judge and prosecutor were often confused, the legal distinction between them was recognized and maintained. In the Hutchinson case a shocking miscarriage of justice was committed when Winthrop and his fellow magistrates undertook to serve as both judges and prosecutors. That they should have done so without a jury to examine and amend their conclusions was

doubly shocking and finally overthrew any sem-
blance of justice the proceeding might have offered.

In recent years the search for motivation has
fastened much attention on the social composition
of dissident groups. It was Bernard Bailyn who first
noticed that Mrs. Hutchinson's following contained
a large component of merchants from the Boston
community.[90] A more detailed analysis of the Antinomian movement has indeed revealed that a
remarkably large percentage of persons occupying a
high secular status were disposed to follow Mrs.
Hutchinson. Though only 39 per cent of the Boston
church members gave continued and open support
to the movement, 65 per cent of the affluent church
members did so, and 69 per cent of those church
members who held governmental office did so.
Those church members who were merchants or
craftsmen were more than twice as likely to join
Mrs. Hutchinson as those who were not. It further
appeared that if the merchants and craftsmen were
successful in their secular roles (i.e., if they were
"rich"), they were even more likely to support Mrs.
Hutchinson. In other words, these entrepreneurial
roles seem to have made the incumbents susceptible
to Mrs. Hutchinson's appeal, and the more inten-
sively they pursued the demands of the roles the
more susceptible they seem to have become.[91]

There is a convenient stereotype in the portfolio
of the social and religious historian that defines

[90] Bernard Bailyn, *The New England Merchants of the Seventeenth Century,* (Cambridge, Mass., 1955), p. 40.

[91] Emery Battis, *Saints and Sectaries: Anne Hutchinson and the Antinomian Controversy in the Massachusetts Bay Colony,* (Chapel Hill, 1962), ch. xvii.

pietistic movements as deriving their support from the "disinherited." However pertinent the formula may have been elsewhere it cannot be so loosely applied to the Antinomian movement. Although some of the disinherited were among Mrs. Hutchinson's disciples, the backbone and sinew of the movement was drawn from an altogether dissimilar social element. They were men and women of affluence, eminence and prestige in the community, people of education and gentle breeding who were not normally given to emotional excess. The reasons for their commitment may be found partially in the social tensions of the period. The present writer has elsewhere summed up his conclusions on this point as follows

One of the major conflicts in the colony at this time was between mercantile and agricultural elements over the problem of economic regulation. A majority of the population, engaged primarily in agricultural pursuits, had sought means to control an inflationary spiral that seemed to be pressed upward by labor costs and imported commodity prices. The gentry and yeomanry who dominated the General Court, moved by an organic social philosophy and a substantial body of English legislative precedent, had experimented with various regulatory measures, none of which proved successful. In their endeavors these men had enjoyed the unequivocal support of the clergy who insisted on an organic social ethic as an intrinsic part of the Puritan moral code and demanded strict compliance in evidence of a regenerate state. This policy placed the merchants and craftsmen of the colony, particularly those of Boston, in an awkward position. Most of them were church members and were resentful when their professions of faith were called into question because they entertained an economic code held objectionable by the rest of the colony. If they were to maintain their spiritual status without abandoning their social and economic values, it was necessary to reinterpret the doctrine of assurance in such a way as to circumvent the orthodox insistence on a narrowly construed organic philosophy. Mrs. Hutchinson filled their need by reasserting the primacy of the Covenant of Grace, the essential Witness of the Spirit. True assurance of grace, she had insisted, is essentially a mystical experience which precedes and precludes any consideration of moral effort on the part of the believer. Although neither she nor her companions were prepared to abandon the basic moral pattern of the community, this altered perspective allowed greater latitude within which to define what was morally sound and what was not. It permitted them to rest confident in their regeneration despite all contrary claims based on empirical data.[92]

True, the Antinomian Controversy was essentially concerned with theological matters. But for the Puritan, doctrinal debate was not an intellectual game; it was the definitive mode of comprehending the concrete data of human existence. It is understandable, therefore, that the Hutchinsonians should examine their secular concerns in religious terms. To them the problem was a religious one, but to the historian their religious and secular motivations appear to have been so closely intermingled as to be practically indistinguishable.

- vi -

In this latter part of the twentieth century the Antinomian Controversy, with its layer upon layer of theological jargon, may seem curiously remote

[92] *Ibid.*, p. 263.

and esoteric to the casual observer. But a second
and closer look suggests that it has a peculiar
pertinence to Americans of our time. Now, perhaps
more than ever before, American society is beset
with Antinomianism and separatism. The massive
cultural changes of recent decades have left a
residue of frustration or apprehension in many
quarters. The complexity of the democratic process
has impeded the performance of many vital social
tasks. Scarcely a day passes without report of individuals or groups who, protesting the injustice of
the law or the illegitimacy of the "establishment"
slash violently at the Gordian knot that binds their
hopes. Others, like Roger Williams before them,
seek only escape from the dung heap of this earth.
Almost invariably the protestants strive for the
apocalypse as though theirs was a gift of grace
which peculiarly exempts them from the ordinary
workings of the law.

Edmund Morgan has suggested that the problem
central to Puritanism and to its greatest leader,
John Winthrop, was—what is the responsibility of
the righteous man toward society?[93] How can one
hold together a community of imperfect beings and
still do God's work? Winthrop viewed society as an
organic whole wherein the fortunes of each were
indissolubly bound up with the good of all. What
must a man do if society pursues a course that he
regards as morally wrong? Should he withdraw and
maintain the integrity of his principles? Should he
pit his own principles against the law and will of the
community? Or should he stay and work as best he

[93] Edmund S. Morgan, *The Puritan Dilemma: The Story of John
Winthrop*, (Boston, 1958), p. xii.

can to reshape the finite materials at hand? Winthrop had learned not to expect perfection in his fellow men and he saw that there was no escape from the dung heap of this earth. His choice was "to march in company with other sinners" and to "restrain the overzealous from setting for the community a standard of godliness that would deny the humanity of human beings."[94]

The dilemma of John Winthrop is the dilemma of every American today. The choice should be made as thoughtfully.

---

[94] *Ibid.*, p. 76.

SELECT BIBLIOGRAPHY

The chief autobiographical materials on Charles Francis Adams, Jr. are *An Autobiography* (Boston, 1916) and the as yet unpublished letters, Diary and Memorabilia in the Adams Papers of the Massachusetts Historical Society. *The Letters of Henry Adams*, 2 vols., (Boston, 1930–1938) and *A Cycle of Adams Letters, 1861–1865* (Boston, 1920) both edited by Worthington Chauncey Ford, contain much of relevance. An excellent brief biography which quotes extensively from Adams' private writings has been written by Edward Chase Kirkland, *Charles Frances Adams, Jr., 1835–1915: The Patrician at Bay* (Cambridge, Mass., 1965). James Truslow Adams, *The Adams Family,* (Boston, 1930), contains a brief section on the latter-day Adamses.

The Charles Francis Adams, Jr. bibliography contains over four hundred and fifty items. Mrs. Garrett Wendell has provided an annotated checklist of the published works in Massachusetts Historical Society, *Proceedings,* 72 (1957–1960), 238–93. Adams' chief works pertaining to the history of colonial New England are *Three Episodes of Massachusetts History* (Boston, 1892), *Massachusetts, Its Historians and Its History: An Object Lesson* (Boston, 1894), "Some Phases of Sexual Morality and Church Discipline in Colonial New England," Massachusetts Historical Society, *Proceedings*, 2nd Series, VI (1891), 477–516, and the "epochal" Weymouth Address reprinted in *Proceedings on the Two Hundred and Fiftieth Anniversary of the Permanent Settlement of Weymount, with an Historical Address by Charles Francis Adams, Jr., July 4th, 1874* (Boston, 1874). Adams also edited Thomas Morton, *The New English Canaan* (Boston, 1883) and *Antinomianism in the Colony of Massachusetts Bay, 1636–1638* (Boston, 1894). Of particular interest in the shaping of Adams' thought is his address to the Wisconsin Historical Society, "The Sifted Grain and the Grain Sifters" in *The American Historical Review*, VI,2 (Jan. 1901), and his Presidential Address to the American Historical Association, "An Undeveloped Function," American Historical Association, *Annual Report*, I, (1901), 47–93.

To give the Antinomian Controversy its due the scholar should delve deeply into the voluminous theological literature of the time. However, the source materials which directly pertain to the conflict may be listed in brief compass. "The Short Story of the Rise, Reigne and Ruine of the Antinomians . . . (presumed to be from the pen of John Winthrop) is one of a number of basic documents included in Charles Francis Adams, Jr., *Antinomianism in the Colony of Massachusetts Bay, 1636–1638*, (Boston, 1894). A variant transcript of Mrs. Hutchinson's civil trial appears in the Appendix to Volume II of Thomas Hutchinson, *History of the Colony and Province of Massachusetts Bay*, ed. by Lawrence Shaw Mayo (Cambridge, Mass., 1936). "A Report of the Trial of Mrs. Anne

Hutchinson Before the Church of Boston" appears in Massachusetts Historical Society, *Proceedings,* 2nd Series, IV (1889), 159–191. Pertinent legislative and judicial proceedings are recorded in Nathaniel B. Shurtleff, ed, *Records of the Governor and Company of the Massachusetts Bay,* Vol. I (Boston, 1853). Governor Winthrop offers his personal account in John Winthrop, *Winthrop's Journal: "History of New England, 1630–1649",* ed. James Kendall Hosmer, 2. vols. (New York, 1902) and many relevant letters and documents are included in *Winthrop Papers,* 5 vols. (Boston, 1929–1947). Volume III includes Winthrop's position in his debate with Henry Vane. A reply is found in Henry Vane, "A Brief Answer to a Certaine Declaration", *Hutchinson Papers,* ed. W. H. Whitmore and W. S. Appleton, (Prince Society Publications, 2 vols, [1865]) I, 84–96. John Wheelwright's position is outlined in *John Wheelwright, His Writings, Including His Fast Day Sermon, 1637, and His Mercurius Americanus,* 1645, ed. Charles Bell (Boston, 1876).

Aside from Winthrop's treatment of the subject the most important seventeenth and eighteenth century accounts of the Antinomian Controversy appear in Edward Johnson, *Wonder Working Providence of Sions Saviour in New England* (Andover, 1867), William Hubbard, *A General History of New England from the Discovery to 1660* (Cambridge, Mass. 1815), Cotton Mather, *Magnalia Christi Americana or the Ecclesiastical History of New England* (Hartford, 1853), and Thomas Hutchinson, *The History of the Colony and Province of Massachusetts Bay,* ed. by Lawrence Shaw Mayo, 2 vols. (Cambridge, 1936).

The filiopietistic viewpoint of the nineteenth century is most preeminently evident in John Gorham Palfrey, *History of New England*, 5 vols. (Boston, 1858–1890), George Ellis, *The Puritan Age and Rule in the Colony of Massachusetts Bay, 1629–1685* (Boston, 1891) and George Ellis, *The Life of Anne Hutchinson* (Boston, 1845). Prior to the publication of *Three Episodes . . .* dissenting views were submitted by Peter Oliver, *The Puritan Commonwealth* (Boston, 1856) and Brooks Adams, *The Emancipation of Massachusetts, The Dream and the Reality* (Boston, 1887).

The twentieth century "progressive" attitude toward Puritanism and Antinomianism is exemplified in James Truslow Adams Pulitzer prizewinning *The Founding of New England* (Boston, 1921), Vernon L. Parrington, *Main Currents of American Thought* (New York, 1927) and is continued in somewhat modified form by Thomas Jefferson Wertenbaker, *The Puritan Oligarchy* (New York, 1947). The progressive viewpoint—or at least a notable antipathy toward Puritanism and sympathy for its first female victim—is conspicuous in Helen Augur, *An American Jezebel, The Life of Anne Hutchinson* (New York, 1930), Edith Curtis, *Anne Hutchinson* (Cambridge, Mass. 1930) and Winifred King Rugg, *Unafraid, A Life of Anne Hutchinson* (Boston, 1930).

Samuel Eliot Morison, *Builders of the Bay Colony* (Boston, 1930) contributed mightily to revision of attitudes toward Puritanism. Many of the writings of Perry Miller furthered and deepened our understanding of the Puritan culture. Most important of these for insights on the Antinomian Controversy are *Orthodoxy in Massachusetts, 1630–1650* (Cambridge, Mass, 1933), *The New England Mind: The Seventeenth Century* (New York, 1939), "The Marrow of Puritan Divinity" in *Errand Into the Wilderness* (Cambridge, Mass. 1956) and "Preparation for Salvation in Seventeenth Century New England," *Journal of the History of Ideas,* IV (1943), 253–86. The important problems of preparation and the qualifications for church membership have been further and more fully developed by Norman Pettit, *The Heart Prepared: Grace and Conversion in Puritan Spiritual Life* (New Haven, 1966) and Edmund S. Morgan, *Visible Saints,* (New York, 1963). Edmund Morgan has contributed a useful chapter on the controversy in *The Puritan Dilemma: The Story of John Winthrop* (Boston, 1958) and the views of the present author may be found in *Saints and Sectaries: Anne Hutchinson and the Antinomian Controversy in the Massachusetts Bay Colony* (Chapel Hill, 1962). Kai T. Erikson, *Wayward Puritans, A Study in the Sociology of Deviance* (New York, 1966) examines the controversy as an example of the social function of deviance.

THE
ANTINOMIAN
CONTROVERSY

by

Charles Francis Adams

THE ANTINOMIAN CONTROVERSY.

CHAPTER I.

THE REV. JOHN WHEELWRIGHT OF "THE MOUNT."

THOMAS MORTON'S house at Merry-Mount was burned to the ground in December, 1630, and its occupants were driven away. For several years thereafter the region between the Neponset and the Monatoquit — the seaward slope of the Blue Hill range — was without other inhabitants than the few Indians of Chickatabot's following, who, the sole representatives in those parts of the Massachusetts tribe, flit to and fro across the pages of the record, and haunt "the Massachusetts Fields," the mere ghosts of their race.

Indeed, for a short space of time, and yet one measured by years, the Neponset seems to have been looked upon as practically the southern boundary of Massachusetts. Starting from Salem, and making their first lodgment on the shores of Boston Bay at Charlestown, the outposts of what is known in New England history as the Great Migration had pushed their way up the valleys of the Charles and the Mystic, and south as far as the Neponset; but at the Neponset the southerly movement paused. It was a barrier in the way, — the first and the smallest of many barriers of the same kind which New England civilization was destined to surmount.

It was in this unoccupied region — a region some
five miles or so across, between Dorchester on the
north and Wessagusset on the south — that in 1634
Alderman of Bear Cove, as Hingham was then called,
losing his way, wandered through woods and swamps
for three days and two nights without encountering
a human being;[1] for, though it was known to have a
fertile soil, clear of trees, and to be well adapted to
farming purposes, the border land, as it then was,
seems to have been under a sort of ban.   Morton's
doings had given it an evil name.   It was no fit home
for godly families.

This state of affairs was not likely to continue long.
The early settlers of Massachusetts Bay, unlike those
of Plymouth, were many of them men of substance.
At home the associates of Carver and Bradford had
been plain people, while, of those who came with
Winthrop and Saltonstall, many had belonged to the
gentry; and these last brought with them to the New
World the English passion for landed possessions, —
that land-hunger which they inherited direct from
Germanic and Norman ancestors, and which they
left unimpaired and unsatisfied to their descendants.
Every man of mark among them was eager, as soon
as he set foot in New England, to secure a domain for
himself and his descendants.   The peninsula of Boston was small, — "too small to contain many," as
Wood described it only three years after the settlement; so that those living there were "constrained to
take farms in the country."   Accordingly, Governor
Winthrop had the Ten-Hill farm of 600 acres in
Medford, besides some 1,200 acres more "about six
miles from Concord northwards."   Governor Dudley

[1] *Supra,* 337.

had 1,700 acres, — 200 on the west side of the Charles
over against Cambridge, 500 on the easterly side of
the river, above the falls, and 1,000 from Concord
northwards. Sir Richard Saltonstall had 1,600 acres,
part in Watertown, part in Natick, and, later, part in
Springfield. So it went on; and it naturally resulted
that, as immigration increased, the land-hunger, which
was quite as well developed in the new as in the old
comers, could find in more remote parts only that on
which to feed.

Then it was that people began to look across the
Neponset; and accordingly, at the session of the General Court, held in May, 1634, it was ordered "that
Boston shall have convenient enlargement at Mt.
Wollaston." Six months later that territory was
formally annexed to Boston as a sort of outlying de-
pendency, Dorchester intervening between the two,
and the process of dividing it up among private own-
ers, in estates of from 200 to 700 acres, was begun.
On the 14th of December a committee of five was
appointed to go out and assign "what may be sufficient for William Coddington and Edmund Quincy
to have for their particular farms there." Quincy
was the progenitor of the family after a member of
which the town in which the Mount lay received its
name a century and a half later; Coddington afterwards became the father of Rhode Island. The Mt.
Wollaston bay-front was now assigned to the two, —
the place where Morton's house had stood subsequently
falling to Coddington, though it finally passed by pur-
chase and descent into the hands of a Quincy.

Allotments to others were at the same time made,
but they are not to the present purpose. It is necessary to pass over a couple of years before coming to

two names — William Hutchinson and John Wheelwright [1] — which are associated not only with holdings
at the Mount, but with controversies that for a time
seemed to threaten the very existence of the colony.
Its life was spared; but through more than a century
and a half its history bears the deep pit-marks of
those controversies, much as men of those early days
bore from childhood scars of the smallpox.

Theological controversies are as a rule among the
most barren of the many barren fields of historical
research; and the literature of which they were so
fruitful may, so far as the reader of to-day is concerned, best be described by the single word impossible. Among modern writers Hallam had to acquaint
himself with it in at least a general way; and even
Hallam, who was not wont to flinch at an array of
books and authors, was appalled, not more by the
mass than by the aridity of those devoted to this
particular branch of learning. More than once he
refers to the subject, with a touch of sadness as well
as a warmth of imagery not usual with him. " Our
public libraries," he in one place remarks, " are cem-
eteries of departed reputation; and the dust accumulating upon their untouched volumes speaks as

---

[1] The allotment to William Hutchinson was made by votes of Jan-
uary $\frac{4}{14}$, 1636 and January $\frac{9}{19}$, 1637, and included 600 acres of land,
lying in what is now North Quincy, "betwixt Dorchester bounds and
Mount Woollistone ryver." (*Second Report of Boston Record Com's,*
(1877), 7, 14.) The Wheelwright allotment was made by vote of
$\frac{\text{February 20}}{\text{March 2}}$, and April $\frac{3}{12}$, 1637. It included 250 acres lying south of Mt.
Wollaston, and "extended into the countrye." (*Ib.* 15, 17, 45, 46.)
The Rev. John Wilson's and the Rev. John Wheelwright's holdings
at "the Mount" seem to have been contiguous, and what Lechford remarked of Blackstone and Williams might have been remarked of Wheelwright: — "He lives neere master *Wilson,* but is far
from his opinions." (*Supra,* 325.)

forcibly as the grass that waves over the ruins of
Babylon ; " and again, speaking of the wordy " champions of a long war," he declares of their writings that
" they belong no more to man, but to the worm, the
moth, and the spider. Their dark and ribbed backs,
their yellow leaves, their thousand folio pages, do not
more repel us than the unprofitableness of their substance."

So far as its substance was concerned, the great
New England religious controversy of 1637 forms no
exception to the general truth of Hallam's criticism.
Not only were the points in dispute obscure, but the
discrssion was carried on in a jargon which has become unintelligible; and, from a theological point of
view, it is now devoid of interest. At most, it can
excite only a faint curiosity as one more example of
that childish excitement over trifles by which communities everywhere and at all times are liable to be
swept away from the moorings of common sense. But
the, so-called, Antinomian controversy was in reality
not a religious dispute, which was but the form it
took. In its essence that controversy was a great deal
more than a religious dispute ; it was the first of the
many New England quickenings in the direction of
social, intellectual and political development, — New
England's earliest protest against formulas. The
movement of sap in a young tree was not more natural,
and the form the quickening took, and the individuals
who participated in it were the only matters of chance.
It was designed by no one. No one at the time realized its significance. It was to that community just
what the first questioning of an active mind is to a
child brought up in the strictest observance of purely
conventional forms. So viewed, the mis-called Anti-

nomian controversy becomes, in the light of subsequent history, full of interest.   As an illustration of the men and manners and modes of thought of a civilization wholly unlike any which now exists, it is replete with life and incident.

John Wheelwright was the third minister of the gospel who regularly preached within the limits fixed in the Massachusetts patent south of the Neponset. William Monell and Joseph Hull of Weymouth alone preceded him; and when Wheelwright's voice was first heard in that wilderness, the voice of Monell had been silent for more than twelve years, while Hull had taken up his work only a twelvemonth before.   Wheelwright was in his day esteemed a learned and eloquent divine, and he was also a very famous one ; for it was his fortune, by a discourse delivered on a day of public fasting and prayer in January, 1637, to throw the Massachusetts community into a state of commotion without a parallel in its history.   It was, perhaps, the most momentous single sermon ever preached from the American pulpit; and, indeed, in this respect to be compared only with the yet more famous Sacheverell sermons, preached seventy years later in London.

The author of this memorable fast-day deliverance was born in 1592 at Saleby, a little hamlet of the market-town of Alford, some twenty-four miles from the English Boston, in the region known as the fens of Lincolnshire.   This region has the reputation of being one of the least interesting in England.   Saturated with water through one half of the year, through the other half it is a dreary flat; and yet, towards the close of the sixteenth century, the fens of Lincolnshire seem to have been somewhat prolific of men destined to play prominent parts in the settlement of America.

The names of all the fen hamlets terminate with *by*, indicative of their Danish origin ; and at Willoughby, only a few miles from Saleby, and a little over thirty from the yet more famous Scrooby, in the next county of Notts, John Smith was born thirteen years before Wheelwright. Of the latter's youthful days not much is known. His father, a landholder of the middle class, gave the son a good education, and in due course of time he became a student at Cambridge. There is a tradition that he and Oliver Cromwell knew each other well in their college days. The story is to the effect that in later years the Protector once said : — " I remember the time when I was more afraid of meeting Wheelwright at football than I have been since of meeting an army in the field, for I was infallibly sure of being tripped up by him." This, like most utterances resting on tradition, has an apocryphal ring ; but it is an established fact that Cromwell esteemed Wheelwright highly, and showed him marked favor at a subsequent time.[1] Taking his degree at Cambridge in 1618, Wheelwright five years later, in 1623, having married in the meanwhile, succeeded his wife's father in the vicarage of Bilsby, one of a cluster of hamlets close to the spot of his birth. The great religious movement against dogmas and ritualism was then fast developing in England, and assuming more and more strongly the Puritan phase. Wheelwright was married, possessed of some property, and secure in a comfortable living ; but he was a born controversialist, and seems to have entered into the spirit of the rising protest with all the superfluous energy of

---

[1] Bell, *John Wheelwright*, Prince Society Publications. Where other authorities are not specified, reference for statements relating to Wheelwright should be made to Bell's work.

youth. Before 1633 the crisis with him had come ; he
was already silenced for non-conformity, and, though
he had neither resigned nor been removed, his vicarage had been treated as vacant, and into it a successor
inducted. During the next three years he ministered
privately, but with an ever-increasing reputation, and
in April, 1636, embarked for New England.

Before this Wheelwright's first wife had died, and
he had married Mary, a daughter of Edward Hutchinson of Alford, and sister of one William Hutchinson. This William Hutchinson had, with his wife
Anne, gone to America in 1634, and landed in Boston
in September, thus preceding Wheelwright by about
two years. Arriving on the $\frac{26th}{6th}$ of $\frac{June}{July}$, 1636, on the $\frac{12th}{22d}$
of the next month Wheelwright was admitted to the
church, being then in his forty-fifth year. In 1636,
and, indeed, for years after that, there was but one
meeting-house in Boston, — the rude, one-story bar-
rack already described. In this edifice were gathered
together each Sabbath and lecture-day all the inhabitants of Boston who were neither too young profitably
to attend divine worship, nor incapacitated for some
good and sufficient reason. The Rev. John Wilson,
first pastor of the church, ministered to the flock,
though somewhat overshadowed by the greater eminence in public estimation of his colleague, — or teacher, as he was called, — the Rev. John Cotton.

Wheelwright had not been many weeks a member
of the church before some of its more active members
began to agitate the question of installing him by
Cotton's side as an additional teacher. The suggestion was first publicly made on Sunday, November $\frac{2}{12}$,
1636, at the church-meeting which regularly followed
the services ; and a week later it assumed formal shape.

A decided opposition was at once developed, at the
head of which were Wilson, the pastor, and Winthrop,
the ex-governor, while the whole movement, as was
natural enough in so small a community, soon connected itself with the political situation.   To understand how this came about, and the close bearing it
had on all that followed, a retrospect is necessary.

The popularity of Winthrop, not only in the colony
at large but in his own town and church of Boston,
had for some time been on the decline.   This was due
to no fault of his; but would rather seem to have
been one of those inexplicable, temporary eclipses
which nearly every prominent public man is at some
time in the course of his career fated to pass through.
With or without cause the community wearies of him,
and then, perhaps, presently returns to him; nor in
either case can any one say why.   The smaller the
community, also, the more liable it is to this ebb and
flow of popular favor.   Accordingly, at the election of
1634, the freemen, without ostensible reason, but in
supposed reply to a famous discourse of John Cotton's
on the tenure of office by magistrates, had quietly relegated Winthrop to private life, and chosen Dudley
governor in his stead.   A year later again they chose
Haynes, who had then only recently come over, to
succeed Dudley.

Among the many newcomers during the terms of
these two governors were three persons destined to play
parts of especial prominence in the early history of
the colony ; these three were Anne Hutchinson, Henry
Vane and Hugh Peters.   It will be necessary to speak
in some detail of Mrs. Hutchinson at a later point in
the narrative, and her presence in Boston was not at
once felt.   With the other two it was different.   From

the moment they set foot on Massachusetts soil, both Vane and Peters became leading factors in the development of the colony.

Naturally enough both the people of Massachusetts and Massachusetts writers have always taken a peculiar interest in the younger Vane. He figures in the list of those who were governors of the Colony and the State, and not only was he subsequently prominent among the statesmen of the English Commonwealth, but the romance which hangs about his death on the scaffold casts a strong gleam of light as well as a tragic shadow upon what is otherwise rather a matter of fact and commonplace record of names, few indeed of which are more than locally remembered. The hand of either the assassin or the headsman is apt, also, to exercise a perturbing and, at times, even a transmuting influence on the judgments of history; and this has been especially so in the case of Vane. At best, his personality is far from being of the distinct kind; if, indeed, so far as Massachusetts is concerned, he has not so long been held up as the ideal of an etherealized Puritan, youthful and poetic, gracefully wearing his halo of martyrdom, that at last effusiveness of sentiment has had more to do with the popular estimate in which he is held, than calm judgment backed by adequate knowledge. Judged, on the other hand, in the ordinary way and by what he did and what he left behind him, "young Sir Harry Vane " was a born parliamentary leader, and an administrator who on occasion did not fear to combine with his energy a sufficiency of guile; while, as a thinker and writer, he was undoubtedly a man of large and aspiring mind, nourishing lofty ideas far in advance of his time, but with a faculty of expression by no means equal-

ling the fineness of his thought. Consequently his
writings are not only mystical, but they are so involved and dull that Hume was fully justified in pronouncing them unintelligible and devoid of common
sense ; and now they are read only by the closest stu-
dents of political history, nor always clearly understood even by them. In the minds and memories of
the great majority of well-informed persons of his own
country, Vane is associated chiefly with the sonnet addressed to him by Milton, and with Cromwell's ejacu-
lation, as characteristic as it was contemptuous, when
he turned the Long Parliament out of doors. It is
also remembered that he met with calm courage a
death no less cruel than early and undeserved.

When he landed in Boston, in October, 1635, young
Vane was scarcely more than a boy. He would seem
to have been what in ordinary life is known as an
ingenuous youth, in eager sympathy with the most
advanced thought of his day. As such he was full of
high purpose ; but his judgment was by no means
mature, and accordingly he was petulant and indiscreet, — at times overbearing. From the outset he
impressed himself deeply on the colonists. There
was a glamour about him. A solemn sedateness of
manner was then in vogue ; but the winning faculty
none the less made itself felt, and Vane was in person
a handsome young patrician, — a man of unusual aspect, as Clarendon phrases it. His zeal and youthful
piety, his manifest simplicity and directness of purpose, won all hearts. Furthermore, at this time Massachusetts was sorely pressed by the machinations of
Gorges and Laud, and stood in utmost need of friends
at court ; Vane was the son of a privy-councillor, one
of the King's most influential advisers, and, naturally

enough, the colonists, overwhelmed by a sense of their own littleness, were inclined to magnify out of all due proportion any possible influence at Whitehall. Everything therefore contributed and combined to lend importance to young Vane. His father's son, he represented also Lords Brooke and Say, the Puritan patentees of Connecticut; and he had come to New England upon the express license and command of King Charles. The result was, that before this "noble young gentleman of excellent parts," as Winthrop describes him, had been two months in America, the inhabitants of Boston, at a general meeting upon public notice, agreed that none of them should sue one another at law " before that Mr. Henry Vane and the two elders have had the hearing and deciding of the cause, if they can." It is no matter for wonder if such adulation turned the head of the recipient, especially when that recipient was a youth yet in his twenty-fourth year.

Hugh Peters, the companion of Vane in his outward voyage, was a man of wholly different stamp. While " young Sir Harry " was innately a patrician, Peters, though he had been educated at Cambridge, was of the people. There was more than an absence of natural fineness in his composition ; he was coarsegrained. Over ten years Vane's senior, tall and thin, nervous and active both in mind and in body, Peters was voluble in speech and afraid of nothing. With his strong voice and fiery zeal, he was looked upon in his day as the typical Puritan fanatic and preacher ; and already, before coming to New England, he was famous for the success with which he swayed great audiences. He had himself experienced persecution ; yet it was not in his nature to brook opposition from

others.   Not long after his arrival at Boston, the banishment of Roger Williams made vacant the Salem
pulpit, and Peters was called to fill it.   This he did
most acceptably through five years, making himself
conspicuous not only for the strict church discipline
he enforced upon his people, but for the bustling out-
door energy with which he devised new business out-
lets for them.   Subsequently, in 1641, he was sent back
to England as a sort of agent of the colony, and during the Civil War he became a fighting chaplain in the
army of the Parliament.   Eliot says that he then " beat
the pulpit drum " for Cromwell ; and Burnet describes
him as " a sort of an enthusiastical buffoon preacher."
He certainly fought, preached and carried despatches
by turns; now stimulating the soldiery by his wild
eloquence, and now rushing in with them to the sack
of Winchester and Basing House.   When Laud, a
broken, weak old man, was leaving the peers' chamber after his arraignment, Peters overwhelmed him
with abuse, and, had he not been restrained, would
have struck him.   He preached by special appointment before Cromwell and the Commons at the Solemn
Fast during the sittings of the High Court of Justice,
and during the trial he was conspicuous for his exer-
tions among the soldiery to incite them to clamor for
the execution of the King.   Whatever it may have been
at Salem, his oratory at this time was famous for its
extravagance of language, and for the coarse, familiar
interpretations of Scripture by means of which he
was wont to stir his audience and raise a solemn
laugh.   At the funeral of the Protector, he walked by
Milton's side.   Thus, when the Restoration took place,
he had won for himself a dangerous prominence, and
was even looked upon as " the most notorious incen-

diary of all the rebels." As such he was marked for
destruction. His trial may be read among those of
the Regicides, and he was butchered at Charing Cross
on the 16th of October, 1660.[1]

Landing in Boston in October, Vane was admitted
to membership of the Boston Church on the 1st/11th of
November, and during the same month Peters was
preaching a sort of commercial crusade in Boston and
at Salem, moving the country to organize a fishing
company. In January the two, acting apparently in

---

[1] The word " butchered " is here used advisedly, for the details
of the execution are incredible in their brutality. John Cook and
Hugh Peters were tried and executed together. They were dragged
from the gaol to the scaffold on hurdles, the head of Harrison, who
had been executed before, being fastened on Cook's hurdle, looking
towards him. Peters' courage, alone of those that suffered, did not
rise to the occasion. " He was in great amazement and confusion,
sitting upon the hurdle like a sot all the way he went, and either
plucking the straws or gnawing the fingers of his gloves; " and " he
was observed all the while to be drinking some cordial liquors to keep
him from fainting." Cook suffered first, bearing himself exultingly,
but expressing the wish that Peters " might have been reprieved for
some time, as not being prepared or fit to die." When Cook was
" cut down and brought to be quartered, one they called Colonel Tur-
ner called to the sheriff's men to bring Mr. Peters near, that he might
see it, and by and by the hangman came to him, all besmeared in
blood, and rubbing his bloody hands together, he (tauntingly) asked,
' Come, how do you like this, Mr. Peters ? How do you like this
work ? ' To whom he replied, ' I am not (I thank God) terrified at
it, you may do your worst.' " Presently he ascended the ladder, and,
" after he had stood stupidly for a while, he put his hand before his
eyes and prayed for a short space ; and the hangman often remembering him to make haste by checking him with the rope, at last, very
unwillingly he was turned off the ladder."

Another account says that " he smiled when he went away," but
what he said " either in speech or prayer, it could not be taken, in
regard his voice was low at that time, and the people uncivil."

Such was a public political execution at Charing Cross, in the most
crowded streets of London, in the year of grace. 1660. See, also, on
this subject note (5) in Baxter's *Memoir of Sir Ferdinando Gorges*, 6.

concert, went still further in their efforts for the well-being of the colony. "Finding some distraction in the Commonwealth, arising from some difference in judgment, and withal some alienation of affection among the magistrates and some other persons of quality, they procured a meeting at Boston of the governor [Haynes], the deputy [Bellingham], Mr. Cotton, Mr. Hooker, Mr. Wilson, and there was present Mr. Winthrop, Mr. Dudley and themselves." The real cause of the trouble thus mysteriously referred to, though well understood by all, could not readily be set forth in an open, public way, for it was nothing more nor less than Dudley's jealousy of Winthrop. This had broken out as early as 1633, and had then culminated in the famous interview at Charlestown, at which the former charged the latter with exceeding his authority as governor. Winthrop, in reply, challenged his critic to show wherein he had so exceeded, "and speaking this somewhat apprehensively, the deputy began to be in a passion, and told the governor that, if he were so round, he would be round too. The governor bad him be round, if he would. So the deputy rose up in great fury and passion, and the governor grew very hot also, so as they both fell into bitterness." A half reconciliation was then effected through the mediation of the clergy, but the two men were of different disposition, and Dudley could not well help criticising Winthrop; for while Winthrop, of a calm temper and naturally tolerant, inclined to the ways of mercy and forbearance, Dudley, a man of thoroughly intolerant nature, was ever harsh and severe. Narrow in mind and rough of speech, with all a narrow-minded man's contempt for opinions different from his own, " the deputy" was as outspoken as he was courageous. Accordingly in the Charlestown interview of 1633 he had not hesitated to attack Winthrop for the too great leniency of his administration. Heavier fines, severer whippings, more frequent banishments, were called for; and as this view strongly commended itself to the average Puritan, and especially to the average Puritan divine, it had contributed in no small degree to the decline of Winthrop's popularity, and Dudley's final substitution for him in the position of governor.[1] And so, as Winthrop put it, " factions began to grow among the people, some adhering more to the old governor, and others to the late governor, Mr. Dudley, — the former carrying matters with more lenity, and the latter with more severity."

The meeting now arranged by Vane and Peters

---

[1] Winthrop has been regarded by most of the native New England historians, and notably by Palfrey, with a veneration which has impaired respect for their judgment whenever the authority of the first governor is invoked. They see things only through his eyes, and the ordinary scrutiny of modern historical criticism is laid aside where he is involved. Repeated instances of this indiscriminate adulation will be referred to in the course of this narrative. Nevertheless the difficulty of Winthrop's position, and the skill and high-minded rectitude with which he on the whole demeaned himself, should always be borne in mind. On this point the evidence of a foreign student and investigator carries more weight than that of one to the manor born : — " Every page in the early history of New England bears witness to the patience, the firmness, the far-seeing wisdom of Winthrop. But to estimate these qualities as they deserve, we must never forget what the men were with whom, and in some measure by whom, he worked. To guard the Commonwealth against the attacks of courtiers, churchmen and speculators, was no small task. But it was an even greater achievement to keep impracticable fanatics like Dudley and Endicott within the bounds of reason, and to use for the preservation of the state those headstrong passions which at every turn threatened to rend it asunder." Doyle, *English in America; the Puritan Colonies,* i. 165.

with a view to healing these factions was highly characteristic. The Lord was first sought. The prayer
over, Vane declared the occasion of the meeting and
the result sought to be obtained from it; which he
described as "a more firm and friendly uniting of
minds, especially of Mr. Dudley and Mr. Winthrop."

It must at first have been somewhat awkward for
the officious youth, as both Winthrop and Dudley professed an utter unconsciousness of any ill-feeling or
jealousy. They did not deny that there had been
something of the sort long previous, but Winthrop
professed "solemnly that he knew not of any breach
between his brother Dudley and himself:" while Dudley comfortably remarked "that for his part he came
thither a mere patient; and so left it to others to
utter their own complaints." Fortunately for Vane,
the existing governor, Haynes, then came to his aid,
and, after a certain amount of clumsy circumlocution,
proceeded, "as his manner ever was," to deal with
Winthrop "openly and freely," specifying certain
cases in which the latter had, as he expressed it,
"dealt too remissly in point of justice." To this
Winthrop replied, and, after partly excusing and explaining, came at last to the real point at issue. He
"professed that it was his judgment that, in the infancy of plantation, justice should be administered
with more lenity than in a settled state, because people
were then more apt to transgress, partly of ignorance
of new laws and orders, partly through oppression of
business and other straits; but, if it might be made
clear to him that it was an error, he would be ready
to take up a stricter course." The aid of the clergy
was then invoked. The matter was referred to the
ministers present, — Cotton, Hooker and Wilson, —

to be considered overnight, and the next day they were to report a rule for the future guidance of the magistrates; and this they did, all agreeing in one conclusion, "that strict discipline, both in criminal offences and in martial affairs, was more needful in plantations than in a settled state, as tending to the honor and safety of the gospel." Winthrop thereupon professed himself satisfied. He admitted that he had theretofore "failed in overmuch lenity and remissness," but promised that he would "endeavor (by God's assistance) to take a more strict course hereafter. Whereupon there was a renewal of love amongst them."

This took place on January $\frac{18}{28}$ and $\frac{19}{29}$, 1636, and in the following May young Vane was chosen governor to succeed John Haynes. He was chosen on the 25th of the month, or what is now the 4th of June. The day following John Wheelwright landed in Boston.

CHAPTER II.

MISTRESS ANNE HUTCHINSON.

WHEN Wheelwright found himself on New England soil, it must have been to the house of his brother-in-law, William Hutchinson, that he first directed his steps. It was the reunion of a family; for not only was Mrs. Wheelwright a sister of Hutchinson, but their mother also had now come over. Nor was Wheelwright himself welcomed there as a relative merely; he was looked upon as another eminent man added to the colony, — a new pulpit light. He at once plunged into whatever of religious or political life the little settlement contained; for of that life the house of William Hutchinson, or rather the house of his wife, Anne Hutchinson, had then for some time been the centre.

It has already been mentioned that the Hutchinsons had come over to New England in 1634, about two years before Wheelwright. Of this couple their contemporaries tell us that the husband was "a man of very mild temper and weak parts, and wholly guided by his wife;" while she was a woman "of a haughty and fierce carriage, of a nimble wit and active spirit,[1] and a very voluble tongue, more bold than a man, though in understanding and judgment inferior to many women." This vigorous bit of portraiture is from the pen of the Rev. Thomas Weld,

---

[1] "Of a ready wit and bold spirit." Winthrop, i. 239, 296.

the unfortunate gentlewoman's most malignant enemy, and it is not necessary here to inquire as to its truth to nature.   Suffice it now to say that during the two years which intervened between her own arrival in Boston and the arrival of her husband's brother-in-law, Mistress Anne Hutchinson, as she was called, slowly, skilfully, conscientiously, had been accumulating, in the heart of the little, nascent community into which she had come, that mass of combustible material which was soon to kindle into a fierce blaze. Wittingly or unwittingly, though probably the latter, she had entered upon a desperate undertaking, which she was destined to carry forward with a degree of courage and persistence, combined with feminine tact, which made the infant commonwealth throb through its whole being.   She had attempted a premature revolt against an organized and firmly-rooted oligarchy of theocrats.

The early Massachusetts community was in its essence a religious organization.   Church and state were one ; and the church dominated the state.   The franchise was an incident to church membership. The minister — the " unworthy prophet of the Lord " — was the head of the church.   There was a deep significance, as there may have been a bitter sneer, in Blackstone's parting shot as he left Boston, in which the " lord-bishops " were joined with " the lord-brethren."   At the point it had now reached, the Reformation of the previous century had resulted in practically substituting for a time many little popes and little bishops for the one pope and the few great bishops.   The fundamental principle of that Reformation had been the paramount authority of the Holy Scriptures as a rule or guide in life, as opposed to the

dictation of popes, synods and councils. The human
mind after centuries of implicit obedience had re-
volted ; and, in the revolt, the reaction as usual was
complete. Instead of unquestioning submission to
human authority, no human authority whatever was
allowed to intervene between man and God's Word.
The issue could not be put more forcibly than it was
by John Knox in one of his discussions with Queen
Mary. She said to him : — "You interpret Scripture
after one manner, the Pope and cardinals after another ; whom shall I believe, or who shall be judge ? "
— and Knox at once replied — " Ye shall believe God,
that plainly speaketh in His Word ; and further than
the Word teaches you, ye neither shall believe the
one nor the other. The Word of God is plain ; and
if there appear any obscurity in one place, the Holy
Ghost, which is never contrarious to Himself, explains
the same more closely in other places ; so that there
can remain no doubt but unto such as obstinately
remain ignorant."

Thus God's Word was beyond question, and it only
remained to interpret it and declare its meaning in
any given case ; but the interpreting and the declaring were the function of the clergy. The " lord-brethren " had thus been substituted for the " lord-bishops,"
— many local popes for the one at Rome. The casuistry to which the early New England clergy gravely
had recourse in defending the position thus assumed
might have moved the admiration of a Jesuit. When
earnestly adjured by brethren, more liberal as well as
more logical, not to make men hypocrites by compelling an outward conformity, thus practising that in
exile which they themselves went into exile to escape,
— when thus adjured, they replied that they had fled

from man's inventions; but there was a wide difference between man's inventions and God's institutions,
and they compelled a conformity only to the latter.
The institution being of God, the sin was not in the
magistrate who compelled, but in his perverse will
who stood in need of compulsion.[1] And so the final
" thus saith the Lord" had passed from Rome to
Massachusetts. Priest and inquisition had given way
to bishop and high-commission, and they in their turn
to minister and magistrate.

It is true, this system, unlike that of Rome, carried
within it the seeds of its own decay, for it rested on
discussion, and no final, inspired authority was recognized when irreconcilable differences of opinion arose.
The minister carried with him only such weight as
belonged to his individual character and learning,
and to his ordained position; though " the unworthy
prophet of the Lord," God had not touched that
prophet's lips with fire, nor did he claim to be in
direct communication with Him. Neither were any
intermediates recognized. Early New England ab-
jured all Saints. But when it came to the interpretation of the Scriptures, — the inspired Word, the
one guide both on earth and heavenward, — though
open and almost endless discussion was allowed and
even encouraged, and that discussion, bristling with
dialectics and casuistry, was overlaid with a rubbish
of learning, yet it has not in the result always been
at once apparent wherein the minister differed from

---

[1] " Christ doth not persecute Christ in New England. . . . For
though Christ may and doth afflict his own members; yet he doth
not afflict (much less persecute) Christ in them, but that which is
left of old Adam in them, or that which is found of the seed of
the serpent in them." Cotton, in *Publications of Narragansett Club*,
ii. 27–8.

the priest. Both priest and minister had recourse to civil persecution to compel religious conformity ; and, while the fagots that consumed Servetus and Savonarola were not unlike, they forever bear witness to a strong family resemblance between Romish cowl and bands of Geneva.

Not unnaturally, therefore, it has of late been somewhat the fashion to ignore this difference between priest and clergyman, and, indeed, some have even been disposed to deny its existence. Like Milton, they have claimed that after all, — "New Presbyter [was] but old Priest writ large." And yet, practically and in point of fact, the difference was not to be measured, for in itself it was great, and in its logical consequences vital. It was the same difference in spiritual matters which exists politically between an absolute ruler under right divine, and a civil authority exercised under the restrictions of a written constitution. In the spiritual contests of the sixteenth and seventeenth centuries the Pope represented divine right ; the Bible, the written constitution. The constitution was, it is true, indisputably vague, and everything depended on the construction given to its provisions. Except in certain small localities like Holland, or among a few most advanced thinkers of the day, who, like Roger Williams, were looked upon as visionaries, the conception of spiritual freedom and religious toleration had no more footing in the mind of the seventeenth century than the idea of freedom in crime and immunity from its legal penalties has now. Human thought had not yet grasped the distinction between personal liberty where the rights of others are not involved, and license where those rights are involved ; so far, indeed, from having grasped this distinction, one of the plainly stated contentions of the more advanced advocates of religious tolerance was, if a man conscientiously disbelieved in the right of any human authority, he ought not to be forced to obey it. None the less, the first great step towards educating the human mind to the difference between spiritual freedom and criminal license was taken when Bible law was substituted for papal dictum. The written word then became matter for judicial construction; but, like any other written law, when once construed and its meaning ascertained by competent and recognized authority, it was held by common consent to be the rule in force. It only remained to compel obedience to it, just as now obedience is compelled to the criminal law. When, therefore, Cotton argued that, while it was wrong to persecute man against conscience, no man's conscience compelled him to reject the truth; and therefore to force the truth upon him could be no violation of conscience, — when he argued in this way he uttered that which to us is foolishness; but, from his standpoint of time and light, he was merely asserting that on points of doubtful construction the law must be established by the tribunal of last resort, and, when once established, must be uniformly obeyed by all or enforced upon all. The fallacy which lurked between his premises and his conclusion did not suggest itself to him. A spiritual authority and a spiritual law were deemed just as necessary as a criminal authority and a criminal law.

Nevertheless, though the divine of the reformed church of the sixteenth century did set himself up as the ordained expounder of the written law, the importance of the ground gained when a written law was

substituted for an inspired dictum must not be lost
sight of. All else followed in due time. In the
searching discussion which ensued, the learning, the
common sense, and finally even the authority and
commission of those who comprised the tribunal, were
questioned ; and at last the law itself, and the necessity
of any law, or of general conformity to it, was openly
denied. " This was some time a paradox, but now
the time gives it proof ; " but two centuries and a half
ago, to the early New England Puritans, it was worse
than a paradox, — it was a blasphemy. As well doubt
the existence of God himself as question the binding
authority of His Word.

The Hebrew Bible was, then, the fundamental religious law — the spiritual constitution, as it were —
of the Puritan community. The clergy were the ordained and constituted expounders of that law, — the
Supreme Theological Court. Before them and by them
as a tribunal each point at issue was elaborately and
learnedly discussed ; reasons were advanced and authorities cited for each decision they rendered. Behind
their decisions was the Word ; and behind the Word
was God and His Hereafter. The spiritual organization was complete.

The religion of the Puritan was, also, realistic in all
its parts, — so realistic, indeed, as to be a practical
piece of machinery, — human, mundane machinery.
There was God, the Constitution and the Court —
and the clergy were the Court. But to the men and
women composing the Puritan community, the Court
was no more a reality — hardly more a visible thing
— than the Supreme Being himself ; for in those days
religion meant a great deal. It was no sentiment or
abstraction. The superstition which prevailed is to

the modern mind well-nigh inconceivable. All shared
in it. Sleeping and waking, at bed and board, in the
pulpit, in the field or at the work-bench, God and his
providences, the Devil and his snares, were ever present. Their direct interposition was seen in events
the most trivial. A harmless reptile crawls bewildered among the elders at a synod and is killed by
one of them, "and out of doubt the Lord discovered
somewhat of his mind in it; " so the serpent personi-
fied the Devil, and the synod the churches of Christ,
while Faith was represented by that elder who crushed
the head of the Evil One. There takes place "a great
combat between a mouse and a snake, in the view of
divers witnesses; " and the pastor of the first church
of Boston interprets the portent to his people, while
the governor of the colony records his words. The
snake is again the Devil, while the mouse becomes
"a poor contemptible people, which God had brought
hither, which should overcome Satan here and dispos-
sess him of his kingdom." Two unfortunate men are
drowned while raking for oysters; "it was an evident
judgment of God upon them, for they were wicked
persons." The hand of God was heavy also on those
who spake "ill of this good land and the Lord's people here; " some were taken by the Turks, and they
and their wives and their little ones sold as slaves;
others were forsaken of their friends, or their daugh-
ters went mad or were debauched, or their children
died of the plague, or their ships blew up with all on
board. Soon or late, some ill befell them or theirs;
and through that ill the finger of the Lord was revealed. A poor barber, called hastily to perform a
dentist's office, and bewildered in a storm of snow
between Boston and Roxbury, is found frozen to

death ; and presently it is remembered he had been
a theological adherent of Mrs. Hutchinson. There
befalls a great freshet, and the Indians " being pow-
wowing in this tempest, the Devil came and fetched
away five of them." A father, industrious or inter-
ested in his task, works one hour after Saturday's
sunset, and the next day his little child of five years
is drowned ; and he sees in his misfortune only " the
righteous hand of God, for his profaning His holy
day against the checks of his own conscience." A
wife is suspected of the murder of her husband, a
mother of killing her illegitimate child, and as they
touched them " the blood came fresh " into the dead
faces, and the bodies " bled abundantly." And when
the most terrible misfortunes incident to maternity befell Anne Hutchinson and her friend, the no less unhappy Mary Dyer, the grave magistrates and clergy,
gloating in blasphemous words over each lying detail
of the monstrous fruit of their wombs, saw therein
" God himself bring in his own vote and suffrage
from heaven."

But it is needless to multiply instances. The
records of the time are full of them ; for even angry
men in their disputes would treasure up in memory
every trivial or ludicrous mishap which befell their
opponents, and, while so doing, they were said to be
busy " gathering Providences." The finger of an om-
nipresent Almighty was thus visible everywhere and
at all times ; now meting out rewards and punishments while reversing the action of the wind and
tide, and then revealing itself in terror through
strange portents in the sky.

Among a people educated to this high pitch of fervor, theological controversy was the chief end towards

which the higher branches of education were directed.
The Scriptures, and the volumes of commentary upon
them, were the sole literary nutriment; while they
were studied only that scholars might, with gloomy
joy, dispute over the unknowable.   Not that there were
then no other books in the world.   It is true, there
was no light current literature in the modern sense of
the term; but the great body of the classics existed,
and every man and every woman of good education
had a familiarity with them now possessed by few.
They were "the humanities" of the time.   Of the
great names in modern letters, also, the greatest were
already known.   Boccaccio, Dante, Ariosto and Tasso
were familiar in the Italian.   Don Quixote is alluded
to in the New Canaan as a book with which every
one was acquainted.   Rabelais had died nearly a
century before, and the third reprint of Montaigne's
Essays, in its English translation, had appeared in
1632.   Bacon, Shakspeare, Spenser and Ben Jonson
had done their work; Milton was doing his, for it was
in 1634 that Comus was set upon the stage: but, to
the New England Puritan, Spenser was an idle rhyme-
ster, Jonson a profane scoffer, and Shakspeare a wanton playwright.   As to Boccaccio and Rabelais, copies
of their works would in primitive Massachusetts have
been rooted out as Devil's tares.   That there were
French books, as well as Latin, in Governor Winthrop's library, we know; and it is possible to imagine him sitting in his library in primitive Boston
with a volume of Montaigne in his hand: but to Endicott or Dudley and the rest, while those writings of
Cotton, which to us are as devoid of life as they are
of value, were full of interest, the pages of the French
humorist would have seemed idle words.   Fanaticism

is no less destructive to the capacity of general literary enjoyment than a diseased appetite is to a delicate
taste.   Drunkards crave alcohol, and communities ex-
alted with religious fervor care only for books on
theology.   Early New England had no others.   Some
adequate idea of the utter intellectual aridity which
consequently prevailed may be derived from the Sewall diary.   Sixty years after the Antinomian controversy, Pole's Synopsis, and the expositions of Calvin
and Caryl, were the companions of the reading man's
leisure, while the Theopolis Americana and the Magnalia were the ripe fruits of the author's brain.

Fortunately, the New Englander came of a hard-
headed stock.   Though individuals at times lashed
themselves into a state of spiritual excitement bor-
dering close upon insanity, and occasionally crossed
the line, this was not common.   When all was said
and done, there was in the early settlers a basis of
practical, English common sense, — a habit of composed thought and sober action, which enabled them
to bear up with steady gait under draughts of fanaticism sufficiently deep and strong to have sent more
volatile brains reeling through paroxysms of delirium.
Only twice or thrice in all their history have New
Englanders as a mass lost their self-control; and because they lost it then, other communities, with whom
losing it has been matter of too frequent occurrence
to excite remark, have never forgotten those occa-
sions, nor allowed New Englanders to forget them.
Such an occasion was the Antinomian controversy,
and such again was the witchcraft mania.

Among this people, — strong, practical, self-contained and tenacious, burning with a superstitious zeal
which evinced itself in no sharp, fiery crackle, but in a

steady glow, as of white heat, which two centuries did
not suffice wholly to cool, — among this people stood
the clergy, a class by themselves, almost a caste.
Learned in things theological, highly moral, deeply im-
bued with a sense both of the dignity and the duties
of their calling, the first generation of New England
divines was no less bigoted as a class than men with
minds at once narrow and strong are wont to be. That
they were to the last degree intolerant needs not be
said, for all men are intolerant who, in their own con-
ceit, know they are right; and upon this point doubt
never entered the minds of the typical divines of that
generation. Their pride of calling was intense. Not
only in their pulpits, but in their daily lives they
were expected to and did make a peculiar sanctification obtrusively manifest. They were not as other
men ; and to this, not only their garments, but their
Scriptural phrase and severe visage bore constant witness. And in these last characteristics — the dress,
the speech and the faces of the clergy — lay the heart
and the heat of the great Antinomian controversy.
The ministers were the privileged class of that community, — " God's unworthy prophets," as they phrased
it. Living in the full odor of sanctity among God's
people, — His chosen people, whom He " preserved
and prospered beyond ordinary ways of Providence,"
— they constituted a powerful governing order. And
now, suddenly, a woman came, and calmly and persistently intimated that, as a class, God's prophets in
New England were not what they seemed. No longer
were they unworthy in their own mouths alone.

Though she is said to have been a cousin of John
Dryden, little is known of Mrs. Hutchinson's ante-
cedents in England ; nor is it necessary that much

should be known. Her husband was the owner of an
estate at Alford, and descended from a family the
genealogy of which has since been traced with results
more curious than valuable. Though Alford was so
far from the English Boston that Mrs. Hutchinson
could hardly have been a constant attendant at St.
Botolph's Church, she seems to have been such an
ardent admirer of the Rev. John Cotton that, when
" he kept close for a time, and fitted himself to go to
New England," she prepared to follow. Born about
the year 1600, during the time she lived in Boston —
a little less than four years — Anne Hutchinson was
a woman in the full vigor of life. She had a strong
religious instinct, which caused her to verge closely on
the enthusiast, and a remarkably well-developed controversial talent. But above all else Anne Hutchinson, though devoid of attractiveness of person, was
wonderfully endowed with the indescribable quality
known as magnetism, — that subtle power by which
certain human beings — themselves not knowing how
they do it — irresistibly attract others, and infuse them
with their own individuality. Among the many well-
known phases of emotional religion, that of direct intercourse with the Almighty has not been the least
uncommon ; and, if Mistress Hutchinson did not actually pretend to this, she verged dangerously near it.
She certainly in moments of deep spiritual enthusiasm
felt movements which she professed to regard as direct
divine revelations. Not that she actually claimed to
be inspired, or to speak as one prophesying ; but at
intervals she professed to feel that the Spirit of God
was upon her, and then she was not as her ordinary
self, or as other women. The exact line between this
and inspiration is one not easy to draw ; yet probably

some shadowy line did exist in her mind. However
this may be, the mere suggestion of such a thing was
enough with the early Massachusetts divines. The
doctrine of an inward light was to them peculiarly
hateful, and they regarded such a light rather as a
gleam of hell fire than as a heaven-born beam. That
they themselves were not in any way inspired was a
cardinal point in their religious faith.[1] They had for
their guide the written Word; and that only. For
any one to claim to have more, — to be in direct spiritual communication with the Almighty, — was to assert a superiority in what was the very soul of their
calling. They were "unworthy prophets" of the
Lord; and here was one who claimed to be more
nearly than they in the Master's confidence. But the
God they worshipped was that same Jehovah with
whom direct and personal intercourse had been held
by the prophets of old. He was not a metaphysical
abstraction. Freely pictured in glass and on canvas,
the awe with which a finer sense has since surrounded
Him did not surround Him then. Always present,
always in that human form in which He revealed himself to Moses, his face might well be seen at any
moment, even as his voice was often heard and his
hand felt. But to them, his servants, He had given
only his Scriptures through which to ascertain his
will. When, therefore, Mistress Hutchinson claimed,
through a process of introspection, to evolve a know-

---

[1] This was explicitly set forth in the Westminster Confession of
1643: "The whole Council of God concerning all things necessary
for his own Glory, Men's Salvation, Faith and Life, is either expressly
set down in Scripture, or by good and necessary Consequence may be
deduced from Scripture: Unto which nothing at any time is to be
added, whether by new Revelations of the Spirit, or Traditions of
Men." See, also, Ellis, *The Puritan Age in Massachusetts*, 124–166.

ledge of the divine will from her own inner conscious-
ness, she not only, in the eyes of the ministers, began
to share in the blasphemies of Knipperdolling and
John of Leyden, but she did so through the assertion
of a most impudent and irritating superiority.　If she
did not directly say it, her every act was a repetition
of the phrase, " I am holier than thou! "

Thus Mrs. Hutchinson's whole course in Massachusetts was a direct and insulting challenge to the body
of the clergy.　Bad enough in itself from their point
of view, it was aggravated by the feminine ingenuity
with which she made herself disagreeable.　She belonged to a type of her sex for the production of
which New England has since achieved a considerable
notoriety.　She seems to have been essentially transcendental.　She might perhaps not inaptly be termed
the great prototype of that misty school.　She knew
much; but she talked out of all proportion to her
knowledge.　She had thought a good deal, and by
no means clearly; having not infrequently mistaken
words for ideas, as persons with more inclination than
aptitude for controversy are wont to do.　To confute
her was not easy, for her disputation was involved in
a mist of language which gave the vagueness of a
shadow to whatever she might be supposed to assert.
Nevertheless, here was this eloquent mystic lifting up
her voice under the very eaves of the sanctuary, and
throwing the subtle charm of her magnetism over the
hearts of God's people.

Boston was in 1637 the village capital of an infant
colony.　It was a very small place, — so small that
when Josselyn visited it, a year later, he spoke of it as
containing not above twenty or thirty houses.　In this
he must have been mistaken, as a stranger often is, in

roughly estimating the size of a town new to him; for, even then, Boston must have numbered about two thousand inhabitants of all ages.[1]   The original huts and cabins, of rough-hewn logs, were fast giving place to a better class of frame houses, the Elizabethan fronts and overhanging gables of which looked out on crooked, unpaved lanes, something more than cow-paths, but not yet streets.   No building in the town was eight years old, and the new brick house of Mr. Coddington, the treasurer of the province, was the only one of the kind.   It was a. hard-working little community; but, when work was done, only religion remained upon which social and intellectual cravings could expend themselves.   There were no newspapers, — no dances, parties, concerts, theatres or libraries. They had the Sabbath services, followed by the church-meetings, and the Thursday lectures.   The wedding was a civil service; the funeral a sombre observance.[2] In a state of society such as this it was inevitable that the love of excitement, common to all mankind, should take a morbid shape.   There must be religious sensations, seeing there could be no other; and the place

[1] It is difficult to see how, with the strict church attendance then exacted, so large a population could have been accommodated in one meeting-house.   Yet in 1638 Boston was called upon to furnish twenty-six men for the Pequot War, out of a total levy of one hundred and sixty.   The population of Massachusetts in 1637 could not well have been less than twelve thousand. (See *supra*, 340, n.)   It was probably more than that.   If the levy was proportional, it would indicate for Boston a population of at least one thousand nine hundred and fifty.

[2] "Marriages are solemnized and done by the Magistrates, and not by the Ministers.   At burials, nothing is read, nor any funeral Sermon made, but all the neighborhood, or a good company of them, come together by tolling of the bell, and carry the dead solemnly to his grave, and there stand by him while he is buried.   The ministers are not commonly present." Lechford, *Plain Dealing*, 94.

was so small that a moderate-sized sensation absorbed
it wholly.   Though the stage was far from large, Mrs.
Hutchinson found it admirably prepared for her; the
audience craved excitement, every eye was upon her,
her voice filled the theatre.

During her earlier life in Boston she seems to have
acquired a well-deserved popularity by her considerate
spirit and skill as a nurse and adviser in cases of child-
birth, and ailments peculiar to her sex.   She was evidently gentle, and by nature sympathetic.   Then she
began to meddle with theology, to which, from the
first, she had shown herself much inclined.   Even on
her voyage her utterances had excited doubts as to her
orthodoxy in the mind of the Rev. Zachariah Symmes, a
devout man who had come with her; and his warnings
to the magistrates for a time delayed her admission to
the church.   But admitted she was at last, and about
two years later she began to make her presence felt.
Her husband's house stood in what might be called
the fashionable quarter of the town, — a good stone's
throw to the south of the church and behind it, not far
from the town spring, and nearly opposite the house
of Governor Winthrop.[1]   Here, and at the homes of
certain of her acquaintances, she presently began to
hold a series of exclusively female gatherings, and
later of gatherings composed of both sexes.   At the
earlier of these she herself presided, and in all she was
the leading spirit.   These meetings were numerously
attended, and at those held exclusively for women,
forty, sixty, and even eighty would be present.   The
original idea was to recapitulate, for the benefit of

---

[1] It occupied the Old Corner Bookstore lot, now so called, on Wash-
ington and School streets, extending up the latter to the present City
Hall enclosure.   *Memorial History of Boston*, i. 174, n., 579, n.

such as had been unable to attend Sabbath services,
the substance of the recent discourses of the clergy,
and more particularly of Cotton.   Small private gatherings of a similar character had been not uncommon
ever since the beginning of the settlement; but, though
the idea was not new with Mrs. Hutchinson, she developed it.   Under her inspiration the germ grew
rapidly ; or, as she might herself have said, it came
up in a night, even as the gourd came up which God
prepared for Jonah.   The woman was in fact a born
social leader.   Her meetings were the events of a primitive season.

At first the elders and magistrates favored them
and smiled upon her.   It looked like an awakening;
souls were being drawn to Christ.   It soon became
what would now be known as a revival.   But Anne
Hutchinson was light-headed as well as voluble.   She
had an unruly tongue as well as an insatiable ambition,
and, not long contenting herself with the mere repetition of sermons, she began to comment upon them, to
interpret and to criticise.   In other words, she set up
as a preacher on her own account.   The women were
not accustomed to hear one of their own sex "exercise," and she was popular among them ; so they
flocked to her more and more.   A community living
in a state of religious exaltation is of course predis-
posed to mental epidemics.   Accordingly, to the utter
dismay of the clergy and the old magistrates, every one
near enough to feel her influence was soon running
after the new light.   "It was a wonder," wrote Winthrop, "upon what a sudden the whole church of Boston (some few excepted) were become her new con-
verts, and many also out of the church, and of other
churches also ; yea ! many profane persons became of

her opinion." And in another place he asserts that " she had more resort to her for counsell about matter of conscience than any minister (I might say all the elders) in the country." To the same effect the Rev. Thomas Weld declared that she " had some of all sorts and quality in all places to defend and patronize " her opinions ; " some of the magistrates, some gentlemen, some scholars and men of learning, some burgesses of our General Court, some of our captains and soldiers, some chief men in towns, and some men eminent for religion, parts and wit." Then Mrs. Hutchinson's head turned. She had a calling to be a religious enthusiast, and it would seem that visions of political greatness also began to float before her. In imagination she saw her husband seated in the chair of Winthrop and of Vane, with herself by his side, " a prophetess, raised up of God for some great work now at hand, as the calling of the Jews."

Unfortunately for Mistress Hutchinson, what has since been known as " the emancipation of woman " had not in the first half of the seventeenth century been formulated among political issues, and the more conservative soon began to look upon her much as Governor Winthrop subsequently looked on crazy Mistress Ann Hopkins, — " a godly young woman and of special parts," who had lost her understanding " by occasion of her giving herself wholly to reading and writing ; " whereas, " if she had attended her household affairs, and such things as belong to women, and not gone out of her way and calling to meddle in such things as are proper for men, whose minds are stronger, etc., she had kept her wits, and might have improved them usefully and honorably in the place God had set her."

But at first Mrs. Hutchinson was encouraged. In modern language, she was even fashionable ; her *sé-ances* were in vogue. Not only did the thoughtful and the half-crazed, but the very parasites flocked to them. Side by side with young Harry Vane were Richard Gridley, " an honest, poore man, but very apt to meddle in publike affaires, beyond his calling or skill," and canny Jane Hawkins, " notorious for familiarity with the Devil." [1] Indeed, there have not come down to us from those times many touches of nature more life-like than Wheelwright's description of the grounds of " goodwife Hawkins's " Antinomianism. The Rev. Thomas Weld had accused her, in the language just quoted, of being a witch ; whereupon Wheelwright very sensibly replied that she was —

" A poore, silly woman, yet having so much wit as, perceiving Mrs. Hutchinson ambitious of proselytes, to supply her wants she attended on her weekly lecture (as it is called), where, when Mrs. Hutchinson broached any new doctrine, she would be the first would taste of it : And being demanded whether it were not clear to her, though she understood it not, yet would say, *Oh yes, very clear.* By which means she got, through Mrs. Hutchinson's affection to her, some good victuals, insomuch that some said she followed Christ for loaves. Now seeing those things were so, me thinks our Author need not have been so rigid in his opinion of her . . . when, as it appears, she complied with her patroness, not so much out of love to her positions as possets, — being guilty, I think, of no other sorcery, unless it were conjuring the spirit of Error into a Cordial." [2]

[1] Weld, *Short Story*, 31. The unfortunate Jane Hawkins' proclivities to the Evil One gave Governor Winthrop much trouble ; for " she grew into great suspicion to be a witch " (Winthrop, i. *263). Where no other sources of information are cited, Winthrop's *History*, and Weld's *Short Story* are the authorities for the narrative.

[2] Bell, *John Wheelwright*, 198.

For the severe old theocrats it was a serious matter to have a school of criticism — a *vivâ voce* weekly religious review, as it were — thus spring into life, under the very eaves of the meeting-house. They had been accustomed to have their teachings accepted as oracles ; but those teachings now no longer passed unchallenged, nor were the voices of the critics hushed even at the gates of the tabernacle. On the contrary both Mrs. Hutchinson and her disciples audaciously carried their war into Africa. She herself publicly left the congregation when the pastor, Wilson, rose to preach. Others followed her example, contemptuously turning their backs on their ministers ; while it was plaintively observed that " the most of them were women, and they pretended many excuses for their going out, which it was not easy to convince of falsehood in them, or of their contempt " of the pastor.[1] Yet others boldly and in open meeting challenged the minister's words almost before they had passed his lips. So that the Rev. Thomas Weld was driven lugubriously to exclaim, with a degree of feeling which speaks volumes as to his own individual experiences in that kind, —

" Now, after our sermons were ended at our public lectures, you might have seen half a dozen pistols discharged at the face of the preacher (I mean) so many objections made by the opinionists in the open assembly against our doctrine delivered, if it suited not their new fancies, to the marvellous weakening of holy truths delivered. . . . Now the faithful ministers of Christ must have dung cast on their faces, and be no better than legal preachers, Baal's priests, Popish factors, Scribes, Pharisees, and opposers of Christ himself ! Now they must be pointed at, as it were with the finger, and reproached by name."

[1] Cotton, *Way Cleared*, 61.

The cup was indeed a bitter one. Yet, bitter at best, it was administered with a perverse ingenuity which distilled it to gall. Mistress Hutchinson professed what was called, in the theological parlance of the time, the Covenant of Grace, as distinguished from the Covenant of Works. Without going into any detailed explanation of long-forgotten seventeenth century theology, it is sufficient for present purposes to say that the relations of the Creator with mankind seem in it to have been largely based on the analogy of a human landlord and tenant. To mankind the earth had been given; not outright, but on certain terms and conditions, all of which were expressed in the Hebrew Bible. These terms, as primarily set forth, had been violated by Adam, and the original covenant between Creator and created, known as the Covenant of Works, had then ceased to be binding, **and been** terminated by one party to it. Under this **covenant** all of the seed of Adam would have been **saved, and en**joyed after mundane death an eternity **of heavenly** life. When the original Covenant of **Works was** thus cancelled, the Creator, instead of, so to **speak**, ejecting and destroying Adam, made, out of a spirit of pure mercy, a new covenant with him and his seed, under which not all of the sons of man would be saved, but only such of them as the Creator might see fit to spare, — the Lord's elect. And this was known as the Covenant of Grace.[1]

---

[1] "To open and clear this matter the following *Positions* may be laid down.

1. "*It has pleased God all along from the beginning of the World to transact with man in a Covenant way.* This is an effect of God's good pleasure towards him. God could be no debtor to his creature, till he made himself so by his own *promise.* He might, if he had so pleas'd, stood upon his Sovereignty, and challenged the Obedience

Originally, therefore, for one to be under a Covenant of Works meant to be of those left under the
original and violated compact, and consequently not
included among those admitted to the benefits of the
new compact, or Covenant of Grace. In other words,
those under a Covenant of Works were the unregenerate seed of Adam, — not the Lord's elect; those
under a Covenant of Grace were the regenerate seed.
The whole question went back to the third chapter of
the book of Genesis, — the garden, the serpent, original sin and the fall of man.

The theory of the two covenants, starting from this
far-away origin, underwent during the fierce religious
controversies of the reformation an outward change at

from him that was due to him, without engaging any reward for it.
But to shew his *goodness* and bounty to man, he has been pleas'd to
bind himself to him by Covenant.

2. "*GOD never has made but two Covenants with man:* which are
ordinarily distinguish'd into, the *Covenant of Works,* and the *Covenant
of Grace.* The Covenant of Works, was that which God made with
Adam in a state of Innocence; in which all *his seed* were comprehended with him: and under which, he as their *Head* stood a pro-
bationer for life, upon the condition of perfect obedience. Of this
Covenant we have an account in many places of Scripture. The
Covenant of Grace is with *man fallen:* the first revelation whereof was
made presently after God had past sentence upon him; and the first
account we have of it is in that *promise,* Gen. 3. 15. And was more
and more *explain'd* as God saw fit at *divers times,* and in *divers ways*
to the *fathers* by the *Prophets:* but especially to *Abraham* and the
Church of *Israel;* as the writings of the *Prophets* fully shew." Williams, *Essay to Prove the Interest of the Children of Believers in the
Covenant* (1727), 5–6.

Winthrop says that Mrs. Hutchinson " brought over with her two
dangerous errors: 1. That the person of the Holy Ghost dwells in a
justified person. 2. That no sanctification can help to evidence to us
our justification. From these two grew many branches; as, 1, Our
union with the Holy Ghost, so as a Christian remains dead to every
spiritual action, and hath no gifts nor graces, other than such as are
in hypocrites, nor any other sanctification but the Holy Ghost himself." (i. *200.) This is Winthrop's first mention of Mrs. Hutchinson.

the hands of Luther. It was, indeed, a necessary part
of the reaction against mediæval Romanism that heart-
piety and spiritual exaltation, or justification by faith
as it was termed, should be opposed to the tests of
confession, penance, pilgrimages, legacies to the church,
masses, Ave Marias, etc., all constituting justification
by works. In the theological parlance of the sixteenth
and seventeenth centuries, therefore, neither grace nor
works, as applied to the two covenants, signified what
they signified in the beginning, or what they signify
now.   Grace was no longer an act of supreme mercy,
as at first, nor was it conscientious carriage in life, as
now ; but it implied a certain vague and mystic exaltation and serenity of soul arising from the conscious-
ness of a Heaven-directed heart, — a serenity not to
be attained by the most exact observance of the for-
malities of religion ; the word works, on the other
hand, did not imply, as now it would, the idea of a
life devoted to good deeds, as distinguished from one
of mere empty professions, but it meant simply a rigid
and exact compliance with the forms of pietism, — its
fastings, its prayers, its sanctimoniousness and harsh
discipline, — in a word, with all external observances
involving continuous mortification of soul as well as
body.[1] Viewed from a modern point of view the seventeenth century Covenant of Grace was as mystic, indefinable and delusive as its Covenant of Works was
harsh, material and repulsive.

Nevertheless, there the two covenants were, the very
corner-stones of theology, — recorded and set forth
from the beginning of the world, accepted by all. The
single question was as to the elect, — which among

[1] This difficult subject is fully discussed by Dr. G. E. Ellis in his
Puritan Age in Massachusetts, 300–362.

the living seed of Adam were, through the Covenant
of Grace, to enjoy life everlasting? — and which, walking under the Covenant of Works, were damned to an
eternity of Hell fire? When, dead in the flesh, the im-
mortal soul of the believer appeared before God's judgment seat, how justify the life which had been lived?
What pleas for salvation would be listened to? And
one class of religionists insisted that a record of faithfully observed rules of conduct, a careful regard for
the decalogue, alms, fasts, Sabbath attendance, — all
this was but to claim the advantage of the abrogated
Covenant of Works. Hell yawned for such. On the
other hand was infinite faith, a love of Christ un-
limited, an inward sweetness and light, — and these,
in their case they proclaimed, meant a justification
through Grace.

The only certain elements in the awful problem were
death and the judgment. The situation, accordingly,
is not one conceivable now; but it was very real among
those dwelling in Massachusetts in 1636, when Mistress
Anne Hutchinson proceeded to draw the line. With
her it may be said to have been a question of afflatus,
for she contended that the divine spirit dwelt in every
true believer; but that the fact of any single person
— even though such person might be a minister of the
gospel, of extraordinary gifts — being a true believer,
could not with any certainty be inferred either from a
demeanor of sanctity or from conduct in life. Mrs.
Hutchinson's Covenant of Grace is, perhaps, most
nearly expressed in modern religious cant as a " condition of true inwardness." But with her it further
implied the actual indwelling of the Spirit of the
Lord. He in whom that Spirit dwelt was of the elect.
He in whom it did not dwell might be a very worthy

man, and what we would call a good conventional minister; but God's seal was not on his lips.

The conclusion to be drawn from all this was painfully apparent. To say that a grave divine was under a Covenant of Works was a gentle paraphrase for calling him a "whited sepulchre." This certainly was bold enough; but Mrs. Hutchinson did not stop here. With great cunningness of aggravation — with an almost unsurpassed faculty of making herself innocently offensive — she then proceeded, not to designate particular divines as being under a Covenant of Works, but to single out two of their whole order as walking in a Covenant of Grace. These two were John Cotton, and, after his arrival, John Wheelwright. The others were necessarily left to make the best of an obvious inference.

Looked at even after the lapse of two centuries and a half, and in the cold perspective of history, it must be conceded that this was more than the meekest of human flesh could be expected quietly to endure; but the early clergy were not conspicuous for meekness. Nor had they come to New England with this end in view. On the contrary, they had come expecting God's people to be there ruled by God's Word; and that Word God's ministers were to interpret. And now, on the very threshold of this theocracy, the sanctity of His mouthpiece was disputed. They loved controversy dearly; but this was no case for controversy. God's kingdom was threatened from within; the serpent was among them. The head of the serpent must be crushed. So they sternly girded themselves for the fray: and opposed to them was one woman only; but her tongue was as a sword, and she had her sex for a shield.

CHAPTER III.

A QUARREL IN A VESTRY.

It was not until it reached its later stages that what has passed into New England's history as the Antinomian controversy involved the whole province of Massachusetts. At first it was confined to the church in Boston, — a family affair, so to speak. Mrs. Hutchinson, like many other women before and since, did not fancy her minister. He failed to appeal to her. The cause of her dislike is not known. Most probably it lay upon the surface and was of a personal character; for the Rev. John Wilson, though doubtless in his way a worthy, well-intentioned man of the commonplace, conventional kind, had about him little that was either sympathetic or attractive. Harsh in feature and thick of utterance,[1] he was coarse of fibre, — hard, matter-of-fact, unimaginative. In his home and church life he is reputed to have been a not unkindly man, and a " devoted friend and helper to those who needed his love and care;" while in his pulpit he was more remarkable for his strength of faith and zeal for ordinances than for his talents as a preacher. On the other hand, he was by nature stern, unrelenting, bigoted; a man " than whom orthodoxy in New England had no champion more cruel and more ungenerous." [2] Of his conduct and bearing in the Antinomian con-

[1] Johnson, *Wonder-Working Providence*, 40.
[2] J. A. Doyle, *English in America: The Puritan Colonies*, i. 419.

troversy of 1637 much will need to be said in these
pages, while in the Baptist persecution of twenty years
later his zeal and passion led him to revile and even
strike prisoners being led away from the judgment
seat;[1] and, in 1659, when the two Quakers, William
Robinson and Marmaduke Stevenson, were hanged on
Boston Common, the aged pastor of the First Church
not only denounced them fiercely from his pulpit, but
he even railed at them from the foot of the gallows.[2]

[1] " Upon the pronouncing of [my sentence] as I went from the Bar,
I exprest myself in these words : ' I blesse God I am counted worthy to
suffer for the name of Iesus ; ' whereupon Iohn Wilson (their Pastor as
they call him) strook me before the Iudgment Seat, and cursed me,
saying, ' The Curse of God, or Iesus, goe with thee ; ' so we were carried to the Prison.'' Letter from Obadiah Holmes in *Ill Newes from
New England*, IV. *Mass. Hist. Soc. Coll.* ii. 47.

[2] With these two was Mary Dyer, who will be often referred to in
this narrative. She was reprieved, and, when the others were hanged,
sat on the steps of the scaffold. The story is most characteristic of
the time and people under discussion, but can only be told in the
quaint language of the original chronicle : —

" Then Mary Dyar was called, and your Governour said to her, to
this effect, — Mary Dyar, you shall go to the place whence you came,
and from thence to the place of Execution, and be hanged there until
you are Dead : — To which she replied, The Will of the Lord be
done. — Then your Governour said, Take her away, Marshal : She
Answered, Yea, joyfully shall I go. — So she was brought to the
House of Correction again, and there continued, with her other two
Friends, in Prison, till the 27th of the same Month ; . . . And on the
27th of the 8th Month, aforesaid, ye caus'd the Drums to beat, to
gather your Soldiers together for the Execution ; and after your Worship was ended, your Drums beat again, and your Captain, James Oliver, came with his Band of Men, and the Marshal, and some others,
to the Prison, and the Doors were opened, and your Marshal and Jay-
lor call'd for W. Robinson and M. Stevenson, and had them out of the
Prison, and Mary Dyar out of the House of Correction, . . . and your
Captain, with his Band of Men, led them the back way (it seems you
were afraid of the fore-way, lest it should affect the People too much)
to the Place of Execution, and caused the Drums to beat, when they
attempted to speak (hard Work) and plac'd them near the Drums, for
that purpose, that when they spake, the People might not hear them,

In such a man as this, however useful he might be
for much of the coarser though necessary work of life,
there was little to attract a person of delicate percep-

who in great Multitudes flock'd about them. . . . I say, your Captain
caused his Drums to Beat, when they sought to speak ; and his Drums
he would not cease beating, tho' they spake to him, whilst they were
speaking. (A Barbarous Inhumanity never heard of before in the
English Nation, to be used to suffering People.) And as he led them
to the place of Execution, your old bloody Priest, Wilson, your High-
Priest of Boston (who was so old in Blood, that he would have had
Samuel Gorton, and those with him, long ago to be put to Death, for
their Differing in Religion ; and when but one Vote parted it, was so
Mad, that he openly inveighed against them who did it, saying in the
Pulpit, Because thou hast let go the Man, whom I have appointed to
Destruction, Thy Life shall go for his Life, and thy People for his
People ; Preaching from that Text, who said, — He would carry Fire
in one Hand, and Faggots in the other, to Burn all the Quakers in
the World. — Who having some of those Peoples Books in his Hand,
as they were burning the Books of Friends by your Order, threw them
in the Fire, saying, — From the Devil they came, (Blasphemous
Wretch !) and to the Devil let them go. — He who said to ye, when
ye sat on the Blood of these Men, — Hang them,[1] or else (drawing
his Finger athwart his Throat, so making Signs for it to be cut, if ye
did it not) I say, this your bloody old High-Priest, with others of his
Brethren in Iniquity, and in persecuting the Just, met them in your
Train-Field ; and, instead of having a sense upon him suitable to such
an Occasion, and as is usual with Men of any Tenderness, he fell a
Taunting at W. Robinson, and shaking his Hand in a light Scoffing
manner, said, — Shall such Jacks as you come in before Authority
with your Hats on ? — with many other taunting words.   To which
W. Robinson replied, — Mind you, mind you, It is for the not putting
off the Hat, we are put to Death. — And when W. Robinson went
cheerfully up the Ladder, to the topmost round above the Gallows,
and spake to the People, — That they suffered not as evil Doers, but
as those who testified and manifested the Truth, and that this was the
Day of their Visitation, and therefore desired them to mind the Light

---

[1] " This is that Priest Wilson, whom C. Mather, in his late History of New England, so much commends, and with his Brother in Iniquity, John Norton (of whom
more hereafter) ranks with John Cotton (a Man of a better Spirit, in his Day) under the Title of Reverend and Renowned Ministers of the Gospel, comparing him
to David and John the Apostle ; and calls, That Great Saint and Worthy Man, that
was such an irreverent, unworthy and blood-thirsty Persecutor of the People of
God : But, let him know, That Sinners are no Saints ; nor, no Murtherer hath Eternal Life abiding in him, 1 John 3. 15."

tion like Mistress Hutchinson, — nay, more, there
must have been in him much that was absolutely repulsive to her. The antipathy clearly was not on the
pastor's side. Indeed, at first, in his heavy, mannish
way, he seems to have been disposed to patronize his
female parishioner, so much his intellectual superior.
He encouraged her meetings, manifesting his good-
will whenever occasion offered, and bearing cheerful
witness to the ways of free grace. He was not a man
to entertain a secret, instinctive distrust; for, though
compounded of a clay less fine, he was by nature
frank, open and outspoken. Presently his suspicions
were aroused. He was human, too, and undoubtedly
he began to feel jealous. To the pastor, this constant and public adulation of the teacher could not be
altogether grateful. Indeed, it was plainly meant to
be otherwise than grateful to him. To bear and for-
bear was not in the man's nature; so by degrees he
passed from open approval to silent disapproval, and
then it was not long before he began to speak out.
So far as his side of the case was concerned, this did

that was in them, the Light of Christ, of which he Testified, and was
now going to Seal it with his Blood. — This old Priest in much Wicked-
ness said, — Hold thy Tongue, be silent, Thou art going to Dye with
a Lye in thy Mouth. . . . So, being come to the place of Execution,
Hand in Hand, all three of them, as to a Wedding day, with great
cheerfulness of Heart; and having taken leave of each other, with
the dear Embraces of one another, in the Love of the Lord, your Exe-
cutioner put W. Robinson to Death, and after him M. Stevenson . . .
and, to make up all, when they were thus Martyr'd by your Order,
your said Priest, Wilson, made a Ballad of those whom ye had Martyr'd. . . . Three also of Priest Wilson's Grand-Children died within a
short time after ye had put these two Servants of the Lord to Death,
as something upon his Head, who cared not how he bereaved the Mother, of her Son, and the Children, of their Father, and the Wife, of
her Husband. The Judgment of the Lord in . . . which, is to be taken
Notice of." *New England Judged* (1661,) pp. 122–5, 126, 136.

not mend matters ; for as an antagonist — in what might be called the socio-parochial fence of that day — John Wilson was wholly at the mercy of Anne Hutchinson. She was as quick as he was clumsy, and his grave censure was met with a contempt which was at once ingenious and studied. Presently she found that he stood in her way. In Boston there was but one church ; and clearly that church was not large enough for both. Cotton was Mrs. Hutchinson's favorite preacher. At his feet she had sat at home; when he came to New England she soon followed. Next to Cotton's, she set most store on the teachings of her husband's kinsman, Wheelwright ; and when Wheelwright landed in Boston her influence was at its height.

The church was already split into factions. On the one side was the pastor, supported by Winthrop — then deputy — and a few others ; on the other side was Mrs. Hutchinson, carrying with her the whole body of the members, with the governor, Vane, at their head. The teacher, Cotton, also notoriously inclined to her. The young sap was moving in the tree, and Boston, at least, was ripe for revolt against the old order of men and of things ; but hostilities had not yet begun.

The coming of Wheelwright brought on a crisis. It was Mrs. Hutchinson, doubtless, who now conceived the idea — if indeed she had not already for some time been entertaining it — of having Wheelwright installed as an assistant teacher by Cotton's side. This could not, of course, be agreeable to Wilson, who for some time must have had cause to realize that his own religious influence was on the wane ; just as he had seen the political influence of his life-long friend and patron, Winthrop, wane before. He and his friends accordingly, if they did not actually oppose the suggestion, received it with coldness. Then Mrs. Hutchinson seems to have begun hostilities. She struck; and she struck none the less hard because the blow was given in a woman's way. She intimated that the pastor of the church was, after all, not an able minister of the New Testament; he was not sealed with the spirit; he was under a Covenant of Works. The conflict now began to rage fiercely all through the little town. Wilson was struggling for what to him was worth more than life, — a minister, he was struggling to sustain himself in his pulpit and before his people. With him was Winthrop. Opposed to him was all Boston. Indeed, the members of his parish seem even now to have been as men infatuated; they acted as those might act who were subject to the wiles of a sorceress.

Meanwhile, outside of Boston all was comparatively quiet. The contagion of the new opinions had, indeed, spread to Roxbury and a few other of the neighboring towns, church-members of which had doubtless attended Mrs. Hutchinson's gatherings; but, as a whole, the rest of the province pursued the even tenor of its way, though the air was full of rumors as to the strange uproar going on in Boston, — the new ideas advanced there, the dissensions in the church, the quarrel between Mr. Wilson and his people, the dubious attitude of Cotton. The sympathies of the other ministers were wholly with Wilson. Not only was he a member of their order of the regular, conventional type, but he was receiving harsh treatment; for the course of Mrs. Hutchinson and those who followed her was as unprovoked and cruel as it was ingenious and feminine.

Presently, therefore, the ministers of the outlying towns determined to intervene, in their brother's behalf, and endeavor to restore peace to his distracted church.   A meeting of the General Court was to take place in October, and it was arranged that the ministers should then come to Boston and hold a conference on these matters among themselves and with the members of the Court.   They did so Tuesday, the 25th, and, Cotton and Wheelwright both taking part with the rest, some progress into the incomprehensible was made.   They agreed on the point of sanctification, " so as they all did hold that sanctification did help to evidence justification ; " but they were not all of a mind as to the "indwelling of the person of the Holy Ghost ; " and none of the ministers were disposed to go the length of asserting " a union of the person of the Holy Ghost, so as to amount to a personal union ; " though it was understood that Mrs. Hutchinson and Governor Vane held even this advanced tenet.   However unintelligible the discussion might be in other respects, one thing was clear, — if the last proposition was admitted, inspiration followed.   The way was open for the appearance of a brood of God's prophets in New England.

The conference resulted in nothing, and the open move, already referred to, was made in favor of Wheelwright as an assistant teacher.   This had already been proposed at the meeting of the Boston church held after the services of the previous Sabbath ; and now on Sunday, the 30th, five days after the conference of the clergy, the proposal was brought up for final action.   The meeting was one of far more than ordinary interest, for it was felt that something decisive was at hand ; and presently, when the ser-

vices were ended, the calling of Wheelwright was formally propounded. It is easy to imagine the silence
which for a brief space prevailed in the crowded meeting-house. It was at last broken by Winthrop, who
rose and said that he could not give his assent to the
thing proposed. He spoke with much feeling, and
referred to the fact that the church was already well
provided with able ministers, "whose spirits they
knew, and whose labors God had blessed in much love
and sweet peace;" while he objected to Wheelwright, as being a man "whose spirit they knew not,
and one who seemed to dissent in judgment." He
then proceeded to specify certain questionable doctrines supposed to be entertained by the new candidate, having reference to a distinction between "creatures" and "believers," and the relations of either, or
both, with the Holy Ghost. Vane immediately followed on the other side, and "marvelled" at the point
just made; quoting the high authority of Cotton in
support of the doctrine in question. This reference
naturally brought Cotton to his feet, who proceeded
to demur and define; and in closing called upon
Wheelwright to explain himself on a few controverted
points of theology. This the latter then proceeded
to do. When he had finished, Winthrop closed the
debate, for the time being, by declaring that, although
he personally felt the utmost respect for Mr. Wheelwright, yet he could not consent to choose him an
associate teacher, "seeing he was apt to raise doubtful
disputations."

The matter was taken up again the next day. In
the little village community, anything which affected
the church affected every member of it. The proposal
to make Mr. Wheelwright an associate teacher, and

the discussion to which it had given rise, had all that
Sunday evening and the next morning been the one
subject talked about in every household and at each
street corner.   A good deal of feeling was evinced
also over the position taken by Winthrop ; and more
yet at the warmth with which he had maintained it.
For the last, when the debate was renewed, he made
an ample apology.   He then went on to state at considerable length his views upon certain " words and
phrases, which were of human invention, and tended
to doubtful disputation rather than to edification."
When he had finished, a profound silence seems to
have pervaded the grave, well-ordered assembly.   No
one rose to reply to him, or to continue the discussion ; and here the whole matter was allowed to drop.
No factious spirit was shown.   According to the rule
of the Boston church, it was sufficient that grave
opposition had been expressed.   The selection of
Wheelwright was urged no further.

But Wheelwright was too active and able a man to
remain long without a call, and a large and very influential'portion of the Boston church was in close
sympathy with him.   Among these were Coddington,
Hutchinson, Hough and others, who held the large
allotments, which have been referred to, at the Mount.
Those dwelling in that region, though few in number,
had for some time been complaining of the hardships
their remote and isolated position imposed upon them.
They were mainly poor men with families.   Ten or
twelve miles from the meeting-house, this distance
they had to traverse each Sabbath, or else fail to par-
ticipate in worship.   Accordingly the gathering of a
new church at the Mount had been for some time
under discussion.   The chief objection was that such

action would apparently defeat the very end for which
Boston had received " enlargement," — the upholding
of the town and the original church, — for the loss of
so many leading members of both, as would move
away if a new society was gathered, could not but be
severely felt.   To meet this objection it had been arranged in the September previous that those dwelling
at the Mount should pay a yearly town and church
rate to Boston of sixpence an acre for such lands as
lay within a mile of the water, and threepence an acre
for such as lay inland.   It was a species of non-resi-
dent commutation tax.   This arrangement imposed in
turn on the Boston church a well-understood obligation to make adequate provision for the spiritual well-
fare of those thus tributary to it.   In the days of
sparse settlement the situation could not but occur,
and the natural way of meeting it was to establish
branch churches, or " chappels of ease," as they were
termed in the English church, for the accommodation
of the outlying precincts.[1]   Some elder, or gifted
brother, was wont to hold forth, or to prophesy, as it
was phrased, at these each ordinary Sabbath, while
the sacrament was administered at stated periods in
the mother church.

As soon as Winthrop's dissent had put a final stop
to the plan of choosing Wheelwright associate teacher,
the friends of the latter from the Mount had recourse
to this plan.   At the very meeting at which Winthrop insisted on his objection, the records of the
First Church show that " Our brother, Mr. John
Wheelwright, was granted unto for the preparing for
a church gathering at Mount Woollystone, upon a
petition from some of them that were resident there."

[1] III. *Mass. Hist. Coll.* iii. 75.

This vote was passed on the 30th of October. On the 20th of February following, an allotment of two hundred and fifty acres of land at the Mount was made to the new pastor, to be located "where may be most convenient, without prejudice to setting up a towne there." Wheelwright seems to have ministered faithfully and acceptably to those settled immediately beyond the Neponset, during a period of almost exactly one year.

Chosen to his ministry, if such it might be called, in what are now the earlier days of November, the new pastor may, during the winter's inclemency, have ministered at the homes of his little congregation, and the following spring and summer preached "abroad under a tree," like Phillips and Wilson at Charlestown seven years before ; but in all probability during the succeeding summer of 1637, for John Wheelwright and under his supervision, the rude meeting-house was built, which afterwards stood for years in Braintree "over the old Bridge" and just south of it, on the rising ground where the road, or trail rather as it then was, between Boston and Plymouth crossed the little streamlet subsequently known as the town brook.[1]

[1] Wilson, 250th *Commemorative Services*, 26, 41 ; *Braintree Records*, 2, 9 ; Pattee, *Old Braintree and Quincy*, 228 ; Lunt, 200th *Anniversary Discourses*, 121-2 ; Adams, *Address in Braintree* (1858), 74.

CHAPTER IV.

A PROVINCE IN A TURMOIL.

THE settlement of Wheelwright at the Mount did
not serve to restore theological tranquillity either to
the Boston church or to the province. On the contrary, the action of the ministers at their October conference, and the sympathy they had then shown for
their brother Wilson, only stimulated Mrs. Hutchinson.
Her tongue was more active than ever, and her followers more noisily aggressive. So far from being
overawed by authority, she met authority with what
sounded very like defiance ; for now she declared that
his brethren were no better than Wilson. None of
them were sealed ; none of them were able ministers
of the New Testament. They, as well as he, were all
under a Covenant of Works ; they were Legalists, to
a man.

During the month of November, 1636, a long controversy was carried on between Vane and Winthrop,
arising out of the discussion at the time of Wheelwright's proposed appointment. Vane, it has been
seen, went with Mrs. Hutchinson the full length of
maintaining " a personal union with the Holy Ghost."
He was not content with Cotton's belief in " the indwelling of the person of the Holy Ghost in a believer." He was apparently disposed .to contend that
a believer, truly justified, was himself the Holy Ghost.
The discussion turned on a metaphysical abstraction,

which the disputants sought to solve by quoting at
each other the English rendering of Hebrew or Greek
texts, and scraps of Patristic learning. Conducted
in writing "for the peace sake of the church, which
all were tender of," it covered the first "three hundred years after Christ" and was, of necessity, absolutely sterile. Both parties to it agreed that the
Holy Ghost was God, and that it dwelt in believers;
but in what way nowhere appeared, "seeing the Scripture doth not declare it." Winthrop, therefore, earnestly entreated Vane that in the phrase "indwelling
of the person of the Holy Ghost" the "word 'person'
might be forborn, being a term of human invention
and tending to doubtful disputation in this case."

As the rumors of this controversy, and of Vane's
ardent support of the new opinions, spread through
the province, Winthrop's popularity underwent a sudden revival. He was recognized as the champion of
the old theocracy, the defender of the true faith, the
clergy and the ancient order of things. His too great
leniency was forgotten. He was the opponent of
Vane; he alone in Boston had been faithful found
among the faithless many. Vane, on the other hand,
was rapidly getting his first lesson in realities, and he
did not relish it. From being the umpire in all disputes, — the blessed peacemaker, — he was now, everywhere outside of Boston, looked at askance, as the
great sower of the seeds of dissension in God's vine-
yard. The most scandalous motives were freely imputed to him; these troubles were all to promote his
selfish ends. Conscious of the purest purpose only,
young Sir Harry was of a sensitive nature, easily
wrought upon. He probably felt his intellectual superiority to those about him; he knew that his views

were broader than theirs; that he had a larger and
firmer grasp of principle. But, after all, a callow
youth, he had yet to learn how to bear up successfully
against the hard, practical tests to which, fortunately,
day-dreams of human progress are wont to be subjected. His nerves, therefore, soon completely got the
better of his judgment; and in December, receiving
letters from England, he informed his brother magistrates that his immediate return was necessary. At
once the General Court was called together to arrange
for his departure.

The magistrates and deputies being assembled at
Boston, on the $\frac{7\text{th}}{17\text{th}}$ of December, the Governor made
known his intentions. The nature of the urgent de-
mands upon him from England were not publicly
stated, but certain of the magistrates to whom the letters had been shown agreed that they were imperative, "though not fit to be imparted to the whole
court." Accordingly the members of the Court, after
looking at one another for some time in grave per-
plexity, decided to hold the matter under advisement
overnight; and so adjourned. When they met the
next morning, one of the magistrates rose and made
a speech expressive of the deep regret felt by all at
losing such a governor in a time of so great peril, referring more particularly to the Pequot troubles then
impending. This either proved too much for the ex-
citable and overwrought Vane, or it afforded him the
opportunity for which he was waiting. Suddenly,
bursting into a flood of tears before the astonished
assembly, he blurted out the true facts in the case,
declaring that the causes assigned for his departure
were not the real causes, — that even though they involved his whole worldly ruin, they would not have

induced him then to depart, if it were not for the
wicked accusations advanced against him, as if he
were the cause of the dissensions and differences
which rent the colony, and which he feared must soon
bring down a judgment of God upon them all. This
singular confession naturally changed the aspect of
the case. Urgent private business in England might
afford a governor sufficient reason for vacating his
office; a conviction on his part of impending public
disaster was wholly another thing. Accordingly,
when Vane had calmed himself and wiped away his
tears, the deputies very properly said that if such
were his reasons for going, they did not feel bound to
give their assent. Vane then went on to protest that
what had escaped from him during his recent outburst
had been dictated rather by feeling than judgment, —
that the private reasons contained in his letters seemed
to him imperative, and that he must insist upon receiving leave to depart.

There can be little question that a large majority
of the Court were quite willing events should take
this course, and, indeed, would have been only too
glad to be thus rid of their too impressionable governor. Accordingly a general and respectful silence
indicated that assent which it would have been awkward, at least, formally to announce. After some further debate it was then decided to choose a new governor in Vane's place, instead of having the deputy
succeed him, and that day week was fixed for holding
the court of elections. The matter seemed to be disposed of, and the way was open for the conservatives
quietly to resume political control. Winthrop was to
replace Vane.

This arrangement wholly failed to meet the views

of the friends of Mrs. Hutchinson.   No sooner, therefore, were the tidings generally known in Boston,
than the town was alive with excitement.   A meeting
of certain of the more prominent among the church-
members was at once held, and it was decided that
Vane must not be permitted to go, — that they did
not apprehend the necessity of his departure upon the
reasons alleged ; and a committee was appointed to
wait upon the Court, and present this view of the
case.   Whereupon Vane, whether quietly or with
more tears and passion does not appear, " expressed
himself to be an obedient child to the church, and
therefore, notwithstanding the license of the court,
yet, without the leave of the church, he durst not go
away."   But the fact would seem to be, that Vane's
somewhat transparent *coup de théâtre* failed.   The
deputies evinced an unanticipated readiness to take
him at his word ; and so his friends of the church had
to help him out of an awkward predicament.

When the day fixed for the new election came, it
was merely voted not to proceed, and the election was
deferred until the regular time in May.   Meanwhile
Vane's troubles were by no means lessened by his va-
cillating and puerile course.   The clergy whom he had
offended might be narrow-minded bigots ; but they
were none the less men, stern and determined.   A
number of them had come to Boston, at the time the
new election was to have taken place, to advise with
Winthrop and their other friends in the Court as to
what course should now be pursued to put an end to
the dissensions.   They were especially anxious to win
Cotton over from the Opinionists, as the followers of
Mrs. Hutchinson were called.   They were anxious to
win him over for two reasons : not only was he the

most eminent man of their order, and as such respected and even revered by them all, but his great
name and authority were a tower of strength to their
opponents, making their cause respectable and shield-
ing it from attack. So Weld, Peters and the rest
now drew up under specific heads the points on which
it was understood Cotton differed from them, and submitted the paper to him, asking for a direct answer
of assent or dissent on every point. Cotton took the
paper and promised a speedy reply.

When Vane heard of this meeting he was deeply
offended, for it had been held without his knowledge.
A day or two later the ministers and the Court met
to consider the situation. The Governor of course
presided, and opened the proceedings by stating in a
general way why they were there gathered. Then
Dudley and others, after the usual practice, exhorted
all to speak freely ; whereupon Vane pointedly remarked, from his place at the head of the table, that,
for his part, he would be content to do so, but that he
understood the ministers were already settling matters
in private and in a church way, among themselves.
Then another scene took place. Hugh Peters stood
up and proceeded sternly to rebuke the Governor.
In language of the utmost plainness he told Vane that,
with all due reverence, it " sadded the ministers' spirits " to see him jealous of their meetings, or apparently
seeking to restrain their liberty. As the loud-voiced
fanatic began to warm in his exhortation, the unfortunate young Governor realized the mistake he had
made and tried to avert the gathering tempest ; he
explained that he had spoken unadvisedly and under
a mistake. Peters could not thus be stopped, and
what ensued was intensely characteristic of the Pres-

byterian and Puritan times. It vividly recalls to mind
those parallel scenes, which only a few years before had
been so common between the ministers of the Scottish
Kirk and the son of Mary Stuart, when they were
wont to scold him from their pulpits, and bid him " to
his knees ; " so that once when — as Vane had now
done — James complained of some meeting of theirs as
being without warrant, " Mr. Andrew Melville could
not abide it, but broke off upon the King in so zealous, powerful and unresistible a manner that, howbeit
the King used his authority in most crabbed and
choleric manner, yet Mr. Andrew bore him down,
and uttered the commission as from the mighty God,
calling the King but ' God's silly vassal ; ' " and,
taking him by the sleeve, told him that there were
" two kings and two kingdoms in Scotland. There
is Christ Jesus the King, and his kingdom the kirk,
whose subject James the Sixth is, and of whose kingdom not a king, nor a lord, nor a head, but a member." And all this he had said to him " divers times
before." So now in New England, Hugh Peters —
speaking, it may safely be assumed, after his wont,
with much vehemency — plainly told Governor Vane
that until he came, less than two years before, the
now troubled churches were at peace. Again the
Governor broke in with the text that the light of the
gospel brings a sword. In reply Peters besought
him " humbly to consider his youth and short experience in the things of God, and to beware of peremp-
tory conclusions, which he perceived him to be very
apt unto." Then the Salem minister launched into
a long discourse on the causes of the new opinions
and divisions, leaving the discomforted chief magis-

trate of Massachusetts to meditate on the consequences
of juvenile indiscretion.[1]

Later in the proceedings Wilson rose and seems to
have relieved his feelings by what Winthrop describes
as " a very sad speech." It would appear indeed to
have been a veritable jeremiad. The pastor of the
church of Boston deplored the condition of things,
and predicted the disintegration of the settlement
unless existing troubles were speedily settled. He
touched upon doctrinal points, and took direct issue
with Cotton, who only that very day had, in a sermon
before the Court, laid down the principle that "sanctification was an evidence of justification." Wilson
now denied this, — though apparently the metaphysical issues involved became at this point too subtle to
be grasped by Winthrop, who alone has given an
account of the debate ; and it is obvious that in this
regard the ordained theological combatants were quite
as much in the dark as those of the laity who strove
to follow them. While one learned divine asserted
a thesis beyond human intelligence to comprehend,
another denied it ; and the lay members of the congregation listened, and tried to look wise over the
spiritual issues involved. As to the practical issues,
no illumination was needed and, in regard to them,
all were sufficiently in earnest ; for, when it came
to trouble in the churches, Mr. Wilson had ground
to stand upon. That did exist ; especially, as his
listeners knew, in his own church. And he attributed
it all to the "new opinions risen up amongst us."
At the conclusion of this diatribe, which evidently

[1] Subsequently in England, during the time of the Commmon-
wealth, Vane and Peters would seem to have sustained very friendly
relations towards each other. (Yonge, *Life of Peters*, 5.)

called forth marks of decided approval from the audience, some expression of opinion was taken, and it was found that all the magistrates excepting Vane, Coddington and Hough, and all the ministers excepting Cotton and Wheelwright, were in sympathy with the Boston pastor.

In the way of conferences this month of December, 1636, was a busy time in Boston. Not content with dealing first with Cotton and then with Vane, the visiting clergy appear to have gone to the fountain-head of the trouble, seeking an exchange of views with Mrs. Hutchinson herself.[1] She was nothing loath, and the occasion could not have been otherwise than edifying in the extreme. Being summoned to the place where the ministers were already met, she there found Wilson, Peters, Weld and others of those opposed to her; and of her friends, Cotton, Wheelwright, Leverett (the elder of the Boston church) and a few more. Peters acted as spokesman for the ministers, while Wilson busied himself with taking notes. Addressing Mrs. Hutchinson " with much vehemency and intreaty," Peters urged her, as the source from which all difference had arisen, to explain why she conceived that he and his brethren were different from Cotton

---

[1] This must have been the time of the meeting, though the date of it nowhere appears. Peters, however, in his evidence, says: — " We did address ourselves to the teacher of the church [Cotton] and the court then assembled . . . our desire to the teacher was to tell us wherein the difference lay between him and us. . . . He said that he thought it not according to God to commend this to the magistrates, but to take some other course, and so . . . we thought it good to send for this gentlewoman." (Hutchinson, ii. 490.) Here is a very distinct reference to the conference between his brother ministers and Cotton, which took place, as appears in the text, on December $\frac{12}{22}$ or $\frac{13}{23}$, 1636, and was followed immediately by the interview, described at the trial, between them and Mrs. Hutchinson.

in their ministry, and why she so openly asserted that
they taught a Covenant of Works. At first Mrs.
Hutchinson would seem, as well she might, to have
been somewhat appalled at the presence in which she
found herself, and the directness of her arraignment.
She was even disposed to deny what was charged.
But, when they offered proof, she presently recovered
her courage, and even assumed her rôle of prophetess,
exclaiming, — "The fear of man is a snare; why
should I be afraid?" Then, in reply to Peters' questions, she asserted that there was indeed a wide and
broad difference between Cotton and the others, that
he preached a Covenant of Grace, and they a Covenant of Works; and, moreover, that they could not
preach a Covenant of Grace, because they were not
sealed, and were no more able ministers of the gospel than were the disciples before the resurrection of
Christ. Cotton, in whose presence all this was said,
found his position becoming uncomfortable, and accordingly broke in, objecting to the comparison. But
she insisted upon it. Then she instanced Shepard of
Cambridge and Weld of Roxbury, as neither of them
preaching a Covenant of Grace clearly. The former,
she said, was not sealed. "Why do you say that?"
he asked. "Because," she replied, "you put love for
an evidence." Presently Mr. Phillips of Watertown,
observing how reckless her criticisms were, and bethink-
ing himself that she had never heard him preach,
asked her in what his ministry differed from that of
Cotton. She apparently asserted that he too was not
sealed. As Peters afterwards remarked : — "There
was a double seal found out that day," — a broad seal
and a little seal, — "which never was." Then the discussion seems to have run off into the unintelligible;

and, when at last they parted, all were not quite clear
whether what had taken place tended, as a whole, to
allay exasperation or to increase it.

But no such doubt rested on Wilson's speech before
the General Court. That had amounted to nothing
less than an angry arraignment of almost the whole
body of his own people, including both Cotton and
Vane. It excited, therefore, great anger among them,
and at once the contest was transferred back from the
General Court to the Boston church. It was there
proposed to admonish him. Again Winthrop came
to his defence, claiming that, whatever the pastor
might have said before the Court, it was general in
its application, and of a privileged nature. When
called upon to explain what he meant by his statements, and to name those he referred to in them, Wilson did not appear well. He equivocated, in fact,
most barefacedly, professing that he had not intended
to reflect on the Boston church or its members, any
more than upon others. Every one who listened to
him knew that this was not so. Vane and Mrs.
Hutchinson were members of his church. It was
they to whom he had referred ; and what he now said
was not true.

It was at last determined to proceed against him
publicly, and on Tuesday, the $\frac{31st}{10th}$ of $\frac{January}{February}$, the Boston
pastor was arraigned before his flock and in his own
meeting-house. Vane led the attack ; and, after his
nature at that time, he did it violently. Then the
whole congregation followed, pouring bitter and reproachful words upon their minister's head. Winthrop and one or two others alone said anything in
the pastor's behalf, and in his journal Winthrop remarked that " it was strange to see how the common

people were led by example to condemn him in that
which, it was very probable, divers of them did not
understand, nor the rule which he was supposed to
have broken ; and that such as had known him so long,
and what good he had done for the church, should fall
upon him with such bitterness for justifying himself in
a good cause." Wilson bore the ordeal meekly, answering as best he could, but to little purpose. The
great majority were in favor of immediately passing a
vote of censure. Throughout Cotton had sympathized
with the church, expressing himself with a good deal
of feeling ; but he had not failed to preserve a certain judgment and moderation. He now intervened,
saying that he could not at that time proceed to
censure, as the usage of the Boston church required
unanimity, and some were opposed to it ; nevertheless
he did administer a grave exhortation. That the
teacher should thus rebuke the pastor, in the presence
of the whole congregation, was probably a thing un-
exampled, and a picture at once suggests itself, of a
venerable man standing up, with white hair uncovered
before his people, to be reprimanded by his junior. It
is, therefore, well to bear in mind that the facts were
quite otherwise. Though Wilson was pastor and Cotton teacher, the former was a man not yet fifty, and
with a large share of health and vigor ; while the latter was not only several years the older of the two,
but recognized by all as much the more eminent.
Nevertheless, the proceeding was outrageous and unjustifiable. Deeply mortified as he must have been,
Wilson bore himself with manly dignity. He took
his scolding before his flock in silence, and, going
quietly on in his duties, he bided his time. And his
time came.

Throughout the next forty days the storm continued to rage with ever-increasing violence. Winthrop
and Cotton engaged in a written controversy over the
proceedings in Wilson's case, which correspondence
Winthrop says was loving and gentle, though in it he
" dealt very plainly " with the teacher. A whole brood
of new heresies was meanwhile currently alleged to
be cropping out in Boston. It was even asserted that
such opinions were publicly expressed, " as that the
Holy Ghost dwelt in a believer as he is in heaven ;
that a man is justified before he believes ; and that
faith is no cause for justification." That heresies
such as these should be tolerated in any well-ordered
Christian community was looked upon by the body of
the clergy as wholly out of the question. After due
consultation among themselves, therefore, they determined to labor with Cotton once more. He himself
afterwards asserted that, through all these times, Mrs.
Hutchinson seldom resorted to him, and was never in
Vane's confidence or in his. Indeed, he added, probably with a good deal of insight into the woman's
character, even when Mistress Hutchinson " did come
to me, it was seldom or never, that I can tell of, that
she tarried long. I rather think she was loath to resort much to me, or to confer long with me, lest she
might seem to learn somewhat from me."[1] But the
general report was otherwise; and so his brethren
drew up another schedule of differences, this time
under sixteen heads : —

This they " gave to him, entreating him to deliver his
judgment directly [on the sixteen points ;] which accordingly
he did, and many copies thereof were dispersed about.
Some doubts he well cleared, but in some things he gave

[1] *Way Cleared*, 88.

not satisfaction.   The rest of the ministers replied to these answers, and at large showed their dissent, and the grounds thereof ; and, at the next General Court, held 9th of the 1st, they all assembled at Boston, and agreed to put off all lectures for three weeks, that they might bring things to some issue."

CHAPTER V.

SUCH was the condition of affairs in Boston and in the province of Massachusetts when the year 1637 opened. "Every occasion," says Winthrop, "increased the contention, and caused great alienation of minds; and the members of Boston [church], frequenting the lectures of other ministers, did make much disturbance by public questions, and objections to their doctrines, which did any way disagree from their opinions; and it began to be as common here to distinguish between men, by being under a Covenant of Grace or a Covenant of Works, as in other countries between Protestants and Papists."

From the depths of one of the now forgotten controversies in which Luther was a chief participant, the Orthodox faction had exhumed a term of opprobrium to be applied to their opponents; for then to say that a man was an Antinomian or an Anabaptist was even more offensive and injurious than it would be in the present day to speak of him as a communist or a free-lover. It was merely another way of calling him a lawless libertine or a ferocious revolutionist. It would be mere waste of space to go into the history of a religious sect which seems to have existed from the earliest days of the Christian era; suffice it to say that the name Antinomian was coined by Luther and applied to the adherents of John Agricola. It meant,

as its derivation implies, that those designated by it
set themselves against and above law and denied its
restricting force, — though law, it should be added,
meant in the religious disputations of the days of
Luther the Mosaic code as revealed in the Old Testament, and more especially set forth in the decalogue.
In other words, Antinomianism was merely another
phase of the same old dispute over the one true and
only path to salvation. The idea of the arraignment
at the bar of final judgment, universally accepted in
those days and that community, has already been
alluded to. It was in no way vague, remote or mystical as it has now become. The doctrine that a pure,
straightforward, conscientious performance of duty in
this life is the best preparation for the life to come,
which, under these conditions, may safely be left to
take care of itself, — this modern doctrine of justification and salvation had then no vogue. On the
contrary the judgment seat was a sternly realistic,
matter-of-fact tribunal, fashioned on human models,
but never absent from thought, — a living, abiding
terror. It was, in the minds of the men and women
who then lived, just as much an ordeal to be looked
forward to and be prepared for as, with certain classes,
the admission to an academy or college or a profession is looked forward to and prepared for now: only,
in the former case the question at issue was all-important, and the decision was one from which there was
no appeal; for behind the judgment seat were the
gates of Heaven and Hell, — life everlasting or endless torments. As already has been said, — What plea
in justification would be accepted at that tribunal? —
The Church of Rome preached the doctrine of works,
— obedience to the law as expounded by authority,

observance of ceremonies, conformity in life : — the
Lutheran, on the other hand, abjuring all forms and
ceremonials, put his trust in faith, implicit and unquestioning, and in divine grace.

So far all was simple. The issue was easy to comprehend. But the revealed Word now presented itself, and to it the pitiless logic of Calvin was applied.
The biblical dogmas of creation, original sin and re-
demption through God's grace had to be brought into
some accordance with the actualities of this life and
the revelation as to the life to come ; omnipotence,
omniscience, prevision and predestination were to be
accepted and disposed of. Logic gave way under the
strain, and human reason sought refuge in the inconceivable. What was right and good and just among
men was, necessarily, neither just nor good nor right
with God. He was a law unto himself.

Then followed the dogma of the elect. As pre-
science was a necessary, and so admitted, attribute of
the omnipotent God, everything was ordained in advance, and consequently all men were predestined
from the beginning, — many would be lost, a few
would be saved ; — but, whether lost or saved, the decision had been reached from the beginning and could
in no way be influenced. It is difficult to see how
what was called Antinomianism did not follow of
necessity from these premises. The elect were superior to the restraints of law; and this Luther distinctly asserted. Antinomianism was therefore the
refuge of the libertine : — if he was destined to be
saved, he would be saved, all possible misdeeds to the
contrary notwithstanding; if he was doomed to be
lost, the rectitude of a life of restraint would avail
him nothing.

As applied to Anne Hutchinson, Henry Vane and John Wheelwright the term Antinomian was, therefore, an intentional misnomer.[1] About them there was no trace of license, no suggestion of immorality or hypocrisy; nor, it must be added, was there any disposition to protestantism, or even increased liberality in religion. They accepted both law and gospel. They denied none of the tenets of Calvin. They merely undertook to graft upon the stern, human logic of those tenets certain most illogical, spiritual offshoots of their own. In other words, they also, like their teacher and prototype the transcendentalists of that earlier day, were in their own estimation the elect of God. Conscious of the indwelling of the Holy Ghost, they, and they only, could look forward with confidence to the inevitable time when, standing before the judgment seat, they should plead in justification the Covenant of Grace.

Such was New England Antinomianism and such was the spiritual issue the Antinomian presented, — an issue harmless enough in our days, though not so wholly devoid of harm then; an issue not easy now to comprehend, nor calculated to excite a feeling of sympathy. Ordinarily it would be dismissed as merely one more phase of religious exaltation. But in the case of Anne Hutchinson and her following, with the spiritual was combined a political issue, and with both yet other issues, social, parochial and individual, until together they made up a drama in which almost no element was wanting. The theological struggle was

---

[1] In his Fast-day sermon, now to be referred to, Wheelwright expressly enjoined his hearers and sympathizers " to have care that we give not occasion to others to say we are libertines or Antinomians." Bell, *Wheelwright*, 175.

between Anne Hutchinson and John Wilson, and it
was over Cotton ; the political struggle was between
Vane and Winthrop. Cotton, both factions hoped
to secure. That he now sympathized with those who
preached the new Covenant of Grace, or the Antinomians as their opponents designated them, was apparent; but his brother ministers looked upon him as
a very precious brand which it might yet be given
unto them to snatch from the burning. Anne Hutchinson, with whom the church-people of Boston were
literally infatuated, outside of Boston was regarded
with hate, — and a hate not of the mere conventional
kind, but of that exquisitely rancorous description
which has been set apart by itself and regularly classi-
fied as the *odium theologicum.* Though Wheelwright
had moved to Mount Wollaston, and for several weeks
been ministering to the scattered farmers thereabouts,
his position in the controversy was well understood.
Too sensible and cool-headed to go the whole length
Mrs. Hutchinson went, he did not believe in her misty
transcendental revelations ; but, as regards the dogmas of sanctification and the personal presence of the
Holy Ghost in the true believer, he stood in advance
probably of Cotton, and by the side of Vane. None
the less, by classing him with Cotton, as alone being
sealed and preaching a Covenant of Grace, his sister-
in-law had conferred on the minister at the Mount a
dangerous prominence. His position was not like that
of Cotton. He did not enjoy the same reputation or
equal authority. He did not even have a distinct settlement of his own. He rested moreover under the
imputation of inclining to novel and questionable
doctrines. Everything combined, therefore, to centre
upon Wheelwright the angry eyes of his brethren.

He was the representative, the kinsman, the favored
preacher of her whom they called the " virago," the
" she-Gamaliel," the " American Jezebel." She was
a woman, and her sex could not but shield her somewhat. He was a man, and a contentious one ; and as
such he invited assault. So over his head the clouds
began to gather, black and ominous. An occasion
for their bursting only was needed ; and for that his
enemies had not long to wait.

On the $\frac{19th}{29th}$ of January a solemn fast was held, because of " the miserable estate of the churches in Germany " and in England, the growing Pequot troubles,
and the dissensions nearer home. Wheelwright may
have preached to his own people at Mount Wollaston
on the morning of that day ; but later he seems to
have gone to Boston, where in the afternoon he attended church services and listened to a discourse
from Cotton. After Cotton had finished, Wheelwright
was called upon " to exercise as a private brother ; "
and he improved the occasion by delivering his famous
sermon.[1] There is strong presumptive evidence that,
even on this day of penitential humiliation, certain of
God's unworthy prophets were cunningly lying in wait
one for another ; for, as he held forth, some one
among those who listened to him was rapidly taking
down a verbatim report of all that he uttered.

Once hostilities are decided upon, a pretext for open
war is never far to seek. In itself there was assuredly
nothing in that Fast-day sermon which would have.
attracted any general public notice. It had a very
direct bearing on things then exercising the public
mind ; but this is usual in occasional discourses. As
a matter of taste, so sharp an arraignment of those

[1] Bell, *Wheelwright*, 13, 15, notes 21 and 25.

walking in a Covenant of Works was at that time
decidedly out of place, especially when preached from
Mr. Wilson's pulpit. Though the congregation, with
less than half a dozen exceptions, entirely sympathized
in it, yet they all knew, and Mr. Wilson knew, that
he, the minister of the church, was receiving an exhortation. It was this apparently which gave the
affair what zest it had. In fact the whole thing would
seem to have been arranged beforehand between Mrs.
Hutchinson and Wheelwright. It bore on its face
traits highly suggestive of her handiwork. The Lord,
it was seen, might be made to deliver Wilson into the
hands of his enemies on the Fast-day; and so Wheelwright stood ready to smite, and spare not.

In common with most writers of his time, and especially theological writers, Wheelwright was always
involved and obscure in expression. How, in fact,
the congregations of those days understood and followed the pulpit utterances is incomprehensible now.
Possibly there was an inspiration of fanaticism then
about, which has since passed away; but, more probably, much that was said was not taken in at all, and
religious fervor supplied the place of comprehension.
The Fast-day sermon is no better calculated for easy
comprehension by an audience, or for that matter by
a reader even, than are the other productions of
Wheelwright's pen. Couched in that peculiar scriptural language in which the Puritan and the Covenan-
ter delighted, and of which the most familiar specimen
— *plus Arabe que l'Arabie* — is the address of Eph-
raim McBriar after the skirmish at Drumclog, it is,
except in parts, a very dull performance; and, if delivered to a modern congregation, would hardly excite
in those composing it any sensations except curiosity,

soon followed by drowsiness and impatience. But, so far as phraseology and the corresponding delivery of the speaker are concerned, the following extracts from Wheelwright's discourse might well have been the original which inspired the more brilliant imitation of Scott : —

"The way we must take, if so be we will not have the Lord Jesus Christ taken from us, is this, — We must all prepare for a spiritual combat, — we must put on the whole armor of God, and must have our loins girt and be ready to fight. Behold the bed that is Solomon's ; there is threescore valiant men about it, — valiant men of Israel. Every one hath his sword in his hand and, being expert in war, hath his sword girt on his thigh, because of fear in the night. If we will not fight for the Lord Jesus Christ, Christ may come to be surprised. Solomon lyeth in his bed; and there is such men about the bed of Solomon ; and they watch over Solomon, and will not suffer Solomon to be taken away. And who is this Solomon but the Lord Jesus Christ; and what is the bed but the church of true believers ; and who are those valiant men of Israel but all the children of God ! They ought to show themselves valiant; they should have their swords ready ; they must fight, and fight with spiritual weapons, for the weapons of our warfare are not carnal but spiritual. And, therefore, wheresoever we live, if we would have the Lord Jesus Christ to be abundantly present with us, we must all of us prepare for battle, and come out against the enemies of the Lord ; and, if we do not strive, those under a Covenant of Works will prevail. We must have a special care, therefore, to show ourselves courageous. All the valiant men of David and all the men of Israel, — Barak, and Deborah, and Jael, — all must out and fight for Christ. Curse ye Meroz, because they came not out to help the Lord against the mighty ! — Therefore, if we will keep the Lord Jesus Christ and his presence and power amongst us, we must fight. . . .

" When Christ is thus holden forth to be all in all, — all
in the root, all in the branch, all in all, — this is the gospel.
This is that fountain open for the inhabitants of Judah and
Jerusalem for sin and for uncleanness ; and this is the well,
of which the wells under the old testament were certain
types. This same well must be kept open. If the Philis-
tines fill it with earth, with the earth of their own inventions, those that are the servants of Isaak, — true believers,
— the servants of the Lord, — must open the wells again.
This is the light that holdeth forth a great light, that lighteth
every one that cometh into the world. And if we mean to
keep Christ, we must hold forth this light.

.   .   .   .

" The second action we must perform and the second way
we must take is, — When enemies to the truth oppose the
ways of God, we must lay hold upon them, we must kill
them with the Word of the Lord. The Lord hath given
true believers power over the nations, and they shall break
them in pieces as shivered with a rod of iron. And what
rod of iron is this but the word of the Lord ; — and such
honor have all his saints. The Lord hath made us as
threshing instruments with teeth, and we must beat the
hills as chaff. Therefore, in the fear of God handle the
sword of the spirit, the word of God ; — for it is a two-
edged sword, and this word of God cutteth men to the
heart." [1]

---

[1] In his references to Wheelwright and the Fast-day discourse, Dr.
Palfrey, in his History, evinces even more than his usual spirit of reverence for the fathers of New England, and less than his usual accuracy. He speaks of the sermon as " a composition of that character
which is common to skilful agitators. Along with disclaimers of the
purpose to excite to physical violence, it abounds in language suited
to bring about that result. . . . Another art of demagogues Wheelwright perfectly understood. By exhorting his hearers to prepare
themselves to be martyrs, he gave them to understand that they were
in danger of being so, and that, if they preferred not to be, they must
take their measures accordingly." (i. 479, n.) He also remarks that
" it was perhaps well that this sermon was delivered at Braintree, and

Though at the time of their delivery these utterances do not seem to have excited any particular remark, they did soon after afford a pretext for open
strife between the factions into which the province
was divided. As the weeks passed on, it became
apparent that a struggle was to take place in the next
General Court. This met on the $\frac{9\text{th}}{19\text{th}}$ of March, nearly
seven weeks after the fast, and was attended by an
advisory council of clergymen. It has been seen that
all lectures were then deferred for three weeks, that

that the angry men whom it stimulated did not pass Winthrop's house
in returning to their homes."

The fact is, the sermon was delivered, not at Braintree, but in Boston, and within a stone's throw of Winthrop's house; while there can
be very little doubt that Winthrop was himself among the audience
which listened to it. In their anxiety to justify the subsequent proceedings of the magistrates and clergy, the New England historians
have imagined a condition of affairs existing in Massachusetts in
1635–7 which the evidence does not warrant. They have transformed
the self-contained little New England community into something very
like a French or German mob. The Wheelwright discourse neither
led, nor was intended to lead, to any outbreak of "angry men." Indeed, it did not at the moment excite enough remark to cause Winthrop, after listening to it, to make any mention of it in his journal.
It dealt in no rhetoric or figures of speech which were not usual in the
pulpit oratory of those days.

That Wheelwright was a strong-willed and ambitious divine, prone
to controversy and eager for notoriety, is evident enough; but the
record of his earlier no less than of his later life stamps him as a
thoroughly pure and conscientious man. Every believing controversialist is of necessity an agitator; but "demagogues" rarely enjoy
convictions for the sake of which they suffer, as did Wheelwright
and his friends, persecution and banishment. In the Antinomian controversy the record of Wheelwright is far more creditable to him
than those of Cotton and Winthrop are to them. Finally, there is no
reason whatever to question the judgment of Mather, pronounced
long after the controversy had subsided, that Wheelwright "was a
man of the most unspotted morals and unblemished reputation;"
and that "his worst enemies never looked on him as chargeable with
the least ill practices."

nothing might hinder the ministers from giving their exclusive attention, during the sessions of the Court, to the one subject uppermost in the minds of all.

Although the opponents of Mrs. Hutchinson controlled every church, and consequently every town in the province outside of Boston, yet the legislature — as then organized under the governorship of Vane — was not unequally divided. A preliminary struggle between the two parties took place over the case of one Stephen Greensmith, who had ventured to express, somewhere and at some time, the opinion that all the ministers, with the exception of Cotton, Wheelwright, "and, as he thought, Mr. Hooker," were under a Covenant of Works, — in other words, were "whited sepulchres." Being adjudged guilty of this sweeping criticism, Greensmith was fined £40, and required to give sureties of £100 for the payment thereof. Who the man was, or why he was thus utilized for example's sake, does not appear. The Court, having in this way indicated its disapproval of the new doctrines, next went on to emphasize its approval of the old. The proceedings of the Boston church against Wilson, because of his jeremiad before the December Court, were reviewed. Winthrop says that they "could not fasten upon such as had prejudiced him," and would seem to imply that it was for this reason — because they could not be fastened upon — that these persons escaped punishment with Greensmith. Yet Winthrop had himself recorded how, on the 31st of December at the church-meeting, "the governor [young Harry Vane] pressed it violently" against the pastor. The chief offender in the case happened, therefore, to be the presiding officer of the Court which thus failed to "fasten upon" him,

Nevertheless the subject was discussed and evidently
with warmth, for the ministers were called on to advise upon it. They took the correct ground, laying
down the principle that no member of a court, and
consequently no person by request advising a court,
could be publicly questioned elsewhere for anything
said to it. The spirit and tenor of Wilson's speech
were then approved by an emphatic majority, this action being, of course, intended as a pointed rebuke to
Vane.

So far it was mere skirmishing. The parties were
measuring strength before they grappled over the real
issue. It had probably now been determined among
the ministers that Wheelwright was to be called to a
sharp account. His position invited attack ; and his
utterances in private, there is every reason to suppose,
as well as in public, afforded ready pretext for it.
He was the man set up against Wilson, by Wilson's
own people, in his own meeting-house. Wilson had
there been called to account for a speech made before
the Court ; and now the Court proposed to call Wheelwright to like account for a sermon delivered before
Wilson's church. No sooner, therefore, had the Court
approved of what Wilson had said in December, than
it went on to consider what Wheelwright had said in
January. The matter of the Fast-day sermon was
brought up. In answer to a summons Wheelwright
presently appeared, the notes of his discourse, taken
at the time of its delivery, were produced, and he was
asked if he admitted their correctness. In reply he
laid before the Court his own manuscript, and was
then dismissed. The next day he was again summoned.

Less than twenty-four hours had elapsed, but during that brief space of time the Court had received a very distinct intimation that the course upon which it seemed to be entering was not to pass unchallenged. It came in the form of a petition, signed by nearly all the members of the Boston church, praying that proceedings in judicial cases should be conducted publicly, and that matters of conscience might be left for the church to deal with. The Court was, in other words, respectfully invited to attend to the matters which properly concerned it, and not to meddle in the affairs of the Boston church. This paper was at once ordered to be returned to those from whom it came, with an indorsement upon it to the effect that the Court considered it presumptuous. The examination of Wheelwright was then proceeded with behind closed doors. His sermon being produced he justified it, and asked to be informed of what, and by whom, he was accused. He was answered that, the sermon being acknowledged by him, the Court would proceed *ex officio*, as it was termed. In other words, it would examine him inquisitorially under oath. This proposal immediately called forth loud expressions of disapproval from those of the members who were friendly to the accused. Voices were heard exclaiming that these were but the methods of the High Commission, and as such were associated in the minds of all with the worst measures of that persecution which had harried them and their brethren out of England. Wheelwright thereupon declined to answer any further questions, and the proceedings for the moment came to a standstill.

The anti-clerical party in the Court now carried their point, in so far that what more was to be done was ordered to be done in public. This decided,

Wheelwright, later in the day, was again summoned.
The room was now thronged, nearly all the clergy of
the colony being among those present, and, his Fast-
day discourse having been again produced, Wheelwright proceeded to justify it, — declaring that he
meant to include in his animadversions "all who
walked in such a way," as he had described to be a
Covenant of Works. The matter was then referred
to the ministers of the other churches, who were
called upon to state whether "they in their ministry
did walk in such a way." As a method of securing
at once evidence, and a verdict upon it, this was ingenious, and worked most satisfactorily. There was
little room for doubt what the answer would be, and
when the Court met the next morning it was ready.
One and all, — Cotton only excepted, — the ministers
replied, they did consider they walked in such a way.

The verdict was thus rendered. But the record was
not to be made up without a further struggle. It yet
remained to declare the judgment of the Court that
Wheelwright was guilty of contempt and sedition.
The doors were again closed, and behind them a debate which lasted two entire days was entered upon.
Nothing is known of its details, except that Winthrop
and Vane were the leaders of the opposing forces, and
the result hung long in the balance. For a time it
seemed as if the extremists would be thwarted by a
small preponderance of voices ; but at last, to quote
the words of one most active in the struggle, "the
priests got two of the magistrates on their side," and
so secured a majority.[1]

The judgment of the Court was announced. But
not even then did Vane abandon the struggle. He

[1] Coddington to Fretwell; cited in Felt's *Eccles. Hist.* ii. 611.

tendered a protest against the action just taken. This
protest the Court refused to spread upon its record, on
the ground that in it the proceedings were condemned
and the convicted divine wholly justified. Another
petition from the church of Boston was now presented,
which, at a later stage of the struggle, came into sin-
ister prominence. It was a singularly well-drawn
paper. Respectful in tone, it was simple, brief, direct
and logical. It was, of course, an earnest protest
against the action of the Court, and breathed a deep
sympathy with the condemned; but at the time no
exception was taken to its tone. It seems to have
been received as a matter of course, and was placed
upon the files of the Court. To it were appended
above threescore names.

The conservatives had carried their point. None
the less, the struggle had been so severe, the resistance at every point so obstinate and the majorities
so small, that the victors were not in a position to
follow up their success. Accordingly the sentence
upon Wheelwright was deferred to the next General
Court, before which he was ordered to appear. So
far as he was concerned, therefore, it only remained
to decide whether he should, during the interim, be
silenced as a preacher. This, also, being a question
of church discipline, the magistrates referred to the
ministers for their advice; and they naturally hesitated to have recourse to a proceeding so irresistibly
suggestive of bitter English memories. Though angry
and bigoted, they were honest; and they could not at
once, even with Hugh Peters and Thomas Weld as
their leaders, introduce into this, their place of refuge
from Laud's pursuivants, the most odious features of
Laud's ecclesiastical machinery. Weld himself, in-

deed, had good cause to know what it was to be silenced. Six years before, in company with Thomas Shepard who now again sat by his side, he had stood before the hated Archbishop, even as Wheelwright now stood before them. With what face could they now measure out to him as "that lion" had then meted out to them? Accordingly the magistrates were advised not to silence Wheelwright, but to commend his case to the church of Boston, to be dealt with spiritually. In view of the remonstrance from members of that church which had just been presented, this course certainly was a forbearing one. It opened a door to conciliation.

As was the custom, the sessions of the Court had been held in Boston. But Boston swarmed like an angry ant-hill with the adherents of those who professed the Covenant of Grace. The influence of an intense local, though outside, public opinion, all setting strongly one way, had made itself unmistakably felt throughout the recent stormy sittings, and had greatly modified the conclusions arrived at by the deputies. Action taken behind closed doors had been met within a few hours by earnest protests over long lists of well-known names. The conservative party, though in the majority, was none the less the opposition, so long as Vane remained governor. Naturally, therefore, those composing it felt anxious to have all further operations conducted amid less uncongenial surroundings. If it was necessary to proceed to extremities, it would be expedient, at least, to secure the removal of the seat of government from Boston to some other place, at any rate for a time. Accordingly, when all other business was disposed of, the final move of that session on the part of the con-

servatives was made in the form of a proposition that
the next General Court should meet at Cambridge,
or Newetowne as it was then called.

Though the suggestion was unprecedented, it was
by no means unjustifiable. It was fairly open to
question whether, under the circumstances of intense
excitement then prevailing, the action of the Court
could be looked upon as wholly free from outside
restraint so long as its sittings were in Boston. It
was true there had been no tumult as yet, and the
law-abiding habits of the people made tumults improbable. But the province, though made up of a
tolerably compact body of settlements, was without
any system of mails or public conveyance, — without
newspaper, newsletter, or printing-press. The only
means of communication was by word-of-mouth, or by
letter sent through chance occasion. The boat, the
saddle and the farm-wagon were the forms of carriage; and he who could command none of these
might either find his way on foot or stay at home.
This was an important fact, not to be disregarded in
any attempt to forecast the result of an impending
election. It was true, the charter-officers of the company were no longer chosen by those only of the freemen who were present and actually voting in the general assembly which elected them. Heretofore this had
been the practice; but, naturally, the inconvenience
incident to such a system had made itself more and
more felt as the settlements spread over a wider ter-
ritorial surface, and this inconvenience had been tem-
porarily met by the passage of a recent law permitting
the freemen to send in their votes by proxy, which
law was now to go into operation for the first time.
Still the votes were not to be cast in the towns where

the freemen dwelt, and then canvassed. They were
simply held in the form of proxies to be used in the
case of formal balloting by a deliberative body. That
the coming election would be hotly contested was well
known. It was to take place, as before, in a general
assembly of the freemen ; and, in the course of a contested election held in this way, it was inevitable that
points of order and procedure would arise. These
points, as they arose, would have to be decided by
those actually present, voting *vivâ voce*, or by count
of uplifted hands. If the election was held in Boston, every Boston freeman would assuredly be present, and his vote would count. The freemen from
the other towns would be in a strange place ; they
would be overawed and silenced by the unanimity of
those who felt themselves at home. If riot or violence should occur, the case would be yet worse, for
every advantage would be on one side ; all the dis-
advantages on the other. Then, after the magistrates
were chosen, the sessions of the Court were to be
held. At these sessions matters were to be discussed
and issues were to be decided in regard to which
intense feeling existed. Under such circumstances, a
legislative assembly, which was supreme, could hardly
be expected to hold its sittings in a place where the
whole public sentiment was bitterly opposed to those
composing a majority of that assembly, and where the
local church constituted itself a sort of board of revision over any action taken.

Though all this was obvious enough, Vane declined
to see it. He was the presiding officer of the Court,
and he met a formal motion for a change of the place
in which its next sessions were to be held, not as a
governor and presiding officer should, but again with

the angry petulance of a displeased boy. He flatly refused to entertain it. Apparently he had not yet learned that those with whom he was dealing were men, — and men quite as decided as he, and a good deal more mature. They were of the class which produced Eliot and Pym, Hampden and Cromwell; and it was not likely they would now be turned from their course by childish opposition: so, when Winthrop, the deputy-governor, hesitated to usurp the presiding officer's functions, upon the ground that he was himself also an inhabitant of Boston, the stern Endicott was equal to the occasion. He submitted the question to a vote, and declared it carried. The Court then adjourned.

CHAPTER VI.

A HOUSE DIVIDED AGAINST ITSELF.

THE charter-election was this year to be held on the $\frac{17th}{27th}$ of May, and the time which intervened between the adjournment of the Court in March and that day was one of great excitement. Not only was each party to the theological dispute striving to secure the control of the government, but the fear of an impending war with the dreaded Pequot tribe was in every mind. So far as the church of Boston was concerned, there were no signs whatever that the dissensions which rent it were subsiding. Mr. Wilson and Mrs. Hutchinson could not be brought together. They were separated by something far more insuperable than even theological tenets, — by an extreme personal antipathy.

As the election day drew near, Winthrop and Vane were put forward as opposing candidates, and the adherents of neither neglected any precaution likely to influence the result; while the deep interest felt in that result of itself insured not only a full vote, but a large personal attendance. Though recorded as of May 17, 1637, it is to be borne in mind that the events now to be described really took place on what is with us the 27th of the month, so that, as spring was merging into early summer, the verdure was far advanced. The day was clear and warm, when at one o'clock the freemen gathered in groups about a large

oak-tree which stood on the north side of what is now
Cambridge Common, where Governor Vane, in English fashion and beneath the open sky, announced the
purpose of the meeting, — the annual charter-election.
Most of the notabilities of the province, whether magistrates or clergy, were among the large number present. As soon as the meeting was declared ready for
business, a parliamentary contest was opened over a
petition offered on behalf of many inhabitants of
Boston. It was in effect an appeal, in the case of
Wheelwright, taken from the deputies to the body of
freemen themselves, in General Court assembled. As
such, its presentation at that time was clearly not in
order; for, as the day was specially set apart for the
choice of magistrates, the choice of magistrates took
precedence over everything. If other business could
be thrust on the meeting first, it was obvious an election might in this way be defeated, and the colony
left without a government. Vane took advantage
of his place as presiding officer to insist upon having
the paper read. To this Winthrop objected, contending very properly that the special business of the day
should first of all be disposed of. As Vane stood
firm, an angry debate ensued, and the significance
of the change in locality became at once apparent.
Had the Court met in Boston, there can be little
doubt that Vane, who had forgotten the magistrate in
the party leader, would have been sustained in his
arbitrary rulings by the voices of those actually present. The position assumed by the youthful governor
was striking and dramatic enough; but it was also
suggestive of memories connected with that greater
and more turbulent forum, in which Gracchus and
Sulpicius appealed directly from the senate to the

people of Rome.   That, under the strain to which
the eager and too zealous patrician now subjected it,
the meeting did not break into riot, was due only to
the self-control and respect for law and form — the
inherited political habit — of those who composed it.

Separated as the two places were by a broad arm
of the sea, and the adjoining flats and marshes, Boston
was then a long way from Cambridge.   Indeed, it is
not easy to realize that the two cities — now so closely
connected by direct, broad thoroughfares, running between continuous rows of buildings — could, even two
centuries and a half ago, have been so far apart that
the passage from one to the other was not only long
and tedious, but at times fraught with peril.   Yet
such was the fact.   Only a few months after the election of 1637, Winthrop recorded how a young man,
coming alone from Cambridge to Boston in a storm,
perished, and was found dead in his boat ; and, more
than sixty years later, the wife of the president of the
college, having her children with her, was in great
danger while making the same passage, and found her
way to Boston at last over Roxbury neck, after being
driven ashore on the Brookline marshes.[1]   On the
4th of July, 1711, Judge Sewall noted down that he
" went to Commencement by Water in a sloop," and
in May, 1637, the most direct way of going to Newetowne from the vicinity of Mr. Wilson's church, at
the head of State Street in Boston, was unquestionably by boat, taken probably at Long Wharf.   In a
good shallop, with a favoring breeze and a flood tide,
it was a pleasant sail ; but if the journey was to be
made by land, it would be necessary to cross over to
Charlestown, or go many miles about by way of Bos-

---

[1] Sewall, *Diary*, ii. 74.

ton neck, through Roxbury and Watertown, for there was as yet no ferry from the foot of the hill below William Blackstone's house. Accordingly, as had doubtless been intended when the place was chosen, it had proved much easier for the freemen of Roxbury, Watertown, Charlestown and the northern towns to assemble on Cambridge Common than for those of Boston; and it speedily became manifest that the larger number of those present sided with Winthrop. This fact held in check the friends of Vane. None the less, threatening speeches drew forth angry words, and a few of the more hot-headed were on the verge of coming to blows; some, indeed, did lay hands upon each other. In the midst of the tumult the pastor Wilson — his gravity of calling, the stoutness of his person and his fifty years of age notwithstanding — clambered up against the trunk of the spreading oak, and, clinging to one of its branches, began vehemently to harangue the meeting, exhorting the freemen there present to look to their charter, and to consider of the present work of the day, which was therein set apart for the choosing their magistrates. In reply to this sudden appeal, a loud cry was raised of " Election! Election!! " in response to which Winthrop, as deputy-governor, cut the knot by declaring that the greater number should decide on the course to be pursued. He then put the question himself. The response did not admit of doubt. The majority were clearly in favor of proceeding to an immediate election.

Vane still refused to comply. Then, at last, Winthrop flatly told him that, if he would not go on, they would go on without him. Remembering how Endicott had dealt with him under very similar circum-

stances only two months before, Vane now gave way
to the inevitable, and the election was allowed to proceed. It resulted in the complete defeat of his party.
He was himself left out of the magistracy, as also
were Wheelwright's two parishioners at the Mount,
Coddington and Hough. The conservative party re-
sumed complete political control under Winthrop as
governor, with the stern and intolerant Dudley as his
deputy. As if also to indicate in a special way their
approval of Endicott's decided course throughout
these proceedings, the deputies, among their first acts
when they met, chose him a member of the standing
council for the term of his life, — an honor which a
year before, in plain defiance of the charter, had been
conferred upon Winthrop and Dudley, the governor
and deputy now elected, and which never was conferred on any except these three. The reaction was
complete.

The freemen of Boston meanwhile had anxiously
watched the election, intentionally deferring the choice
of their own delegates to the new Court, in order that
they might be free to act as events should seem to
make expedient. They now at once, on the morning
of the day after the election, chose as their representatives the defeated candidates for the magistracy, —
Vane, Coddington and Hough. The Court saw fit to
look upon this action as an affront, and, declaring the
election " undue," ordered a new one to be had. A
pretext for this foolish course was found in an alleged
failure to notify two of the Boston freemen of the
meeting to elect. A new warrant was immediately
issued, and notice then given by " private and particular warning from house to house," as a result of
which the contumacious town returned the same three

men. And now the Court, "not finding how they might reject them," admitted them to their seats. This was on the $\frac{19th}{29th}$ of May, two days after the general election, — so simple and prompt was the early procedure.

The Massachusetts General Court of 1637 consisted of eleven magistrates elected by the freemen of the colony at large, and thirty-two deputies chosen by the fourteen towns, and representing them. Magistrates and deputies sat and voted together, — the separation into two chambers, as the result of the controversy between Goodwife Sherman and Captain Keayne over the slaughtered hog of the latter, not taking place until five years later, in 1642. Of this body, consisting, all told, of forty-three members, the opponents of Mrs. Hutchinson had complete control; might was wholly on their side, for the opposition was limited to the three Boston representatives. At first the dominant party used their power sparingly, and an earnest attempt seems even to have been made to put an end to strife. It came, too, from influential quarters. The clergy was not wholly made up of fanatics like Peters, or of bigots like Weld, or of those by nature contentious, like Wheelwright, and the better class of them, men like Shepard and Cotton, now evinced a real desire to reach some common ground. There was no printing-press in the land, and it was only through sermons, lectures, disputations, and manuscript writings circulating from hand to hand, that the discussion could be carried on ; but, by the industrious use of these means, the subtle questions in dispute were reduced to so fine a point that Winthrop, tolerably versed as he was in the metaphysico-theologies of the time, very distinctly intimated that the issues involved were beyond his comprehension. "Except men of good understanding," said he, "and such as knew the bottom of the tenets of those of the other party, few could see where the difference was." Wheelwright even, stubborn as he was, showed some signs of yielding. And thus the stumbling-block, the single obstacle which apparently stood in the way of complete reconciliation, was reduced to this curious thesis, — to the average modern reader, pure foolishness, — "Whether the first assurance be by an absolute promise always, and not by a conditional also ; and whether a man could have any true assurance, without sight of some such work in his soul as no hypocrite could attain unto." Translated into modern speech this meant simply that, Vane and Cotton, representing the Boston church, accepted the Calvinistic tenet of predestination, and denied that conduct in life, or works, could be a plea for salvation. In other words, in the elect, salvation was not conditional; such were born to be saved, else Omnipotence was not prescient. From this logic there seemed, humanly speaking, no escape, and Antinomianism apparently followed ; but it was then added that, practically, no one could be of the elect, or have any real assurance of salvation, without such genuine moral elevation as was wholly inconsistent with hypocrisy or licentiousness in life.

There would seem to be nothing in metaphysical subtleties of this description calculated of necessity to render those who saw fit to indulge in them an element of civil danger in the state. Winthrop seems to have reached some such common-sense conclusion, and at first his councils prevailed. So presently when, in the order of legislative business, Wheelwright's case was taken up, and he again presented himself before the Court, he was merely dismissed until its next session; though with a significant admonition that in the interval it would be well for him to bethink himself of retracting and reforming his error, if he hoped to receive favor. His answer was thoroughly characteristic of the man and of the times. He boldly declared that if he had been guilty of sedition he ought to be put to death; but that, if the Court meant to proceed against him, he should take his appeal to the King. As for retraction, he had nothing to retract.

Although the more moderate portion of the dominant party were reluctant to go to extremes, and still hoped that some way would open itself to peace and reconciliation, they were not disposed to run any risk of letting the fruits of their victory escape them. They held the magistracy, and they did not propose to be driven from it. The franchise, it has already been mentioned, was an incident to church-membership; and all the churches in the province, save one only, could safely be counted upon. Though such a condition of affairs would seem to have afforded assurance enough, it did not satisfy the dominant party; so it was determined to make assurance doubly sure. With this end in view the General Court now passed an alien law, which may safely be set down as one of the most curious of the many curiosities of partisan legislation.

As is usually the case with legislation of this nature, the alien law of 1637 was intended to meet a particular case. Framed as a general law, it was designed for special application. The tide of immigration to New England was then at its flood. With the rest, Wheelwright and his friends were looking for a large addition to their number in the speedy arrival of a

portion of the church of a Mr. Brierly in England,
who possibly may have been Wheelwright's successor
at Bilsby. One party was already on its way; for,
while the Court sat in June, in July, only a month
later, some of Hutchinson's kinsfolk landed with others
at Boston. Not improbably they were of the Brierly
church. Had they been permitted to remain within
the limits of the patent, there can hardly be any question these people would have settled at the Mount,
where Wheelwright ministered and where William
Hutchinson's farm lay. In the existing state of public opinion they could not, indeed, have very well settled anywhere else. It was with a view to this rein-
forcement of the minority that the General Court in
May passed that alien law of 1637, which imposed
heavy penalties in case strangers were harbored or
allowed to remain in the province above three weeks
without a magistrate's permission. The peculiar point
and hardship of the law lay, of course, in the fact that
all the magistrates, without exception, belonged to one
party in the state, and were wholly devoted to it.[1]

---

[1] The original germ of this law is found in the entry of 30th November, 1635, of the Boston records (*Second Report of Boston Record
Commissioners*, 5). But the act passed by the General Court of 1637
is so singular, and so large a body of Massachusetts town legislation
seems to have originated from it, that it is here printed in full. Its
passage led at the time to a series of papers, attacking and defending
it, from the pens of Vane and Winthrop. These are included in the
Hutchinson Papers. There is an abstract of the discussion in Up-
ham's Life of Vane in Sparks' American Biography (N. S. vol. iv.).
The text of the law (*Records*, i. 196) reads as follows : —

"It is ordered, that no towne or person shall receive any stranger,
resorting hither with intent to reside in this jurisdiction, nor shall
allow any lot or habitation to any, or entertain any such above three
weeks, except such person shall have allowance under the hands of
some one of the council, or of two other of the magistrates, upon pain
that every town that shall give or sell any lot or habitation to any

When the body of immigrants from the Brierly church landed, they were confronted with this new ordinance. So far as appeared, they were all God-fearing, well disposed, English men and women, and in Boston their friends were in a large majority; yet their friends could not entertain them above three weeks, nor could Boston give or sell them a lot or habitation, under a heavy and recurring penalty. Presently others came, and among them Mrs. Hutchinson's brother.[1] A delay of four months only in the enforcement of the law could be obtained for them from Winthrop. At the expiration of that time they must be without the jurisdiction. They submitted, for they could not help themselves; nor is it now known where they went, though probably they settled in Exeter, in New Hampshire.

Party feeling already ran dangerously high, evincing itself in ways not to be mistaken. The debates in the General Court had been violent and angry; as Winthrop says, even insolent speeches had been delivered. When the result of the election at Cam-

---

such, not so allowed, shall forfeit £100 for every offence, and every person receiving any such, for longer time than is here expressed, (or than shall be allowed in some special cases, as before, or in case of entertainment of friends resorting from some other parts of this country for a convenient time,) shall forfeit for every offence £40; and for every month after such person shall there continue £20; provided, that if any inhabitant shall not consent to the entertainment of any such person, and shall give notice thereof to any of the magistrates within one month after, such inhabitant shall not be liable to any part of this penalty. This order to continue till the end of the next Court of Elections, and no longer, except it be then confirmed."

[1] Winthrop speaks of "a brother of Mrs. Hutchinson" (i. 278), but he probably meant a brother-in-law. It was apparently Samuel Hutchinson, who received permission to remain in Boston through the winter of 1637 (*Records,* i. 207), and who the next spring accompanied Wheelwright to New Hampshire. (Bell, *Wheelwright,* 34.)

bridge was declared, the sergeants who, as was then
the custom, were in official attendance upon Vane,
armed with swords and halberds, refused to escort
his successor. They were all Boston men, and their
conduct is the best possible evidence of the unanimity as well as the intensity of the feeling there. Laying down their halberds they went home, leaving
Winthrop, the newly elected governor, to do the same,
unattended. When at this time, also, Boston was
called upon to supply her portion of the levy for service in the Pequot campaign, not a church-member
would consent to be mustered; and the refusal was
based on the fact that their own pastor, selected from
among the clergy by lot as the chaplain to accompany
the contingent, walked in a Covenant of Works. Military service, especially of a somewhat desperate character in savage warfare, is not usually coveted, and in
this case a prudent regard for their own scalps may
at the same time have dulled martial ardor and quickened conscientious doubts in the minds of the church-
members in question; but none the less this holding
back made at the time a deep impression throughout
the other towns of the province, giving "great dis-
couragement to the service," and the apologists for
the subsequent persecution have not failed to put due
emphasis on it since.[1]

As the June days passed away, the alien law was
under discussion at Cambridge, and the excitement in
Boston increased rather than grew less. From the
time of his first coming, Vane had always occupied at
church a seat of honor among the magistrates, whether
he was one of them or not. But on the Sabbath after
the election, instead of taking his usual place, he

[1] Palfrey, i. 492.

and Coddington went and sat with the deacons, in a
way calculated to excite the utmost possible public
notice; and when Winthrop, noticing this, cour-
teously sent to them to resume their old places, they
pointedly declined to do so. As governor, Vane had
walked to church in state, accompanied by four of
the town's sergeants. They now refused to attend
Winthrop, alleging that their attendance on his pre-
decessor had been merely out of personal devotion to
him. This could not but have been deeply mortify-
ing to Winthrop; and it occasioned so much scandal
that the colony took notice of it, and offered to furnish men, from the neighboring towns in turn, to
carry the halberds as usual. Upon this Boston professed itself willing to furnish halberd-bearers, though
not the sergeants, and the Governor at last was fain
to use two of his own servants, and so settle the matter. Nor were Vane's discourtesies to Winthrop confined to official acts or questions of church etiquette.
They touched social relations also. It has already been
seen how in June the Governor undertook to give a
dinner party to young Lord Ley, and among others
sent an invitation to Vane; and how Vane declined
to come on the extraordinary ground that " his conscience withheld him; " but, at the time named for
the entertainment, " went over to Noddle's Island to
dine with Mr. Maverick, and carried the Lord Ley
with him." Besides being the recognized leader of
the opposition, Vane was a defeated candidate for
office; and, as such, it was peculiarly incumbent upon
him to behave with dignity and self-restraint. Winthrop had already set him a lofty example in this
respect: but Winthrop never appeared to such advantage as when bearing up against political defeat,

while Vane now demeaned himself rather like an
angry, sulking schoolboy than like the head of a party
in the state ; and his followers undoubtedly imitated
him.   Consequently, all through the summer of 1637
Winthrop's position must have been most trying.
Wilson, who had he been there would have shared
the general opprobrium with him, was absent with the
soldiers of the Pequot expedition.   Hence the Governor found himself in Boston — Boston, his home
and the town he had founded — with the whole community as one man against him.   Vane would not go
to his house.   The town officers refused to attend
upon him.   A bitter controversy was going on over
the alien law, which excited so much feeling that Cotton seriously thought of moving out of the province,
while not even the relief and exultation over the triumphant close of the Pequot war drew men's thoughts
away from it.   Nor was this to be wondered at.   The
news of Mason's victories in Connecticut and the
storming of the Pequot fort reached Boston at the
very time when Winthrop, acting under that alien
law, refused to permit Samuel Hutchinson to remain
in the province.   In the hour of common triumph,
therefore, the people of Boston saw their friends, relatives and sympathizers, who had just finished the
weary voyage which joined them in exile, refused even
a resting-place, much more an asylum, — and refused
it, also, merely on the ground that they were the
friends, relatives and sympathizers of the people of
Boston.   Such a stretch of government authority not
only must have seemed an outrage, but it was an
outrage.   It compelled a denial of those rights of
common hospitality which even savages respect, and
as persecution it was not less bitter than any prac-

tised in England. Looked at even now, after the
lapse of two hundred years and more, to be forced to
send one's brother or sister, at their first coming into
a new land, out into the wilderness — even as Abraham sent Hagar — was a sore test of patience. The
minority in Boston would have been either more or
less than human had they meekly submitted to it.
They did not meekly submit to it; and so, when mid-
summer was come, there were "many hot speeches
given forth," and angry threats were freely made.

Early in August the posture of the opposing factions underwent a change; Wheelwright lost a potent
friend and ally, and the party of the clericals gained
one. On the $\frac{3d}{13th}$ Vane sailed for England, and his
friends took advantage of his departure to make a
political demonstration. The ship he was to go in
lay at anchor well down the harbor, opposite Long
Island. As the hour for embarking drew near, his
political adherents and those who sympathized in his
theological views collected together, and formally accompanied their departing leader to his boat. They
were under arms, and some cannon had been brought
out; and, as the barges bearing him and a company
of friends were rowed out into the stream, they were
saluted again and again by volleys of small arms and
ordnance. Winthrop was not there to bid his rival
farewell; nor, in view of Vane's studied discourtesies
to him, was he to be blamed for his absence. None
the less he was mindful of the occasion and what was
due to it, and, as the party swept by Castle Island,
the salute from the town was taken up by the fort
and repeated.

Vane never came back to Boston; nor, judging
by his course while there, is the fact greatly to be

regretted. Doubtless he improved, and, as he grew
older, he became more self-restrained; none the less
he was born an agitator and always remained one,
and it is of men of this description that new countries
stand in least need. Unquestionably as respects the
issues involved in the so-called Antinomian controversy, Vane was, in the abstract, more — much more
— nearly right than Winthrop. But, while his mind
was destructive in its temper, that of Winthrop was
constructive. In new countries everything is to be built
up, and there is little to pull down. In the Massachusetts of 1637, there was nothing but the clergy.
Vane was the popular leader in the first movement
against their supremacy, and the fight he made showed
he possessed parliamentary qualities of a high order;
but, as was apparent in the result of it, the movement itself was premature. After the failure of that
movement its leader would have proved wholly out of
place in New England, while in England he found
ample field for the exercise of all his powers. In the
world's advance every one cannot be on the skirmish
line; nor is the sharp-shooter necessarily a more useful soldier than he who advances only just in front of
the solid line of battle, — even though the latter be
less keen of sight and wide of vision. As compared
with Winthrop, the younger Vane was a man of
larger and more active mind, of more varied and brilliant qualities. What is now known as an advanced
thinker, he instinctively looked deeper into the heart
of his subject. Winthrop, it is true, shared in the
darkness and the superstition, and even — in his calm,
moderate way — in the intolerance of his time; but
it was just that sharing in the weakness as well as the
strength — the superstitions as well as the faith — of

his time which made him so valuable in the place
chance called upon him to fill. He was in sympathy
with his surroundings, — just enough in the advance,
and not too much. In 1637 — persecution or no persecution, momentarily right or momentarily wrong —
Massachusetts could far better spare Henry Vane
from its councils than it could have spared John Winthrop.

Vane's departure was none the less an irreparable
loss, almost a fatal blow, to John Wheelwright, for
by it he was deprived of his protector, and left, naked
and bound, in the hands of his enemies. Nor did
they long delay over the course they would take with
him. The Pequot war was ended ; for in July the
last remnant of the doomed tribe had been destroyed
in the swamp fight at New Haven, and now grave magistrates and elders were bringing to Boston from the
Connecticut the skins and the scalps of Sassacus and
his sachems, ghastly trophies of the savage fight. They
arrived on the $\frac{5th}{15th}$ of August, Vane having sailed on
the $\frac{3d}{13th}$, and the same day the party of the clericals
was reinforced by the return of Mr. Wilson. Having
been absent some seven weeks, with the Massachusetts contingent under Stoughton's command, he had
been sent for to return at once. In response to the
summons Stoughton — then at New London, and preparing to cross over to Block Island — immediately
dismissed his chaplain, " albeit," he wrote, " we conceived we had special interest in him, and count ourselves naked without him ; " but he bethought himself
that " we could enjoy him but one Sabbath more."
And so Wilson returned by way of Providence, in
company with the Rev. Thomas Hooker and the Rev.
Samuel Stone, respectively the minister and the

teacher of the church at Hartford, both close disputants as well as famous divines.   All the clergy of the
province and neighboring settlements were in fact
now directing their steps towards Boston ; and the
spirit of theological controversy aroused itself, quickened and refreshed by two months of thought diverted
to carnal warfare.   A synod was to be held.

CHAPTER VII.

VÆ VICTIS.

Synods and convocations are the last recourse of
perplexed theologians. A high authority in matters
connected with Puritan history and theology, after
referring to them as "the bane and scourge of Chris-
tendom," adds . that, while "called to promote harmony and uniformity, they have invariably resulted
in variance, discord and a widening of previous
breaches." [1] The synod of 1637 was the first thing of
the sort attempted in America; and, under the circumstances, and in the absence of all the usual machinery for carrying on discussion, it was perhaps
as good a method of bringing opposing parties together as could have been devised. When brought
together, even if no agreement could be reached, they
might at least find out each where the other stood;
and, if the chances were that in its results a synod
would embitter rather than allay strife, this risk had
to be taken. The meeting was fixed for the $\frac{30\text{th}}{9\text{th}}$ of
$\frac{\text{August}}{\text{September}}$, and a busy three weeks, crowded with meetings and lectures, Days of Humiliation and Days of
Thanksgiving, preceded. Some of the elders, evidently much troubled at the gravity of the situation,
busied themselves to bring about an understanding
between Wilson and Wheelwright and Cotton. So
far as Cotton was concerned they were not unsuc-

---

[1] Ellis, *The Puritan Age*, 219; Savage, *Winthrop*, i. *240, n.

cessful, for, now that Vane was gone, the eloquent
teacher of the Boston church began to find his position a trying one. He had, indeed, seriously thought
of turning his back on the dust and turmoil of Boston, — political as well as theological, — and seeking
refuge and quiet elsewhere ; but the idea did not
commend itself to him. He was no longer young,
and, perhaps, his nerves gave way before the pros-
pect of again facing the wilderness, a banished man ;
perhaps also he was over-persuaded by the members
of his church. Accordingly a sensation was excited
in the Boston meeting-house when, on the Sunday
following Wilson's return, Cotton announced to the
congregation that the minister had explained certain
words, used by him in his discourse before the Court
in the previous October, as applying not to any pulpit doctrines uttered by the teacher himself or by
his brother Wheelwright, but to some opinions " privately carried." As it was quite well known that Mr.
Wilson had long before made this very equivocal con-
cession, the sudden change in his own mind, indicated
by Cotton's announcement, excited no little comment.
He was evidently opening a way for retreat.

The following Thursday Mr. Davenport delivered
the lecture at Boston. He was a famous controversialist, and had in Holland borne earnest witness
against what he termed " promiscuous baptism," holding rigidly to the tenet that children of communicants
only should be admitted to that holy institution.
Having only recently come to New England, Mr.
Davenport had no settlement within the patent; but,
nevertheless, out of deference to his great fame, he had
been urged to attend the Synod, and he now lectured
on the nature and danger of divisions, while at the

same time he " clearly discovered his judgment against the new opinions." It was another indication of the set of the tide. The 24th of the month was kept as a Fast-day in all the churches; and on the 26th, amidst much rejoicing, Stoughton and his soldiers returned from their Pequot campaign and were feasted. Then came $\frac{\text{August 30th}}{\text{September 9th}}$, and the Synod.

It met at Cambridge, and was composed of some twenty-five ministers, being " all the teaching elders through the country," with whom were Davenport and others freshly arrived. When to these were added the lay members and the body of the magistrates, it will be seen that the attendance was large. The deliberations were in public. Among those present were some few of Shepard's conciliatory temper, but the majority and the leaders were men of the type of Ward, Weld and Peters. They were there to stamp a heresy out; and they proposed to do it just as effectually in New England as Archbishop Laud, at that same time, was proposing to do it in the mother country. From the first, a well-developed spirit of theological hate showed itself in easy control of everything. Mather says that " at the beginning of the assembly, after much discourse against the unscriptural enthusiasms and revelations then by some contended for, Mr. Wilson proposed: 'You that are against these things, and that are for the spirit and the word together, hold up your hands!' And the multitude of hands then held up was a comfortable and encouraging introduction unto the other proceedings." The other proceedings were in perfect keeping with the introduction. There was in them no trace of wisdom, of conciliation or of charity, — nothing but priestly intolerance, stimulated by blind zeal.

No sooner was it organized and ready for business than the Synod proceeded to throw out a sort of general drag-net designed to sweep up all conceivable heretical opinions. The work was thoroughly done, and soon there were spread upon the record no less than eighty-two " opinions, some blasphemous, others erroneous, and all unsafe," besides nine " unwholesome expressions." [1]   As all the twenty-five ministers — with one exception, or possibly two — were of the same way of thinking, the proceedings were reasonably harmonious. Certain of the lay members from among the Boston delegates were indeed outspoken in their expressions of disgust that such a huge body of heresies should be paraded without any pretence of their being entertained by any one ; but Wheelwright seems discreetly to have held his peace, taking the ground that, as they were not imputed to him, they were none of his concern. Consequently, when the indignant Bostonians got up and left the assembly, he remained behind, nor jarred upon the spirit of unbroken harmony which for a time followed their departure. After every conceivable abstract opinion and expression had been raked up, the entire pile was most appropriately disposed of by the Rev. Mr. Wilson with one sweep of the theological dung-fork.   In reply to the gasping inquiry of one of his brethren as to what should be done with such a dispensation of

---

[1] As the term " unwholesome expressions " hardly conveys a clear idea to modern readers, a statement of one of those now spread upon the record, and of its synodical confutation, may not be out of place :—

"S. Peter more leaned to a Covenant of Works than Paul, Pauls doctrine does more for free grace than Peters.

" ANSW. To oppose these persons and the doctrine of these two Apostles of Christ, who were guided by one and the same Spirit in preaching and penning thereof, in such a point as the Covenant of workes and grace, is little lesse than blasphemy."

heterodoxies, the pastor of the Boston church exclaimed, no less vigorously than conclusively : — "Let them go to the devil of hell, from whence they came!"

Having in this way very comfortably disposed of preliminaries, the Synod settled itself down to real business. The work in hand was to devise some form of words which Cotton and Wheelwright on the one side, and the body of their brethren on the other, would assent to as an expression of common belief. There were five points nominally in question, which were subsequently reduced to three. To appreciate the whole absurdity of the jargon, in which metaphysics lent confusion to theology, these must be stated in full : —

"1. That the new creature is not the person of a believer, but a body of saving graces in such a one ; and that Christ, as a head, doth enliven or quicken, preserve or act the same, but Christ himself is no part of this new creature.

"2. That though, in effectual calling (in which the answer of the soul is by active faith, wrought at the same instant by the Spirit,) justification and sanctification be all together in them ; yet God doth not justify a man, before he be effectually called, and so a believer.

"3. That Christ and his benefits may be offered and exhibited to a man under a Covenant of Works, but not in or by a Covenant of Works."

It is not easy to realize now that strong, matter-of-fact, reasoning men could ever have been educated to the point of inflicting — and, what is far more curious, of enduring — persecution, banishment and torture in the propagation or in the defence of such incomprehensible formulas. They furnish in themselves at once the strongest evidence and the most striking illustration of the singular condition of religious and

theological craze in which early New England existed.
As the modern investigator puzzles over these articles
of a once living faith, in vain trying to find out in
what lay their importance, — even conceding their
truth, — the Synod, and the outcome of its wrestlings,
calls to mind nothing so much as that passage from
the poem of the greatest of its co-religionists, wherein,
with bitter mockery, one portion of " the host of Hell "
is represented as sitting on a hill apart, where they

> " reason'd high
> Of Providence, foreknowledge, will, and fate,
> Fix'd fate, free will, foreknowledge absolute ;
> And found no end, in wand'ring mazes lost."

The difference between Milton's devils and the early
New England divines seems to have been that, while
the one and the other lost themselves in the same
mazes of the unknowable, the former evinced much
the more Christian spirit of the two in their methods
of conducting the debate.   Both were suffering banishment from their former homes ; but, while the
Synod of the fallen angels in their place of exile
amicably discussed points of abstract difference, the
similar Synod of New England ministers betrayed,
throughout their proceedings, all " the exquisite rancor
of theological hate."

After much discussion, written as well as oral, of
the controverted points, Cotton, with a degree of
worldly wisdom which did credit to his head, declared
at last that he saw light.   Whether he really did so
or not is of little consequence.   It is clear that no one
in the assembly had any distinct conception of what
they were talking about ; and it was certainly nothing
against any one that he professed to see the nebulous
idealities, at which they were all gazing through the

dense mist of words, in the same way that the majority saw them. Wheelwright was of a less accommodating spirit. To him the cloud looked neither like a whale nor like a weasel. He would not say that it did. So far as he was concerned, therefore, the Synod resulted exactly as his enemies desired. He was now completely isolated; he had lost Cotton as well as Vane.

The sessions continued through twenty-four days. At first arguments were delivered in writing and read in the assembly, and answers followed in the same way; but as this method of procedure occupied too much time, recourse was had to oral disputation. Then the questions at issue were speedily determined. Finally, all other business being disposed of, Mrs. Hutchinson's female symposiums were voted a nuisance, or, in the language of the day, "agreed to be disorderly and without rule;" and then, on the $\frac{22d}{24}$ of $\frac{\text{September}}{\text{October}}$, the convocation broke up amid general congratulations "that matters had been carried on so peaceably, and concluded so comfortably in all love." The result of it all was that "Mr. Cotton and they agreed, but Mr. Wheelwright did not."

From the day of adjournment onward, therefore, Wheelwright was to confront his opponents alone; and in the number of his opponents were included the whole body of the clergy and the whole body of the magistracy. The Synod had done its work in two ways; not only was Cotton saved, but, the efforts at conciliation having failed, it only remained to leave the refractory to be dealt with by the arm of the civil authority. The General Court, elected at the time of the stormy Cambridge gathering in May, had shown little disposition to grapple in earnest with the Antinomian issue. As often as that issue presented itself it was postponed; and the course of the deputies would seem to warrant an inference that, elected as they had been while the parties were not unevenly divided, the Court contained a representation of each side sufficient to hold the other side in check. Whether this was so or not, on the $\frac{26\text{th}}{6\text{th}}$ of $\frac{\text{September}}{\text{October}}$ — just four days after the adjournment of the Synod — the Court, which had been elected for the entire year, was suddenly dissolved, and a new election ordered.

The cause of so unusual a proceeding can only be inferred; yet it would seem but reasonable to suppose that the legislature, as then made up, was not considered equal to doing the work in hand; and, certainly, the new Court was a very different body from the old one. Of the twenty-seven delegates who met at Cambridge on the day the May Court was dissolved, twelve only were reëlected; and of the thirty-three members of the Court chosen in October, no less than twenty-one were new men. Among those left out was Wheelwright's stanch friend and parishioner, Atherton Hough; but Coddington, Aspinwall and Coggeshall were returned by Boston, and constituted at least a nucleus of opposition.

The new Court met on the $\frac{2\text{d}}{12\text{th}}$ of November. Those composing it found both Wheelwright and Mrs. Hutchinson still obdurate. The former, just as if no Synod had ascertained the whole everlasting truth and expressed it in plain language, was preaching the Covenant of Grace to all who would hear him at the Mount; while the latter continued her weekly female gatherings, and put no bridle on her tongue. With the clouds lowering heavily over them, they maintained a bold front. They did more than this, — they even went out to meet the danger, openly rejecting all

thought of compromise, with a loud assertion that the
difference between them and their opponents was as
that between heaven and hell, — a gulf too deep to
fill, too wide to bridge. In later days, under similar circumstances, persons feeling in this way would
quietly have been permitted to set up a conventicle of
their own, at which they could have mouthed their
rubbish until they wearied. A schism in the church
would have restored quiet to the community. But
this was not the rule of primitive New England. That
rule was one of rigid conformity, — the rule of the
" lord-brethren " in place of the rule of the " lord-
bishops." So, as Winthrop expressed it, those in the
majority, " finding, upon consultation, that two so
opposite parties could not continue in the same body
without apparent hazard of ruin to the whole, agreed
to send away some of the principal." A somewhat
similar conclusion had previously been reached in regard to Spain and the Netherlands by Philip II., and
was subsequently reached in regard to France by
Louis XIV.

Having decided upon extreme measures the leaders
of the dominant party now proceeded in a business-
like manner. Those composing the minority were to
be thoroughly disciplined. There was no difficulty
in dealing with Wheelwright and Mrs. Hutchinson.
They were doomed. But the men who were in the
ascendant — the Welds, the Peters, the Bulkleys and
the Symmes of the colonial pulpit — had no idea of
contenting themselves with that small measure of
atonement. The heresy was to be extirpated, root
and branch. " Thorough " was then the word at
Whitehall; and " Thorough " was the idea, if not the
word, in Massachusetts. But a species of sweep-net

was now needed which should bring the followers no
less than the leaders under the ban of the law.   The
successful prosecution of Wheelwright afforded the
necessary hint.   Wheelwright had been brought within
the clutches of the civil authorities by a species of *ex
post facto* legal chicanery.   Even his most bitter
opponents did not pretend to allege that he had
preached his Fast - day sermon with the intent to
bring about any disturbance of the peace.   They only
claimed that his utterances tended to make such a
result probable, and that his own observation ought
to have convinced him of the fact.[1]   Therefore, they
argued, although it was true that no breach of the
peace had actually taken place, and although the
preacher had no intent to excite to a breach of the
peace, yet he was none the less guilty of constructive
sedition.   Constructive sedition was now made to do
the same work in New England which constructive
treason, both before and after, was made to do elsewhere.   It was a most excellent device ; and a pretext, or " fair opportunity," as Winthrop expresses it,
for its application was found in that remonstrance of
the 9th of the previous March, which, signed by sixty
of the leading inhabitants of Boston, had now quietly
reposed among the records of the colony through
four sessions of two separate legislatures.   The paper
speaks for itself.[2]   The single passage in it to which
even a theologian's acuteness could give a color of

[1] This point is of importance, and Winthrop's language is explicit
in regard to it : — " If his intent were not to stirre up to open force and
armes (neither do we suspect him of any such purpose, otherwise than
by consequent) yet his reading and experience might have told him,
how dangerous it is to heat people's affections against their opposites."
Short Story, 53.

[2] See Appendix to Savage's *Winthrop* (ed. 1853), i. 481–3.

sedition was couched in these words: — " Thirdly, if
you look at the effects of his Doctrine upon the hearers, it hath not stirred up sedition in us, not so much
as by accident; we have not drawn the sword, as
sometime Peter did, rashly, neither have we rescued
our innocent brother, as sometime the Israelites did
Jonathan, and yet they did not seditiously." The last
six words are those which Governor Winthrop, and
the subsequent apologists of what now took place,[1]
dwell upon as in themselves sufficient to make the
drawing up or signing of this paper an offence for
which banishment was a mild and hardly adequate
penalty; and this, too, in face of the fact that the remonstrance immediately went on as follows: — " The
covenant of free grace held forth by our brother hath
taught us rather to become humble suppliants to your
Worships, and if we should not prevail, we would
rather with patience give our cheeks to the smiters."

Even had this paper been of a seditious character,
it was presented to a former Court, and not to the
one which now passed judgment upon it. The Court
elected in November, 1637, had no more to do with
the Boston remonstrance of the preceding March
than with any other paper, the character of which, as
it slept among the dusty archives, some deputy might
chance not to fancy. Those to whom it was addressed
had considered it a respectful and proper document;
and it was reserved for a body to which it was not
addressed to hunt it up on the files, in order to declare it a contempt and make it the basis of a proscription.

The Court met on the $\frac{2d}{12th}$ of November. No sooner
was it organized than it became apparent it was to be

---

[1] Palfrey, i. 492.

purged; in it the elements of opposition were few, but
those few were to be weeded out. It has already been
mentioned that Coddington, Aspinwall and Coggeshall were the deputies from Boston. They were all
three adherents of the Covenant of Grace, friends of
Mrs. Hutchinson and supporters of Wheelwright;
while Coddington's name stood first among those
affixed to the remonstrance now pronounced seditious.
Coddington was a magistrate, an old and honored
official, — a man classed, in popular estimation, with
Winthrop and Endicott as one of the founders of the
colony. Him they did not like to attack; and there
is also reason to believe that Winthrop exerted himself to shield his old associate. No such safeguards
surrounded Aspinwall and Coggeshall. The record of
the Court shows that it was at once demanded of the
former whether he still adhered to the sentiments expressed in the remonstrance. He replied that he did.
A vote expelling him from his seat was immediately
passed. Indignant at the expulsion of his colleague,
Coggeshall then rose in his place and declared his
approbation of the remonstrance, though his name
was not among those signed to it; and he added that,
if the course taken with Aspinwall was to be followed
towards others, they " had best make one work of all."
He was taken at his word, and forthwith expelled.
Other deputies had then to be elected. The freemen
of Boston would have been indeed devoid of any feelings of manliness, much more of pride, had such treatment of their representatives not excited indignation
among them, and at first they proposed to return to
the Court the same deputies to whom seats had just
been refused. This action must at once have brought
on the crisis, and Cotton prevented it; for he was

still looked upon as friendly to the defeated party, —
indeed, in heart, he was so, — and among the church-
members, who alone were freeholders, their teacher's
influence was great.   Instead of Coggeshall and Aspinwall, accordingly, William Colburn and John
Oliver were chosen, and the next day appeared to
take their seats.   But an examination of the remonstrance revealed Oliver's name upon it; and, when
questioned, he justified the paper.   Permission to
take his seat was consequently refused him, and the
election of another in his place ordered.   The freemen of Boston took no notice of the new warrant.

The Court being now purged of all his friends,
Coddington only excepted, Wheelwright's case was
taken up.   He appeared in answer to the summons ;
but, when asked if he was yet prepared to confess
his errors, he stubbornly refused so to do, protesting
his entire innocence of what was charged against
him.   He could not be induced to admit that he had
been guilty either of sedition or of contempt, and he
asserted that the doctrine preached by him in his
Fast-day discourse was sound ; while, as to any individual application which had been made of it, he was
not accountable.   Then followed a long wrangle, reach-
ing far into the night and continued the next day,
during which the natural obstinacy of Wheelwright's
temper must have been sorely tried.   At his door was
laid the responsibility for all the internal dissensions
of the province.   He was the fruitful source of those
village and parish ills ; and every ground of complaint
was gone over, from the lax response of Boston to
the call for men for the Pequot war to the slight
put by his church upon Wilson, and by the halber-
diers upon Winthrop.   To such an indictment de-

fence was impossible ; and so, in due time, the Court
proceeded to its sentence. It was disfranchisement
and exile. As it was already what is the middle of
our November, the date of the exile's departure was
at first postponed until March, when the severity of
the winter would be over; in the mean time, as a
preacher, he was to be silenced. From this sentence
Wheelwright took an appeal to the King, which the
Court at once refused to allow. Twenty-four hours
later, after a night of reflection, he withdrew his appeal, offering to accept a sentence of simple banishment, but refusing absolutely to be silenced. He was
then at last permitted to return to his own house at
Mt. Wollaston, and his sentence stands recorded as
follows : —

"Mr. John Wheelwright, being formally convicted of
contempt and sedition, and now justifying himself and his
former practice, being to the disturbance of the civil peace,
he is by the Court disfranchised and banished, having fourteen days to settle his affairs ; and, if within that time he
depart not the patent, he promiseth to render himself to
Mr. Stoughton, at his house, to be kept till he be disposed
of ; and Mr. Hough undertook to satisfy any charge that
he, Mr. Stoughton, or the country should be at."

Unlike Mrs. Hutchinson and the body of those
who were to follow him into banishment, Wheelwright did not direct his steps towards Rhode Island.
On the contrary, after preaching a farewell sermon
to his little congregation, in which there was no word
of retraction, he turned his face to the northward,
and with all the courage and tenacity of purpose
which throughout had marked his action, in spite of
the inclement season and the impending winter, within
his allotted fourteen days he was on his way to the

Piscataqua. He went alone through the deepening
snow, which that winter lay from November to the
end of March " a yard deep," according to Winthrop,
beyond the Merrimac, and "the more north the
deeper," while the mercury ranged so low that the
exile himself, with a grim effort at humor, drearily
remarked that he believed had he been filled with
" the very extracted spirits of sedition and contempt,
they would have been frozen up and indisposed for
action." [1] Not until April did his wife, bringing with
her his mother-in-law and their children, undertake to
follow him to the spot where he and a few others had
founded what has since become the academic town of
Exeter. It is merely curious now to reflect on the
intense bitterness, and sense of wrong and of unend-
ing persecution which must have nerved the steps of
the former vicar of Bilsby, when, at forty-five years
of age, he turned his back on Mt. Wollaston, and
sternly sought refuge from his brethren in Christ
amid the snow and ice of bleak, unfertile New Hampshire.

[1] *Mercurius Americanus*, Bell, 228.

CHAPTER VIII.

HAVING disposed of Wheelwright's case the General Court, without stopping to take breath, at once proceeded to that of Mistress Hutchinson, — "the breeder and nourisher of all these distempers." In the language of the time, she was "convented for traducing the ministers and their ministry in this country;" and these words most happily set forth her offence. It could not be charged against her that she had signed the remonstrance, for her name was not among those appended to it; she had preached no sedition; being a woman, she could bear no hand in any apprehended tumult. She had criticised the clergy; and for that she was now arraigned.

Though, as will presently appear, the proceedings were in no way lacking in interest, there was about them nothing either solemn or imposing. Indeed, all the external surroundings, as well as the physical conditions, were so very matter-of-fact and harsh, that any attempt at pomp or state would have been quite out of keeping; everything, without as well as within, was dreary and repellent, — in a word, New England wintry. The Court was still sitting at Newetowne, as it was called; for the name was not changed to Cambridge until a year later, though the college was at this very session ordered to be fixed there. It was a crude, straggling settlement,

made up of some sixty or seventy log-cabins, or
poor frame-houses, which only eighteen months before had been mainly abandoned by their occupants,
who, under the lead of their pastor, Thomas Hooker,
had then migrated in a body to the banks of the Connecticut. The Rev. Thomas Shepard, with those who
had just come over with him, had bought the empty
tenements and moved into them. An inscription cut
in the granite foundation wall of a modern bake-
house, on the busy Mt. Auburn thoroughfare, now
marks the spot where the church, or meeting-house
rather, stood on the upland, not far from the narrow
fringe of marshes which there skirted the devious
channel of the Charles. In front of it ran the main
village street, ending in a foot-bridge leading down
to low-water mark at the ferry, while a ladder was
secured to the steep further bank of the river for
"convenience of landing." Close to the meeting-
house, but nearer to the ferry, was the dwelling built
for himself by Governor Dudley in 1630, and in
which, at the breaking-up of the sharp winter of 1631,
he wrote his letter to Bridget, Countess of Lincoln,
"having got no table, or other room to write in than
by the fireside upon my knee." Laid out with some
regard for symmetry and orderly arrangement, Newetowne was looked upon as "one of the neatest and
best compacted towns in New England, having many
fair structures, with many handsome contrived
streets." The river being to the south, on the northern side of the village there stretched away a comparatively broad and level plain, covering many
hundred acres, then used as a common pasture-
ground and fenced in by a paling of a mile and a
half in length. A year or two later, the college build-

ing was erected on the southern limit of this plain; while a third of a mile or so to the north stood the great oak under which had been held that May election which resulted in the defeat of Vane, and in Winthrop's return to office.[1]

Of the meeting-house itself no description has been preserved. It seems to have been a rude frame building, built of rough-hewn boards, the crevices of which were sealed with mud. Its roof, sloping down from a long ridge-pole, on which was perched a bell, had, it is supposed, at first been thatched, but was now covered with slate or boards; and the narrow dimensions of the primitive edifice may be inferred from the fact that when, a dozen years afterwards, it no longer sufficed for a prospering community, the new and more commodious one which succeeded it was but forty feet square. Such as it was, the meeting-house was the single building of a public sort in the place, and within it the sessions of the Court were now held, as those of the Synod had been held there shortly before.

The season was one of unusual severity, and the days among the shortest of the year. Though November, according to the calendar then in use, was not yet half over, there had nearly a week before been a considerable fall of snow, which still whitened the ground, while the ice had begun to make, piling itself up along the river's bank.[2] No pretence even was made of warming the barrack-like edifice; and, dark at best in the November day, it could not be

---

[1] Higginson, 250*th Ann. of Cambridge*, 48; Mackenzie, *First Church in Cambridge*, Lect. II.; Paige, *Cambridge*, 18, 37; Young, *Chron. of Mass.* 402.

[2] Winthrop, i. *243–4, *264.

lighted at all after dusk. Its furniture consisted
only of rude wooden benches, on which the deputies
and those in attendance sat, and a table and chairs for
the Governor and the magistrates. All told, the Court
consisted of some forty members, nine of whom were
magistrates ; but the little church was thronged, for
the outside attendance was large, almost every person
of note in the province being there. Indeed, nothing
in the history of Massachusetts, up to this time, had
ever excited so great an interest. The clergy, in
point of fact not only the prosecutors in the case
but also the witnesses against the accused, were necessarily present in full ranks. Wilson and Cotton
both were there from Boston : the former bent on the
utter destruction of her who, sowing dissension between his people and himself, had, with feminine
ingenuity, strewed his path with thorns ; the latter
not yet terrified into a complete abandonment of those
who looked to him as their mentor. The fanatical
Peters had come from Salem ; and he and Thomas
Weld of Roxbury, having been the most active pro-
moters of the prosecution, were now to appear as chief
witnesses against the accused. With the pastor,
Weld, had come Eliot, the teacher at Roxbury, — now
only thirty-four, and not for nine years yet to begin
those labors among the Indians which were to earn
for his name the prefix of " the Apostle." He too
was unrelenting in his hostility to the new opinions.
There also were George Phillips of Watertown, " one
of the first saints of New England ; " [1] Zachariah

---

[1] George Phillips was the common ancestor of that Phillips family
subsequently so prominent in the history of Boston. Cotton Mather,
with even more than his usual quaintness, says of him that " he laboured under many bodily infirmities : but was especially liable to
the cholick ; the extremity of one fit whereof, was the wind which

Symmes of Charlestown, who himself knew what it
was to suffer for "conscientious nonconformity;"
and finally Thomas Shepard of Cambridge, " a poore,
weake, pale-complectioned man" of thirty-four, but
yet "holy, heavenly, sweet-affecting and soul-ravishing." And indeed Shepard alone of them all seems to
have borne in mind, in the proceedings which were to
follow, that charity, long-suffering and forgiveness entered into the Master's precepts. Winthrop presided
over the deliberations of the Court, acting at once
as judge and prosecuting attorney. At his side, foremost among the magistrates, sat Dudley and Endicott, — men whose rough English nature had been
narrowed and hardened by a Puritan education.

Such was the Court. The culprit before it for trial
was a woman of some thirty-six or seven years of age.
Slight of frame, and now in manifestly delicate health,
there was in her bearing nothing masculine or defiant;
though, seemingly, she faced a tribunal — in which,
so far as now appears, she could have found but two
friendly faces — with calmness and self-possession.
She had no counsel, nor was the trial conducted according to any established rules of procedure. It
was a mere hearing in open legislative session. Of
its details, one — himself an eminent New England
clergyman not versed in legal technicalities or familiar
with rules of evidence or the methods of courts — has
said that the treatment which the accused then underwent "deserves the severest epithets of censure," and
that "the united civil wisdom and Christian piety of
the fathers of Massachusetts make but a sorry fig-

carried him afore it, into the haven of eternal rest, on July 1, in the
year 1644, much desired and lamented by his church at Watertown."
Magnalia, B. iii. ch. iv. § 9.

ure." [1] Certainly, if what there took place had taken place in England at the trial of some patriot or non-conformer before the courts — ecclesiastical, civil or criminal — of any of the Stuarts, the historians of New England would not have been sparing in their denunciations. But the record best speaks for itself. From that record it will appear that the accused, unprovided with counsel, was not only examined and cross-examined by the magistrates, her judges, but badgered, insulted and sneered at, and made to give evidence against herself. The witnesses in her behalf were browbeaten and silenced in careless disregard both of decency and a manly sense of fair play. Her few advocates among the members of the court were rudely rebuked, and listened to with an impatience which it was not attempted to conceal ; while, throughout, the so-called trial was, in fact, no trial at all, but a mockery of justice rather, — a bare-faced inquisitorial proceeding. And all this will appear from the record.

The Court met, and presently the accused, in obedience to its summons, appeared before it. At first, though it must have been manifest she was shortly to become a mother, she was not even bidden to sit down, but soon " her countenance discovered some bodily infirmity," and a chair was provided for her.

---

[1] Dr. George E. Ellis, in the biography of Anne Hutchinson. (Sparks' *American Biography*, N. S. vi. 277.) Dr. Ellis' life of Mrs. Hutchinson was written in 1845 ; in 1888, after an interval of over forty years, he reviewed the whole subject of the Antinomian Controversy in his work entitled *The Puritan Age in Massachusetts* (300–62). He there says (336) : — "We have to fall back upon our profound impressions of the deep sincerity and integrity of [Winthrop's] character . . . to read without some faltering or misgiving of approval, not to say with regret and reproach, the method with which he conducted the examination of this gifted and troublesome woman."

The offence of which she had been really guilty, — the breeding of a faction in the Boston church against the pastor, Wilson, and, when his brethren came to his aid, not hesitating to criticise them also, — this offence it was somewhat embarrassing to formulate in fitting words. It could not well be bluntly charged. Winthrop therefore began with a general arraignment, in which he more particularly accused the prisoner of having meetings at her house, "a thing not tolerable nor comely in the sight of God nor fitting for [her] sex;" and, further, with justifying Mr. Wheelwright's Fast-day sermon and the Boston petition. Mrs. Hutchinson now showed herself quite able to hold her own in the casuistical fence of the time, and this part of the case resulted disastrously for the prosecution. Indeed, the logic made use of by Winthrop was of a kind which exposed him badly. He contended that the accused had transgressed the law of God commanding her to honor her father and mother. The magistrates were the fathers of the commonwealth; and therefore, in adhering to those who signed the remonstrance, even though she did not sign it herself, she dishonored the magistrates, and was justly punishable. Coming from the mouth of the Archbishop of Canterbury in 1637 this would be pronounced sophistical rubbish; it was equally sophistical rubbish when uttered by the Governor of Massachusetts Bay for the same year. Mrs. Hutchinson disposed of the allegation with dignity and point in these words: — "I do acknowledge no such thing; neither do I think that I ever put any dishonor upon you."

The next count in the indictment pressed upon her related to the meetings of women held at her house.

Here, too, the prosecution fared badly. Mrs. Hutchinson was asked by what warrant she held such meetings; she cited in reply the usage which she found prevailing in Boston at her coming, and the Scriptural rule in the second chapter of Titus, that the elder women should instruct the younger. The following altercation then ensued : —

"GOVERNOR WINTHROP. You know that there is no rule [in the Scriptures] which crosses another; but this rule [in Titus] crosses that in the Corinthians. You must therefore take [the rule in Titus] in this sense, that the elder women must instruct the younger about their business, and to love their husbands, and not to make them to clash.

"MRS. HUTCHINSON.   I do not conceive but that it is meant also for some public times.

"GOVERNOR.   Well, have you no more to say but this ?

"MRS. H.   I have said sufficient for my practice.

"GOVERNOR.   Your course is not to be suffered; for, besides that we find such a course as this greatly prejudicial to the State, . . . we see not that any should have authority to set up any other exercises besides what authority hath already set up; and so what hurt comes of this you will be guilty of, and we for suffering you.

"MRS. H.   Sir, I do not believe that to be so.

"GOVERNOR.   Well, we see how it is.   We must therefore put it away from you; or restrain you from maintaining this course.

"MRS. H.   If you have a rule for it from God's Word, you may.

"GOVERNOR.   We are your judges, and not you ours. And we must compel you to it.

"MRS. H.   If it please you by authority to put it down, I will freely let you.   For I am subject to your authority."

For a moment, these words as Winthrop uttered them must have jarred with a strange and yet famil-

iar sound on the ears of the listening clergy, hardly
one of whom had in England escaped being silenced
by the prelates; and now they heard the same principles of rigid conformity laid down in their place of
refuge, — freedom of conscience was once for all there
denied. The preliminaries were now brought to a
close, and the trial proceeded to the real issue involved. The charge was explicit. Mrs. Hutchinson,
it was alleged, had publicly said that Mr. Cotton
alone of the ministers preached a Covenant of Grace;
the others, not having received the seal of the Spirit,
were consequently not able ministers of the New Testament, and preached a Covenant of Works. To this
count in the indictment against her she was at first
invited to plead guilty; which she declined to do.
Governor Winthrop then permitted himself to indulge
in a sneer, which was met with a prompt and digni-
fied rejoinder. Both sneer and rejoinder stand thus
recorded : —

"GOVERNOR WINTHROP. It is well discerned to the
Court that Mrs. Hutchinson can tell when to speak and
when to hold her tongue. Upon the answering of a question which we desire her to tell her thoughts of, she desires
to be pardoned.

" MRS. HUTCHINSON. It is one thing for me to come before a public magistracy, and there to speak what they
would have me to speak; and another when a man comes
to me in a way of friendship, privately. There is a difference in that."

Possibly it was at this point in the trial that, stung
by Winthrop's slur, the anger of the accused flashed
up and found expression in hot words; for Weld tells
us that once, " her reputation being a little touched,
. . . she vented her impatience with so fierce speech

and countenance, as one would hardly have guessed
her to have been an Antitype of Daniel, but rather of
the lions, after they were let loose." However this
may be, the witnesses for the prosecution, Peters,
Weld, Eliot, Symmes and the others, who up to this
time had been watching the case in grim silence, were
now called upon, and, one after another, gave their
evidence. Though the question at issue was sufficiently
plain, the discussion then soon passed into the unintelligible. It has been seen that, at a certain point
in the growth of differences in the Boston church,
the ministers of the adjoining towns had been called
upon to interpose, and a conference had then taken
place between the two sides, — the visiting elders and
Mr. Wilson representing one, and Mrs. Hutchinson,
Cotton and Wheelwright the other.[1] The evidence
now given related to what had then taken place. The
ministers all asserted that the conference was a formal
one of a public nature, and so understood at the time.
This Mrs. Hutchinson denied, — thus making the
point that she had been guilty of no open disparagement of the clergy, but that, whatever she had said,
had been drawn from her in private discourse by
those now seeking to persecute her for it. As to the
Covenant of Works, while they asserted that she had
charged them with being under such a covenant, she
insisted that she had done nothing of the sort ; though
she admitted that she probably had said that they
" preached a covenant of works, as did. the apostles
before the Ascension. But to preach a covenant of
works, and to be under a covenant of works, are two
different things." She did not deny that she had
singled out Mr. Cotton from among them all as alone

[1] *Supra*, 426–8.

being sealed with the seal of the Spirit, and therefore
preaching a Covenant of Grace, which bit of jargon
was explained as meaning that one so sealed enjoyed
a full assurance of God's favor by the Holy Ghost.
Here at last, in this special assurance attributed to
Cotton, was the rock of offence from which flowed
those waters of bitterness, the cup of which Wilson
and Weld and Peters and the rest had been forced to
drain to the last drop.   A woman's preference among
preachers was somehow to be transmuted into a crime
against the state.

It would be neither easy nor profitable to attempt
to follow the trial into the metaphysico-theological
stage to which it now passed.   Cotton Mather says
that "the mother opinion of the [Antinomian heresy]
was, that a Christian should not fetch any evidence of
his good state before God, from the sight of any inherent qualification in him ; or from any conditional
promise made unto such a qualification." [1]   This being
the mother opinion, and itself not translucent, all the
parties to the proceedings now began to obscure it by
talking about " witnesses of the spirit " and " the seal
of the spirit," and " a broad seal " and " a little seal,"
and the " assurance of God's favor " and " the graces
wanting to evidence it," and " the difference between
the state of the apostles before the Ascension, and
their state after it."   The real difficulty lay in the
fact that the words and phrases to which they attached
an all-important significance did not admit of defini-
tion, and, consequently, were devoid of exact meaning.
They were simply engaged in hot wrangling over the
unknowable : but, while Court and clergy and accused
wallowed and floundered in the mire of their own

[1] *Magnalia*, B. iii. P. ii. ch. v. § 12.

learning, belaboring each other with contradictory texts and with shadowy distinctions, under it all there lay the hard substratum of injured pride and personal hate; and on that, as on the rock of ages, their firm feet rested secure.

Six of the ministers testified in succession, Hugh Peters first. Their evidence was tolerably concurrent that Mrs. Hutchinson had at the Boston church conference spoken freely, saying that they all taught a Covenant of Works, — that they were not able ministers of the New Testament, not being sealed, — and, finally, that Mr. Cotton alone among them preached a Covenant of Grace. This testimony, and the subsequent wrangle, occupied what remained of the first day of the trial, before the growing dusk compelled an adjournment. The next morning, as soon as Governor Winthrop had opened the hearing, Mrs. Hutchinson stated that, since the night before, she had looked over certain notes which had been taken at the time of the conference, and that she did "find things not to be as hath been alleged," and accordingly she now demanded that, as the ministers were testifying in their own cause, they should do so under oath. This demand caused much excitement in the Court, and was looked upon as a fresh insult heaped upon the clergy. Winthrop held that, the case not being one for a jury, the evidence need not be under oath; while other of the magistrates thought that, in a cause exciting so much interest, sworn testimony would better satisfy the country. The accused insisted. "An oath, sir," she exclaimed to Stoughton, "is an end of all strife; and it is God's ordinance." Then Endicott broke in sneeringly: — "A sign it is what respect she has to [the ministers'] words;" and

presently again : — " You lifted up your eyes as if
you took God to witness you came to entrap none, —
and yet you will have them swear ! "   Finally, Winthrop, that all might be satisfied, expressed himself as
willing to administer the oath if the elders would take
it ; though, said he, " I see no necessity of an oath in
this thing, seeing it is true and the substance of the
matter confirmed by divers."   The deputy-governor,
Dudley, then turned the discussion off by crying out :
— " Mark what a flourish Mrs. Hutchinson puts upon
the business that she had witnesses to disprove what
was said ; and here is no man in Court ! "   To which
bit of characteristic brutality the accused seems quietly
to have rejoined by saying : —" If you will not call
them in, that is nothing to me."

The ministers now professed themselves as ready
to be sworn.   At this point Mr. Coggeshall, the dismissed delegate from Boston, apparently with a view
to preventing a conflict of evidence, ventured to suggest to the Court that the ministers should confer
with Cotton before testifying.   The suggestion was
not well received, and Mr. Coggeshall found himself
summarily suppressed ; indeed, three of the judges
did not hesitate to deliver themselves in respect to
him and the accused as follows : —

" GOVERNOR WINTHROP.   Shall we not believe so many
godly elders, in a cause wherein we know the mind of the
party without their testimony ?

" MR. ENDICOTT (addressing Mr. Coggeshall).   I will
tell you what I say.   I think that this carriage of yours
tends to further casting dirt upon the face of the judges.

" MR. HARLAKENDEN.   Her carriage doth the same.   For
she doth not object an essential thing ; but she goes upon
circumstances, — and yet would have them sworn ! "

But before the elders were again called on to testify, Mrs. Hutchinson was told to produce her own witnesses. Of these Mr. Coggeshall was one. He rose when his name was called, and his examination is reported in full and as follows : —

"GOVERNOR WINTHROP. Mr. Coggeshall was not present [at the conference between Mrs. Hutchinson and the elders].

"MR. COGGESHALL. Yes, but I was. Only I desired to be silent till I should be called [to testify].

"GOVERNOR. Will you, Mr. Coggeshall, say that she did not say [what has been testified to]?

"MR. COGGESHALL. Yes. I dare say that she did not say all that which they lay against her.

"MR. PETERS (interrupting). How dare you look into [the face of] the Court to say such a word.

"MR. COGGESHALL. Mr. Peters takes upon him to forbid me. I shall be silent."

The first witness for the defence having been thus effectually disposed of, the second, Mr. Leverett, was called. He testified that he was present at the discussion between the ministers and Mrs. Hutchinson ; that Mr. Peters had then, "with much vehemency and intreaty," urged the accused to specify the difference between his own teachings and those of Mr. Cotton ; and, in reply, she had stated the difference to be in the fact that, just as the Apostles themselves before the Ascension had not received the seal of the Spirit, so Peters and his brethren, not having the same assurance of God's favor as Mr. Cotton, could not preach a Covenant of Grace so clearly as he. When he had finished his statement a brief altercation took place between Weld and Mrs. Hutchinson, at the close of which Governor Winthrop called on

Mr. Cotton to give his recollection of what had taken place.

Mrs. Hutchinson had been less fortunate in her management of the latter than of the earlier portions of her case. Since the question had turned on what took place at the conference, she had found herself pressed by evidence, and beyond her depth. As is apt to be the case with voluble persons under such circumstances, she had then had recourse to small points, — making issues over the order in which events occurred, or the exact words used, and pressing meaningless distinctions, — cavilling even, and equivocating. By so doing she had injured her case, giving Peters a chance to exclaim: — "We do not desire to be so narrow to the Court and the gentlewoman about times and seasons, whether first or last;" while Harlakenden had, as it has been seen, broken out in disgust: — "She doth not object any essential thing, but she goes upon circumstances." The demand that the ministers should be sworn was another mistake. It was an affront to the elders, the most revered class in the community, and it both angered them and shocked the audience. A blasphemy would hardly have angered or shocked them more. Not only did it excite sympathy for the prosecutors and prejudice against the accused, but there was nothing to be gained by it. The ministers had not given false testimony; and she knew it. The only result, therefore, of her demand of an oath was that they gave their testimony twice instead of once, and insomuch impressed it the more on the minds and memories of all. Mrs. Hutchinson, consequently, was fast doing the work of the prosecution, and convicting herself.

But her cause now passed into far abler hands. Cotton's sympathies were strongly with her, and he seems to have been quite ready to show it. When called upon to listen to the evidence of his brethren, he had seated himself by Mrs. Hutchinson's side; and he now rose in answer to Winthrop's summons, and proceeded to give his account of what had passed at the conference. Silencing the accused and soothing the Court, he soon showed very clearly that the qualities which made him an eminent pulpit orator would also have made him an excellent jury lawyer. With no little ingenuity and skill he went on explaining things away, and putting a new gloss upon them, until, when he got through, the prosecution had very little left to work on. In summing up, he said that at the close of the conference it had not seemed to him " to be so ill taken as [now] it is. And our brethren did say, also, that they would not so easily believe reports as they had done; and, withal, mentioned that they would speak no more of it. And afterwards some of them did say they were less satisfied than before. And I must say that I did not find her saying they were under a Covenant of Works, nor that she said they did preach a Covenant of Works."

A discussion then ensued between Cotton and the other ministers, — calm in outward tone, but, on their part at least, full of suppressed feeling. Peters took the lead in it; but even he was not equal to an attempt at browbeating the renowned teacher of the Boston church from the witness-stand, as he had browbeaten Coggeshall from it a few minutes before. Finally Dudley put this direct question: — " They affirm that Mrs. Hutchinson did say they were not able ministers of the New Testament." It touched

the vital point in the accusation. The whole audience
must have awaited the response in breathless silence.
It came in these words : — " I do not remember it."

The prosecution had broken down. It apparently
only remained to let the accused go free, or to condemn and punish her on general principles, in utter
disregard of law and evidence. Silence and discre-
tion alone were now needed in the conduct of the
defence. Then it was that, in the triumphant words
of her bitterest enemy, " her own mouth " delivered
Anne Hutchinson " into the power of the Court, as
guilty of that which all suspected her for, but were
not furnished with proof sufficient to proceed against
her." But modern paraphrase cannot here equal the
terse, quaint language of the original reports. Cotton had just sat down, after giving his answer to
Dudley's question. Some among the audience were
drawing a deep breath of relief, while others of the
magistrates and clergy were looking at one another
in surprise and dismay. The record then goes on as
follows : —

" Upon this she began to speak her mind, and to tell of
the manner of God's dealing with her, and how he revealed
himself to her, and made her know what she had to do.
The Governor perceiving whereabout she went, interrupted
her, and would have kept her to the matter in hand ; but,
seeing her very unwilling to be taken off, he permitted her
to proceed. Her speech was to this effect : —

" ' When I was in old England I was much troubled at
the constitution of the churches there, — so far troubled,
indeed, that I had liked to have turned Separatist. Whereupon I set apart a day of solemn humiliation by myself,
that I might ponder of the thing and seek direction from
God. And on that day God discovered unto me the un-

faithfulness of the churches, and the danger of them, and that none of those Ministers could preach the Lord Jesus aright; for he brought to my mind this scripture : — " And every spirit that confesseth not that Jesus Christ is come in the flesh is not of God ; and this is that spirit of antichrist, whereof ye have heard that it should come ; and even now already it is in the world." I marvelled what this should mean ; and in considering I found that the Papists did not deny that Christ was come in the flesh, nor did we deny it. Who then was antichrist ? Was it the Turk only ? Now I had none to open scripture to me but the Lord. He must be the prophet. And it pleased the Lord then to bring to my mind another scripture : — " For where a testament is, there must also of necessity be the death of the testator ; " and he that denies the testament denies the death of the testator. And in this the Lord did open unto me and give me to see that every one that did not preach the new covenant denies the death of the testator, and has the spirit of antichrist. And upon this it was revealed unto me that the ministers of England were these antichrists. But I knew not how to bear this ; I did in my heart rise up against it. Then I begged of the Lord this atheism might not be in me. After I had begged for light a twelve-month together, the Lord at last let me see how I did oppose Christ Jesus, and he revealed to me that scripture in Isaiah : — " Hearken unto me ye that are far from righteousness : I bring near my righteousness ; it shall not be far off, and my salvation shall not tarry ; " and from thence he showed me the atheism of my own heart, and how I did turn in upon a Covenant of Works, and did oppose Christ Jesus. And ever since I bless the Lord, — he hath let me see which was the clear ministry and which the wrong, and to know what voice I heard, — which was the voice of Moses, which of John Baptist, and which of Christ. The voice of my beloved I have distinguished from the voice of strangers. And thenceforth I was more choice whom I heard ; for,

after our teacher, Mr. Cotton, and my brother Wheelwright were put down, there was none in England that I durst hear. Then it pleased God to reveal himself to me in that scripture of Isaiah : ⚓ " And though the Lord give you the bread of adversity and the water of affliction, yet shall not thy teachers be removed into a corner any more, but thine eyes shall see thy teachers." The Lord giving me this promise, and Mr. Cotton being gone to New England, I was much troubled. And it was revealed to me that I must go thither also, and that there I should be persecuted and suffer much trouble. I will give you another scripture : —
" Fear thou not, O Jacob my servant, saith the Lord : for I am with thee ; for I will make a full end of all the nations whither I have driven thee : but I will not make a full end of thee ; " and then the Lord did reveal himself to me, sitting upon a Throne of Justice, and all the world appearing before him, and, though I must come to New England, yet I must not fear nor be dismayed. And I could not be at rest but I must come hither. The Lord brought another scripture to me : — " For the Lord spake thus to me with a strong hand, and instructed me that I should not walk in the way of this people."

" ' I will give you one more place which the Lord brought to me by immediate revelations ; and that doth concern you all. It is in the sixth chapter of Daniel. When the Presidents and Princes could find nothing against Daniel, because he was faithfull, they sought matter against him concerning the Law of his God, to cast him into the lions' den. So it was revealed to me that they should plot against me ; the Lord bade me not to fear, for he that delivered Daniel and the three children, his hand was not shortened. And, behold ! this scripture is fulfilled this day in my eyes. Therefore take heed what ye go about to do unto me. You have power over my body, but the Lord Jesus hath power over my body and soul ; neither can you do me any harm, for I am in the hands of the eternal Jehovah, my Saviour.

I am at his appointment, for the bounds of my habitation are cast in Heaven, and no further do I esteem of any mortal man than creatures in his hand. I fear none but the great Jehovah, which hath foretold me of these things, and I do verily believe that he will deliver me out of your hands. Therefore take heed how you proceed against me ; for I know that for this you go about to do to me, God will ruin you and your posterity, and this whole State.'

" MR. NOWELL. How do you know that it was God that did reveal these things to you, and not Satan ?

" MRS. HUTCHINSON. How did Abraham know that it was God that bid him offer his son, being a breach of the sixth commandment ?

" DEPUTY-GOVERNOR DUDLEY. By an immediate voice.

" MRS. HUTCHINSON. So to me by an immediate revelation.

" DEPUTY-GOVERNOR. How ! an immediate revelation ?

" MRS. HUTCHINSON. By the voice of his own spirit to my soul.

" GOVERNOR WINTHROP. Daniel was delivered by miracle ; do you think to be delivered so too ?

" MRS. HUTCHINSON. I do here speak it before the Court. I look that the Lord should deliver me by his providence." [1]

At once, the current of the trial now took a new direction. The dangerous topics of special revelation and miraculous action had been opened up. The feeling which existed with respect to these in the Puritanic mind has already been referred to.[2] That

---

[1] The utterances of Mrs. Hutchinson as here given are taken from both reports of the trial. That in the *Short Story* is at this stage much the more detailed, and it is supplemented by that in Hutchinson's *History*. Though in this narrative the two reports have been woven into one, nothing has been interpolated, and the original phrases and forms of expression have all been carefully preserved. Some of the texts suggest doubts as to the accuracy of the reports.

[2] *Supra,* 387-9.

it was illogical did not matter. It was there. No one
for an instant doubted the immediate presence of the
Almighty, or his care of his Chosen People, or his
Special Providences which they so much loved to note.
In the minds of Winthrop or Dudley or Endicott, to
question that He was there at that trial in the Cambridge meeting-house, guiding every detail of their
proceedings, would have fallen but little short of blasphemy. Had it chanced to thunder during those
November days, or had the Northern Lights flashed
somewhat brighter than was their wont, His voice
would have been heard therein, and His hand seen.
They fully believed that in the ordinary events of
daily life He shielded some, while on others He visited His wrath. But, when it came to revelations
and miracles, they drew the line distinctly and deep.
Special Providences? yes! Miracles? — no! Portents? — yes! Revelations? — no! Mrs. Hutchinson
accordingly had now opened the vials of puritanic
wrath, and they were freely emptied upon her head.
Nor were they emptied on her head alone. Cotton
himself was no longer spared. At first he took no
part in the broken and heated discussion which followed the prophetic and defiant outpouring of the
accused, but some allusion to him was soon made, and
then Endicott called on " her reverend teacher . . .
to speak freely whether he doth condescend to such
speeches or revelations as have been here spoken of."

Cotton in reply endeavored to discriminate between
utterances which were " fantastical and leading to
danger," and those which came " flying upon the
wings of the spirit." As to miracles, he said that he
was not sure that he understood Mrs. Hutchinson;
but, he added : — " If she doth expect a deliverance

in a way of Providence, then I cannot deny it." Here Dudley interposed, exclaiming : — "No, sir, we did not speak of that." Cotton then added : — "If it be by way of miracle, then I would suspect it." Later on he again recurred to the subject, now speaking of miracles and "revelations without the Word" as things he could not assent to and looked upon as delusions ; adding kindly, "and I think so doth she too, as I understand her." Then Dudley broke rudely in, remarking : — "Sir, you weary me and do not satisfy me." The current had now set strongly in one direction, and Cotton was not only powerless to stem it, but was indeed in some danger, as Dudley's remark showed, of himself being swept away by it. All pretence of an orderly conduct of proceedings was abandoned, and magistrates, clergy and deputies vied with each other in denunciation and invective, Winthrop himself setting the bad example.

"GOVERNOR WINTHROP. The case is altered and will not stand with us now, but I see a marvellous providence of God [it will be remembered that the offence of the accused was looking for a deliverance through a 'providence of God'] to bring things to this pass that they are. We have been hearkening about trial of this thing, and now the mercy of God by a providence hath answered our desires and made her to lay open herself and the ground of all these disturbances to be by revelations, . . . and this hath been the ground of all these tumults and troubles ; and I would that those were all cut off from us that trouble us, for this is the thing that hath been the root of all the mischief. . . . Aye! it is the most desperate enthusiasm in the world, for nothing but a word comes to her mind, and then an application is made which is nothing to the purpose, and this is her revelations ! . . .

"MR. NOWELL. I think it is a devilish delusion.

"GOVERNOR WINTHROP. Of all the revelations that ever I read of, I never read the like ground raised as is for this. The Enthusiasts and Anabaptists had never the like. . . .

" DEPUTY-GOVERNOR DUDLEY. I never saw such revelations as these among the Anabaptists; therefore am sorry that Mr. Cotton should stand to justify her.

" MR. PETERS. I can say the same, and this runs to enthusiasm, and I think that is very disputable which our brother Cotton hath spoken. . . .

" GOVERNOR WINTHROP. It overthrows all.

" DEPUTY-GOVERNOR DUDLEY. These disturbances that have come among the Germans have been all grounded upon revelations; and so they that have vented them have stirred up their hearers to take up arms against their prince and to cut the throats of one another; and these have been the fruits of them. And whether the devil may inspire the same into their hearts here I know not; for I am fully persuaded that Mrs. Hutchinson is deluded by the devil, because the spirit of God speaks truth in all his servants.

" GOVERNOR WINTHROP. I am persuaded that the revelation she brings forth is delusion.

" All the Court but some two or three ministers here cried out, — We all believe it ! We all believe it ! ! . . .

" MR. BARTHOLOMEW. My wife hath said that Mr. Wheelwright was not acquainted with this way until that she imparted it unto him.

" Mr. BROWN. . . . I think she deserves no less a censure than hath been already passed, but rather something more; for this is the foundation of all mischief; and of all those bastardly things which have been overthrown by that great meeting [the Synod]. They have all come out from this cursed fountain."

The Governor now forthwith proceeded to put the question. As he was in the midst of doing it, Mr. Coddington, who had hitherto preserved silence, arose and asked to be heard. Referring then to the meetings at Mrs. Hutchinson's house, he asked whether, supposing those meetings to have been designed for the religious edification of her own family, no others might have been present? "If," replied Winthrop, "you have nothing else to say but that, it is pity, Mr. Coddington, that you should interrupt us in proceeding to censure." But Coddington on this occasion showed true courage; for, though in a hopeless minority, he went on — undeterred by Winthrop's rebuke, and regardless of the impatience of his weary and excited audience — to point out that absolutely nothing had been proved against Mrs. Hutchinson, except that she had asserted the other ministers did not teach a Covenant of Grace so clearly as Cotton, and that they were in the state of the apostles before the Ascension. "Why!" he added, "I hope this may not be offensive nor any wrong to them."

Then again Winthrop broke in, declaring that her own speech, just made in Court, afforded ample ground to proceed upon, even admitting that nothing had been proved. Coddington then closed with these forcible and eloquently plain words: —

"I beseech you do not speak so to force things along; for I do not for my own part see any equity in the Court in all your proceedings. Here is no law of God that she hath broken; nor any law of the country that she hath broken. Therefore she deserves no censure. Be it granted that Mrs. Hutchinson did say the elders preach as the apostles did, — why, they preached a Covenant of Grace. What wrong then is that to the elders? It is without question that the apostles did preach a Covenant of Grace before the Ascension, though not with that power they did after they received the manifestation of the spirit. Therefore, I pray consider what you do, for here is no law of God or man broken."

The Court had now been many hours in unbroken session. The members of it were so exhausted and hungry that Dudley impatiently exclaimed : — " We shall all be sick with fasting ! " Nevertheless the intervention of Coddington, and the scruples of one or two of the deputies, led to the swearing of two of the witnesses for the prosecution, and the colleagues, Weld and Eliot, were called upon by the Governor to take the oath. When they rose and held up their hands, Peters rose and held up his hand also. They testified again that at the meeting in Boston the accused had said there was a broad difference between Cotton and themselves, — that he preached a Covenant of Grace, and they of Works, and that they were not sealed; and, added Eliot, " I do further remember this also, that she said we were not able ministers of the gospel, because we were but like the apostles before the Ascension." " This," said Coddington, " was I hope no disparagement to you. Methinks the comparison is very good." And Winthrop then interjected : — " Well, we see in the Court that she doth continually say and unsay things."

The hesitating deputies now pronounced themselves fully satisfied, and Winthrop put the question. The record closes as follows : —

" GOVERNOR WINTHROP. The Court hath already declared themselves satisfied concerning the things you hear, and concerning the troublesomeness of her spirit, and the danger of her course amongst us, which is not to be suffered. Therefore if it be the mind of the Court that Mrs. Hutchinson, for these things that appear before us, is unfit for our society, — and if it be the mind of the Court that she shall be banished out of our liberties, and imprisoned till she be sent away, let them hold up their hands.

" All but three held up their hands.

" Those that are contrary minded hold up yours.

" Mr. Coddington and Mr. Colburn only.

" MR. JENNISON. I cannot hold up my hand one way or the other, and I shall give my reason if the Court require it.

" GOVERNOR WINTHROP. Mrs. Hutchinson, you hear the sentence of the Court. It is that you are banished from out our jurisdiction as being a woman not fit for our society. And you are to be imprisoned till the Court send you away.

" MRS. HUTCHINSON. I desire to know wherefore I am banished.

" GOVERNOR WINTHROP. Say no more. The Court knows wherefore, and is satisfied."

In the Colony Records of Massachusetts the sentence reads as follows: —

" Mrs. Hutchinson, (the wife of Mr. William Hutchinson,) being convented for traducing the ministers, and their ministry in this country, shee declared voluntarily her revelations for her ground, and that shee should bee delivred, and the Court ruined, with their posterity; and thereupon was banished, and the mean while was committed to Mr. Joseph Weld untill the Court shall dispose of her."

CHAPTER IX.

THE EXCOMMUNICATION.

THE case of Wheelwright had been disposed of by the Court on what was then the 4th and is now the 14th of the month, while that of Mrs. Hutchinson had occupied the 7th and 8th, now the 17th and 18th. During the proceedings in the latter case Wheelwright was at his home at the Mount, and it is small matter for surprise that when he heard of them he made haste to quit the soil of Massachusetts. Less able to face a winter in the wilderness, Mrs. Hutchinson was to wait until spring, not in Boston at her own house and among friends and sympathizers, but at Roxbury, under the watch and ward of Thomas Weld, in the house of his brother Joseph. The remaining events of the controversy can be quickly narrated.

Immediately after passing sentence on Mistress Hutchinson, the Court, worn out with excitement, long sessions, cold and fasting, seems to have indulged itself in a recess of several days. It met again on the $\frac{15\text{th}}{25\text{th}}$, and, refreshed by the brief cessation from labor, took up its work vigorously at the point where it had been dropped. The sergeants, who in the previous May had laid down their halberds when Vane failed of his reëlection, and had refused to attend Winthrop home, were "convented." The names of both were "on the seditious libel called a remonstrance or petition." They were discharged from office, disfranchised, and fined respectively twenty and forty pounds. One of them, Edward Hutchinson, — he who was fined forty pounds, — turned himself contemptuously when his sentence was pronounced, telling the Court that if they took away his means they must support his family. He was promptly imprisoned; but, after a night's reflection, humbled himself and was released. William Balston, the other, was apparently a man of the outspoken English type, with the courage of his convictions. When confronted with his signature to the petition he at once acknowledged it, and bluntly told the Court " that he knew that if such a petition had been made in any other place in the world, there would have been no fault found with it." Subsequently the fines of both were remitted on condition they departed the province; and they were among those who the next March went to Rhode Island.

One after another the signers of the Boston remonstrance of the previous March were then summoned to the bar of the Court. The choice offered them was simple, — they could acknowledge themselves in fault and withdraw their names from the offensive document, or they could pass under the ban of the law. A few, some ten in number, recanted; some five or six of the more obdurate were at once disfranchised. Among these was John Underhill, then captain of the train-band and a salaried officer of the colony. The order now made by the Court in regard to him was terse and did not admit of misconstruction. It ran in these words, — " Capt. Underhill, being convicted for having his hand to the seditious writing, is disfranchised, and put from the captains place "; but ten months were yet to elapse before he was banished.

Throughout, Underhill's case was peculiar, and, as will presently be seen, the solemn way in which Winthrop recorded the man's religious buffoonery throws a gleam of genuine humor over one page at least of a dreary record.

Though not now banished, Underhill's name heads the list of the "opinionists" of Boston, fifty-eight in all, who were, at the same November session of the Court which banished Wheelwright and Mrs. Hutchinson, ordered within ten days to bring their arms to the house of Captain Robert Keayne, and there deliver them up to him. Besides the fifty-eight in Boston, seventeen others, in five different towns, — in all seventy-five persons, — the recognized leaders of the minority, were disarmed, and, under a heavy money penalty, forbidden to buy, to borrow or to have in their possession either weapon or ammunition, until the Court should take further action. The ground for this measure, in which the agitation culminated, was set forth in the order promulgating it. It was a "just cause of suspition, that they, as others in Germany, in former times, may, upon some revelation, make some suddaine irruption upon those that differ from them in judgment." The decree, needless to say, excited deep indignation among those named in it. It was in fact a mild proscription. Those proscribed were powerless, and they proved themselves law-abiding. In the words of Winthrop, — "When they saw no remedy, they obeyed."

Plainly, also, there was "no remedy." Throughout all the proceedings which had taken place, the Boston church had been the stronghold of the secular faction in the state; and now even when generally disarmed and with its leading members disfranchised and marked for exile, there were those in it who were earnest to have their brother Winthrop called to account and dealt with in a church way for his course as governor. Obviously, such an attempt would only have made matters worse, and those of the elders, to whom appeal had been made, showed no zeal in their action, — they were not forward in the matter. Then Winthrop, fully understanding the situation, wisely as well as boldly took the initiative, making a formal address to the congregation. In this he laid down the correct rule clearly and forcibly, with numerous scriptural references to chapter and verse in Luke and Matthew, and fortifying himself with precedents drawn from the action in similar circumstances of Uzzia and Asa and Salam : — if a magistrate, he said, acting in his private capacity, should take away the goods of another, or despoil his servant, the church could properly call him to account for so doing; yet if he was guilty of such conduct in his official character, he was not accountable to the church, no matter how unjust his action might be. In the present case, the Governor went on to declare, whatever he had done had been done by him with the advice and under the direction of Cotton and other of the church's elders, and he would now give but a single reason in his own justification, — that single reason was that the brethren singled out for exile were so divided from the rest of the country in their judgment and practice that their presence in the community was, in his opinion, not consistent with the public peace. "So, by the example of Lot in Abraham's family, and after Hagar and Ishmael, he saw they must be sent away."

This action and discourse of Winthrop's was not without importance, and it bore fruit; for it was the

theocratic period in Massachusetts, and the church
was too much inclined to meddle in the affairs of state.
The clergy were now supreme. They had converted
the General Court into a mere machine for the civil
enforcement of their own inquisitorial decrees; Mrs.
Hutchinson had been banished for "traducing the
ministers," and it was not proposed to allow further
freedom of religious thought in Massachusetts. It
was the clergy, not the churches, who constituted the
power behind the throne. The principle that the
magistrate was not amenable to the church for acts
done in his official capacity was sound, and could be
most appropriately asserted by one speaking with
authority. The enunciation of the further principle,
that the magistrate should be equally free from what
may be called a politico-theological coercion, whether
exercised by priests or ministers, was unfortunately
deferred to a long subsequent period.

Mrs. Hutchinson meanwhile, separated from her
family, was wearing away the long winter in semi-
imprisonment at Roxbury. At first she labored under
a good deal of mental depression, natural enough
under the circumstances; for not only must the reaction from the excitement of the trial have been
great, but she was soon to give birth to a child. Her
despondency did not last long; and, indeed, she was
now thoroughly in her element. Though secluded
from the rest of the world for fear of the injury she
might do in the way of spreading pernicious heresies,
she was still the most noted woman in the province;
and as such she was literally beset by the clergy, and
by Mr. Thomas Weld in particular. They were far
from being done with her yet. After the manner
of their kind also, in every age and in all countries,

the Massachusetts ministers, having secured an absolute supremacy in the state, were now busy hunting out "foul errors" about inherent righteousness, the immortality of the soul, the resurrection, the sanctity of the Sabbath, etc., etc., such heresies being very rife; for, as Winthrop sagely observed, it could not be expected that "Satan would lose the opportunity of making choice of so fit an instrument [as Mistress Hutchinson], so long as any hope remained to attain his mischievous end in darkening the saving truth of the Lord Jesus, and disturbing the peace of his churches." It was now that Cotton not only abandoned his old allies to their fate, but became one of their leading persecutors. He probably knew his brethren. At the trial at Cambridge he had seen it wanted but little to cause Peters and Weld to throw off all restraint, and open the cry on him as they had upon Wheelwright. Indeed both Endicott and Dudley had there addressed him in a way he was little accustomed to, using language both insulting and brow-beating; while Winthrop, on one occasion at least, seemed to feel the necessity of diverting attention from him.[1] Having at the close of the Synod ceased from all antagonism to his brethren, Cotton had since sought to occupy a neutral attitude as peacemaker. He now realized that this was not enough. He had professed he was persuaded; he must furnish proof of it by works also. He made up his mind to do it. One feeble effort, as will be seen, he yet made in behalf of Mrs. Hutchinson, and it was creditable to him; in other respects, from this time onward, the position in the controversy held by the teacher of the Boston church was simply pitiable, — the ignominious

[1] Hutchinson, *Massachusetts*, i. 74.

page in an otherwise worthy life.   He made haste to
walk in a Covenant of Works, — and the walk was a
very dirty one.   None the less he trudged sturdily on
in it, now declaring that he had been abused and
made use of as a "stalking horse," and now bewailing
his sloth and credulity.   And thus " did [he] spend
most of his time both publicly and privately," engaged in the inquisitor's work of unearthing heretics
and heresies.   A little later he even allowed himself
to be put forward as the mouthpiece of his order, to
pass judgment on his old associates and to pronounce
filial sympathy a crime.

Mrs. Hutchinson was soon found to be the one root
from whence had sprung the many heresies now un-
earthed ; when traced, they all ran back to her.   Hereupon the ministers " resorted to her many times,
labouring to convince her, but in vain ; yet they resorted to her still, to the end they might either re-
claim her from her errors, or that they might bear
witness against them if occasion were."   For now a
new ordeal awaited her.   She was to undergo the discipline of the church in which she was a sister.

In careful preparation for this, a species of ecclesiastical indictment was drawn up by the brethren, setting forth the utterances of the prisoner, as taken down
from her own lips.   Containing some thirty several
counts, it was altogether a formidable document.[1]   A

---

[1] A few of these counts will suffice to give a general idea of the
whole : —

" 8. The Image of God wherein Adam was made [Mrs. Hutchinson]
could see no Scripture to warrant that it consisteth in holinesse, but
conceived it to be in that he was made like to Christ's manhood."

" 12. There is no evidence to be had of our good estate, either from
absolute or conditional promises."

" 15. There is first engraffing into Christ before union, from which
a man might fall away."

copy of it was then sent to the church at Boston, and that church in due course applied to the magistrates to allow Mrs. Hutchinson to appear and answer to the accusation. Leave was of course granted, and at length, in what would now be the latter part of March, Joseph Weld's prisoner returned once more to her own house. But her husband was not there to meet her. He and her brother, and indeed all those whom she could look to for countenance and support, were away seeking out a new home, against their impending exile; nor did her opponents fail to attribute their absence to "the good providence of God," who thus removed opposition.

The proceedings were appointed for the $\frac{15th}{25th}$ of March. They excited the deepest interest throughout the colony, and as the day drew near, Boston was thronged with visitors. Not only all the members of the Boston church, but many others were there assembled ; for the whole little community was agitated to its depths. The utter sameness of that provincial life — in which no new excitements followed one upon another, dividing attention and driving each other into forgetfulness — was for once broken. The church was the common family, and from that common family the elders were now to cast out the most prominent, —

"17. That Abraham was not in a saving estate till the 22 chap. of Gen. when hee offered Isaac, and saveing the firmenesse of Gods election, he might have perished, notwithstanding any work of grace that was wrought in him till then."

"21. That an hypocrite may have Adams righteousnesse and perish, and by that righteousnes he is bound to the Law, but in union with Christ, Christ comes into the man, and he retaines the seed and dieth, and then all manner of grace in himselfe, but all in Christ."

"28. That so farre as a man is in union with Christ, he can doe no duties perfectly, and without the communion of the unregenerate part with the regenerate."

the best known of all the sisters. It is necessary to think of the domestic circle to enable men or women of to-day to bring home to themselves the intensity of interest then aroused. An excommunication in church or state, or even socially, is now a small matter comparatively. It causes scarcely a ripple in the great sea of life. The event of to-day, it is barely remembered to-morrow. It was not so then. It was as if with us a daughter, arraigned before brothers and sisters, were solemnly admonished by the venerated father and driven from the hearth at which her childhood had been passed. In that family the event would be the one subject of thought; from the minds and memories of those present no incident of the scene would ever fade. So it was in the Boston church. The members of that church felt and thought as the members of a modern family would think and feel of a similar episode in their home. It would be the event not of a day, but of a life, — the family tragedy.

When, therefore, "one Thirsday Lectuer day after Sermon," the hour fixed for the proceedings to begin was come, the Boston meeting-house was crowded with a devout and expectant audience. The General Court was sitting still at Cambridge, and the time of the church meeting — ten o'clock in the morning — interfered with its sessions; leave nevertheless was specially granted to the governor and treasurer of the province, both members of the Boston church, to absent themselves. They were present with the rest of the church when, two hours earlier than usual, the services began; but she who would have been the observed of all was not there. The seat reserved for her was vacant. Sermon and prayer at length ended, she came in, " pretending," as Winthrop expressed it, " bodily infirmity." When at last she had taken her place, one of the elders arose and broke the silence which prevailed. Calling the sister Anne Hutchinson forth by name, he stated the purpose for which she had been summoned, and read the indictment prepared against her. A copy of it, to which those who were to bear witness to the several counts had subscribed their names, had some days before been put in her hands.

The scene that ensued, though sufficiently interesting, was, from the religious point of view, far from edifying.[1] At first the woman at bay most pertinently asked by what precept of holy writ the elders of the church had come to her in her place of confinement, pretending that they sought light, when in reality they came to entrap and betray her. Then, presently, Wilson, her pastor, — the man she disliked of all men, and for whom even her dislike was probably exceeded by her contempt, — Wilson either took some part in the proceedings or was alluded to; and at once her anger flashed out in stinging words. She denounced him for what he had uttered against her before the Court at the time of her sentence. " For what am I banished ? " — she demanded; declaring the heretical speeches, now attributed to her, the results of confinement. Presently the discussion of the articles was begun, and she was called upon to answer to the first; which was to the effect that " the souls of all men (in regard of generation) are mortall like the beasts." The debate then drifted into that region of barren

[1] A comparatively full report of the church proceedings in Mrs. Hutchinson's case was found in 1888 among the papers of President Stiles in the Yale library, and is printed in *Proc. Mass. Hist. Soc.* Series II. iv. 159–91.

theological abstractions in which those composing the
assembly believed themselves entirely at home.   The
accused cited texts and endeavored to draw distinctions; but in reply the elders — as was natural, she
being one and they many — cited several texts, and
drew an infinite variety of distinctions to each one of
hers.   "She could not give any answer to them, yet
she stood to her opinion, till at length a stranger," the
Rev. John Davenport, "being desired to speak to the
point, and he opening to her the difference between
the Soul and the Life, — the first being a spiritual
substance, and the other the union of that with the
body, — she then confessed she saw more light than
before, and so with some difficulty was brought to
confess her error in that point.   Wherein," as Winthrop goes on to remark, not it would appear without
considerable insight as to Mrs. Hutchinson's foibles,
"it was to be observed that, though this stranger
spake to very good purpose, and so clearly convinced
her as she could not gainsay, yet it was evident she
was convinced before, but she could not give the
honour of it to her own pastor or teacher, nor to any
of the other elders, whom she had so much slighted."

It is not necessary to follow the discussion further.
Three more of the articles were propounded; and
still, in spite of the storm of texts pelted upon her,
Mistress Hutchinson persisted in her errors.   She
even returned "forward speeches to some that spake
to her."   By this time the day was grown old, and
the patience of the elders was exhausted.   The single
woman, quick of tongue though weak of body, seemed
not only disposed to out-talk them all, but to out-
endure them as well; for it was not without reason
she had delayed coming into the assembly until ser-

mon and prayer were over. At length, as it grew towards evening and the fourth of the twenty-nine articles was not yet disposed of, the elders bethought themselves to hasten matters by administering to their erring and obstinate sister a formal admonition, the real purport of which apparently was that she should suffer herself to be convinced more readily. In the course of the proceedings one of her sons had ventured a natural inquiry as to the rule which should guide him in expressing his assent or dissent; and later on Thomas Savage, the husband of her daughter, Faith, did himself honor by rising in his place and saying, — " My mother not being accused of any heinous act, but only for opinion, and that wherein she desires information and light, rather than peremptorily to hold [to it], I cannot consent that the church should proceed yet to admonish her for this." Thereupon Thomas Oliver, one of the ruling elders, after declaring that it was grief to his " spirit to see these two brethren to speak so much and to scruple the proceedings of the church," propounded the following as a solution of the dilemma: —

" Seeing that all the proceedings of the churches of Jesus Christ now should be according to the pattern of the primitive churches ; and the primitive pattern was that all things in the church should be done with one heart and one soul and one consent, that any act and every act done by the church may be as the act of one man ; — Therefore, whether it be not meet to lay these two brethren under an admonition with their mother, that so the church may proceed on without any further opposition."

This novel though drastic parliamentary expedient for securing unanimity evidently commended itself strongly to the judgment of the Rev. John Wilson,

for he at once cried out from his place among the
elders, — " I think you speak very well! It is very
meet!" The motion was then put " and the whole
church by their silence consented." The admonition
was pronounced by Cotton, with whom also it was
left " to do as God should incline his heart " in the
matter of including Mrs. Hutchinson's " two sons or
no with herself." As, in the course of his subsequent
deliverance, the eloquent teacher took occasion to address the " two sons," saying among other things that
" instead of loving and natural children, you have
proved vipers, to eat through the very bowells of your
mother, to her ruin, if God do not graciously prevent," the inference would seem to be inevitable that
when the moment came John Cotton found his heart
inclined from above to include offspring as well as
mother in his admonitory remarks. Winthrop says,
and it may well be believed, that on this occasion
the teacher spoke with great solemnity and " much
zeal and detestation of her errors and pride of spirit."
He spake in this wise; and

" First to her son, laying it sadly upon him, that he would
give such way to his natural affection, as for preserving her
honor he should make a breach upon the honor of Christ,
and upon his covenant with the church, and withal tear the
very bowells of his soul, by hardening her in sin. Then to
her, first, he remembered her of the good way she was in at
her first coming, in helping to discover to divers the false
bottom they stood upon in trusting to legal works without
Christ; then he showed her how, by falling into these gross
and fundamental errors, she had lost the honor of her former
service, and done more wrong to Christ and his church than
formerly she had done good, and so laid her sin to her conscience. He admonished her also of the height of spirit,

and charged her solemnly before the Lord, and his Angels,
and Churches there assembled to return from the error of
her way.   Then he spake to the sisters of the church, and
advised them to take heed of her opinions, and to withhold
all countenance and respect from her, lest they should harden
her in sin." [1]

"So she was dismissed, and appointed to appear again
that day seven-night."

It was eight o'clock of the March evening when the
hungry and wearied congregation at last broke up.
Through ten consecutive hours those composing it had
sat on the hard and crowded benches.   Mrs. Hutchinson had been ordered to return at the close of the

---

[1] It may not be uninteresting to quote from the report of these
proceedings and the admonitory remarks of Mr. Cotton so much as
relates to one point at issue, if only to illustrate the singular logical
intricacies into which the discussion wandered, as well as the character of the treatment to which the accused sister was subjected : —

"MRS. HUTCHINSON : — I desire you to speak to that place in I.
Corinthians xv. 37, 44.   For I do question whether the same body
that dies shall rise again. . . .

"MR. BUCKLE : — I desire to know of Mrs. Hutchinson, whether you
hold any other resurrection than that of . . . Union to Christ Jesus ?
— And whether you hold that foul, filthy and abominable opinion held
by Familists of the community of women.

"MRS. HUTCHINSON : — I hold it not. . . .

"MR. DAVENPORT : — Avoid . . . Mr. Buckles question ; for it is a
right principle.   For, if the resurrection be past, then marriage is
past : for it is a weighty reason : after the resurrection is past, marriage is past.   Then, if there be any union between man and woman,
it is not by marriage, but in a way of community.

"MRS. HUTCHINSON : — If any such practice or conclusion be
drawn from it, then I must leave it, for I abhor that practice." . . .

MR. COTTON in his admonition : — . . . "If the resurrection be past,
then you cannot evade the argument that was pressed upon you by
our brother Buckle and others, that filthy sin of the community of
women ; and all promiscuous and filthy coming together of men and
women, without distinction or relation of marriage, will necessarily
follow ; and, though I have not heard, neither do I think, you have
been unfaithful to your husband in his marriage covenant, yet that
will follow upon it." . . .

meeting to her place of confinement at Roxbury ; but some intimation had been received from those supposed to know, that her courage was giving way under the tremendous pressure to which she had been subjected, and that, if properly labored with now, she might be made to yield. Accordingly, she was permitted to remain at Cotton's house. He probably had managed it, wishing to make one last effort to save, from what he looked upon as perdition, the most gifted of his parishioners. The Rev. John Davenport, that " stranger " to whose authority Mrs. Hutchinson had shown herself not indisposed to succumb in the congregation, was also Cotton's guest; and, during the intervening week, the two divines did not, it would seem, strive with her in vain. Indeed, they so far prevailed that she acknowledged she had been wrong, and even brought herself to the point of agreeing publicly to recant. So, —

" When the day came, and she was called forth and the articles read again to her, she delivered in her answers in writing, which were also read ; and, being then willing to speak to the congregation for their further satisfaction, she did acknowledge that she had greatly erred, and that God had now withdrawn his countenance from her, because she had so much misprised his ordinances, both in slighting the magistrates at the Court, and also the elders of the Church. And she confessed that during her trial by the Court, she looked only at such failings as she apprehended in the magistrates' proceedings, without having regard to their position of authority ; [1] and that the language she then used

[1] " 2. For these scriptures that I used at the Court in censuring the country, I confess I did it rashly and out of heat of spirit, and unadvisedly, and have cause to be sorry for my unreverent carriage to them ; and I am heartily sorry that any things I have said have drawn any from hearing any of the elders of the Bay."

about her revelations was rash and without ground; and she asked the church to pray for her."

"Thus far," says Winthrop, "she went on well, and the assembly conceived hope of her repentance." Indeed, it is not easy to see what more could have been asked of any one. A woman, — full of pride of intellect, and of insatiable ambition, — she had confessed herself in error, and, in the presence of her adherents and the face of the world, humbled herself in the dust before the enemies she despised. With all her feminine instinct in that way, she had herself never devised so bitter a humiliation even for John Wilson. But this was not enough. She was not so to elude the lord-brethren. It is apparent they meant to rid themselves wholly of her; nor was it any longer difficult for them to do so. Having at last found out her weak points they were more than a match for her, for they knew exactly how to go to work to convict her. They had but to provoke her to voluble speech, and she was sure to deliver herself into their hands; nor, indeed, could it well have been otherwise, seeing they were engaged discussing the unknowable, many against one, and that one a loquacious woman.

She read her recantation from a paper, speaking evidently with a subdued voice and bowed head. As soon as she finished Thomas Leverett, the ruling elder, rose, saying it was meet somebody should re-state what she had said to the congregation, which had been unable to hear her; whereupon Cotton reiterated the heads of her "groce and fundamentall Errors," and her humiliating admission that "the Roote of all was the hight and Pride of her Spirit." Then presently Wilson, her pastor, stood up before the silent and spell-bound audience. His hour of

triumph and revenge had come; and, apparently, he
proposed thoroughly to enjoy the first, and to make
complete the last. At the meeting of the previous
week Mrs. Hutchinson had made an issue with Shepard and Eliot. The former of these two divines,
almost alone among his brethren, had in the November trial before the Court shown some degree of Christian spirit towards the accused, and afterwards he and
Eliot had labored long and earnestly with her at the
house of Joseph Weld in Roxbury. In the midst of
Cotton's admonition of the week before, Mrs. Hutchinson had broken in upon him with an assertion that
it was only since her imprisonment at Roxbury that
she held any of the erroneous opinions attributed to
her. No sooner had Cotton finished than Shepard
rose to declare his "astonishment" at "what Mrs.
Hutchinson did last speak, . . . that she should thus
impudently affirm so horrible an untruth and falsehood in the midst of such a solemn ordinance of Jesus
Christ and before such an assembly." And now, a
week afterwards, the recantation being over, Wilson
called attention to the fact of its incompleteness in
that it left this question of veracity between the accused and the two ministers undisposed of. Speaking with great restraint and humility Mrs. Hutchinson
replied that what she had said when she interrupted
Cotton had been spoken "rashly and unadvisedly,"
adding, — " I do not allow the slighting of ministers,
nor of the scriptures, nor anything that is set up by
God : if Mr. Shepard doth conceive that I had any
of these things in my, mind then he is deceived."
This response sounds to a modern reader sufficiently
humble and subdued. It did not so sound to the
Rev. Thomas Shepard when it was uttered in the

Boston meeting-house on what is now the 1st of April, 1638 ; on the contrary, that " sweet affecting and soul-ravishing " divine made haste to declare himself " unsatisfied," saying, — " If this day, when Mrs. Hutchinson should take shame and confusion to herself for her gross and damnable errors, she shall cast shame upon others, and say they are mistaken, and to turn off many of those gross errors with so slight an answer as ' your mistake,' I fear it doth not stand with true repentance."

The following colloquy then took place : —

" MR. COTTON : — Sister, was there not a time when once you did hold that there were no distinct graces inherent in us, but all was in Christ Jesus ?

" MRS. HUTCHINSON : — I did mistake the word ' inherent ; ' as Mr. Davenport can tell, who did cause me first to see my mistake in the word ' inherent.'

" MR. ELIOT : — We are not satisfied with what she saith, that she should say now that she did never deny inherence of Grace in us, as in a subject ; for she being by us pressed so with it, she denied that there was no Graces inherent in Christ himself.

" MR. SHEPARD : — She did not only deny the word ' inherent,' but denied the very thing itself ; then I asked her if she did believe the spirit of God was in believers.

" MRS. HUTCHINSON : — I confess my expressions were that way, but it was never my judgment."

The theological issue involved was unintelligible, and the jargon in which the discussion was carried on completed the confusion. The nominal point in dispute was whether the sister on trial was not, or had not at some time previous been, " of that judgment that there is no inherent righteousness in the

saints, but those gifts and graces which are ascribed
to them that are only in Christ as the subject." But,
while this was the apparent issue, the efforts of the
ministers were really directed towards extorting from
Mrs. Hutchinson a full and unconditioned confession
of error, — a recantation absolute and unequivocal.
Her submission was to be complete. The audience
composed of the members of the Boston church, —
her former admirers and still in their hearts her adherents — were in mind. Before their wondering
eyes and to their listening ears, the woman towards
whom their hearts yet went out was to be broken
down, discredited and humiliated ; and she was to
confess herself so without one syllable of reservation.

That Mrs. Hutchinson now found herself beyond
her depth, is obvious. It is stating the case none too
strongly to say that all the disputants, — ministers,
magistrates, elders and female transcendentalist —
were hopelessly lost in a thick fog of indefinable ideas
and meaningless phrases ; but, while all groped their
way angrily, numbers and the clatter of tongues were
wholly on one side. Apparently, feeling herself hard
pressed by men hateful to her, Mrs. Hutchinson could
not bring herself to yield to them as she had yielded
in public to Davenport, and in private to Cotton. So
she adhered to her statement, — " My judgment is not
altered though my expression alters."

Then at once Wilson gave the signal and the on-
slaught began. In referring to the proceedings during Mrs. Hutchinson's trial by the General Court at
Cambridge in November, 1637, and the treatment
the accused then received, a high authority on matters
of New England history has remarked that the reports of what took place " contain evidence that her

judges did not escape the contagion of her ill-temper." [1] This criticism of those composing the Court in question certainly does not err on the side of harshness ; and not impossibly the same sense of pious devotion to the fathers which manifestly inspired it might now see in the course of those controlling the action of the Boston church only another example of the contagious character of the victim's perverse disposition : but to one endeavoring to look upon a scene of ecclesiastical persecution which occurred in Boston in 1638 with the same eyes with which he looks upon other scenes of the same general character which occurred at about that time in England, in France and in Spain, a wholly different impression is conveyed. In dealing with vexed questions of an historical character it is best always to speak with studied moderation, avoiding metaphor scarcely less than invective ; yet it is difficult to read the report of the closing church proceedings in the case of Anne Hutchinson without the simile suggesting itself of some pack of savage hounds surrounding and mercilessly hunting down a frightened fox, driven from cover and crouching.

It was John Wilson's voice which now seemed to raise the familiar view-hallo, and at once the kennel opened in full cry. Magistrates and ministers vied with each other in passionate terms of hatred, opprobrium and contempt. Dudley, the Deputy Governor, though neither a member of the Boston church nor an elder, — simply a stranger present from curiosity, — Dudley cried out, — " Her repentance is in a paper, . . . but sure her repentance is not in her countenance. None can see it there, I think." Then Peters, the minister of the Salem church, exclaimed, —

[1] Palfrey, i. 486.

"I believe that she has vile thoughts of us, and
thinks us to be nothing but a company of Jews;"
and again, — "You have stept out of your place.
You have rather been a husband than a wife; and a
preacher than a hearer; and a magistrate than a subject; and so you have thought to carry all things in
church and commonwealth as you would." After
Peters, Shepard took up the refrain, saying to the
congregation, — "You have not only to deal with a
woman this day that holds divers erroneous opinions,
but with one that never had any true grace in her
heart, and that by her own tenet. Yea! this day she
hath shown herself to be a notorious impostor." Wilson repeatedly broke in, — "One cause was . . . to
set yourself in the room of God, above others, that
you might be extolled and admired and followed after,
that you might be a great prophetess; . . . therefore
I believe your iniquity hath found you out; . . . it
grieves me that you should so evince your dangerous,
foul and damnable heresies." Then, after taking
breath, he presently began again, — "I cannot but
acknowledge the Lord is just in leaving our sister to
pride and lying. . . . I look at her as a dangerous
instrument of the Devil raised up by Satan amongst
us. . . . Consider how we can, or whether we may
longer suffer her to go on still in seducing to seduce,
and in deceiving to deceive, and in lying to lie, and
in condemning authority and magistrates, still to condemn. Therefore, we should sin against God if we
should not put away from us so evil a woman, guilty
of such foul evils." Then Eliot, "the Apostle," —
"It is a wonderful wisdom of God . . . to let her
fall into such lies as she hath done this day; for she
hath carried on all her errors by lies." Finally Cot-

ton, turning at last fairly against his former disciple, announced that "God hath let her fall into a manifest lie, yea! to make a lie," and Shepard, eagerly catching up the phrase, exclaimed, — " But now for one not to drop a lie, but to make a lie, and to maintain a lie! . . . I would have this church consider, whether it will be for the honor of God and the honor of this church to bear with patience so gross an offender."

And so at last the pitiless chase drew to a close. Throughout all its latter stages, while it was exhausting itself by its own heat, the voice of the accused had not been heard, — evidently she sat there, mute, motionless, aghast. Once, after listening to a furious diatribe from Wilson, the hard-hunted creature seems to have tried to take refuge under Cotton's gown, exclaiming, — " Our teacher knows my judgment, for I never kept my judgment from him!" — but already Cotton, recognizing the inevitable and bowing to it, had abandoned her to her fate. Then she ceased to struggle, and the yelling pack rushed in upon her.

Long afterwards, in reply to the charge that he had contrived to transfer the odious duty of excommunicating his disciple from himself to Wilson, John Cotton asserted [1] that he stood ready to be the mouthpiece of the church in this matter, — no less than he had already been in the matter of admonishment, — had the task been put upon him; and there can be no doubt that, at the time, he gave his open assent before the whole congregation to the course which was pursued, and even silenced the scruples of the few who yet clung to their prophetess, by calling

[1] *Way Cleared*, 85.

to mind the precedents of " Ananias and Sapphira, and
the incestuous Corinthian." The offence now charged
against Mrs. Hutchinson was not heresy, but falsehood persistently adhered to. An impenitent liar was
to be cast out. The matter was one touching morals,
not doctrine; and accordingly, as Cotton claimed, lay
rather within the province of the pastor than the
teacher. It was for Mr. Wilson, therefore, to pronounce the sentence of excommunication; nor was
there any reason for delay. A few voices were,
indeed, heard timidly suggesting that the accused
might be once more admonished, and time for repentance yet given her; but she herself sat silent, asking
no respite. Then Wilson rose, and, in the hush of
the crowded assembly, solemnly put the question
whether all were of one mind that their sister should
be cast out. The silence was broken by no reply;
and, after the custom of that church, this betokened
consent. Then the sentence of excommunication was
pronounced; and Anne Hutchinson, no longer a sister,
listened to these words rolled out in triumph from
the mouth of John Wilson, the pastor, — " Therefore
in the name of the Lord Jesus Christ and in the name
of the church I do not only pronounce you worthy to
be cast out, but I do cast you out; and in the name
of Christ I do deliver you up to Satan, that you may
learn no more to blaspheme, to seduce and to lie;
and I do account you from this time forth to be a
Heathen and a Publican, and so to be held of all the
Brethren and Sisters of this congregation and of
others : therefore I command you in the name of
Christ Jesus and of this church as a Leper to withdraw yourself out of the congregation."

When, in obedience to this mandate, Anne Hutchinson, the outcast, moved through the awe-stricken throng, her disciple and devoted friend, Mary Dyer,[1] rose up and walked by her side, and the two passed out together. As they went forth, one standing at the meeting-house door said to Mrs. Hutchinson, — " The Lord sanctify this unto you;" to whom she made answer, — " The Lord judgeth not as man judgeth. Better to be cast out of the church than to deny Christ." At the same time another, a stranger in Boston, pointing with his finger at Mary Dyer, asked, — " Who is that young woman?" and he of whom he asked made answer, — " It is the woman which had the monster." [2]

The records of the First Church of Boston contain the following entry : —

"The 22d of the 1st Month 1638. Anne, the wife of our brother, William Hutchinson, having on the 15th of this month been openly, in the public congregation, admonished of sundry errors held by her, was on the same 22d day cast out of the church for impenitently persisting in a manifest lie, then expressed by her in open congregation."

[1] *Supra*, 408, n.   [2] Winthrop, i. *263; *supra*, 386.

CHAPTER X.

OF the subsequent fate of Anne Hutchinson and John Wheelwright, little need here be said; their stories, — and that of Mrs. Hutchinson is a sufficiently tragic one, — are told in the biographies which have been written of them. Before her excommunication was an accomplished fact, Winthrop says that Mrs. Hutchinson "seemed to be somewhat dejected." She could hardly have been otherwise; for to her the action of the Boston church, when at the meeting of March 15th Cotton solemnly admonished her, must have been a complete surprise, — a revelation of changed public feeling. During the whole four months which preceded it she had been under restraint at Roxbury, and practically shut off from direct intercourse with the body of her fellow-communicants. When her trial before the Court closed in November she was still the central figure and the animating spirit of a formidable party, which in the town and church of Boston, at least, was wholly and even aggressively predominant. The Boston deputies to the legislature had been elected without opposition to sustain her; and they had sustained her to the extent of their power and to the very end. So strong indeed was the feeling locally that it has been seen how even Winthrop, the governor of the colony, had been in imminent danger of being called to account before the church after the trial, for

his course in connection with it; and had felt it necessary to forestall action by publicly telling the congregation, that as a magistrate he could not hold himself
answerable to a congregation. The elders were on his
side, and the malcontents abandoned their project;
but that they entertained it, and that Winthrop should
have taken such public action to anticipate them,
is complete evidence of how strong and general the
feeling was. During the winter which followed, a
great change had occurred. In the first place the
minority was completely vanquished; in the second
place, a system of terrorism was established. People
no more wanted to be sent into banishment to Rhode
Island or New Hampshire then, than now they would
want to be banished to New Mexico or to Wyoming.
Yet banishment, prompt and perpetual, was the alter-
native to complete submission. The leaders, it was
understood, were to go. So much was settled. Indeed, some of them had already gone, and others were
soon to follow. Public meetings of the dissatisfied
were not tolerated, and their most private utterances
were laid hold of and repeated, in order to be heralded
in public, and stamped out as heresies.[1] Moreover,
the influence and example of Cotton were potent.
After Vane left the colony, Cotton was the virtual
leader of the minority, and those composing it had
sought to shelter themselves under the authority of
his name. But Cotton had now wholly accepted the
situation. He had done even more than this, — he had,
heart and soul, gone over to the other side. He was,
indeed, inquisitor-in-chief, and, " finding how he had
been abused, and made (as himself said) their stalking horse," he spent most of his time discovering

[1] Cotton, *Way Cleared*, 58, 85.

errors and leading back such as were gone astray.[1]
The clergy, therefore, were united as one man. So
was the magistracy. To stand up in that community,
against church and state combined, called for great
moral courage. Not one in a hundred would dare do
it. Under these circumstances, the fact that all opposition ceased calls for no explanation. The silence
which prevailed may have been sullen, but it was complete. The minority surrendered their arms and held
their tongues. Order reigned in Boston.

While Mrs. Hutchinson could have had little idea
of all this when she was brought in from Roxbury to
confront the church, a realizing sense of it must have
come to her when she, whose utterances a few short
months before had been received by all as those of a
prophetess, found not one to oppose her public censure. The utter downfall of her faction and the
collapse of her ambitious projects were apparent. For
the moment her mind must have been crowded with
very mundane misgivings. A wife and the mother of
many children, she was under sentence of banishment;
and even then her husband and brethren were seeking
out a home in some uninhabited place. The marvel
is how a woman in delicate health and of sensitive
organization, burning with religious fervor and soon
once more to become a mother,[2] bore up against such
a sea of troubles.

[1] Winthrop, i. *258.

[2] The miscarriage of Mrs. Hutchinson, over the details of which
Governor Winthrop and Messrs. Weld and Cotton all gloated with
singular pleasure, seems to have occurred in Rhode Island in July
or August, 1638, some four months after her excommunication. Six
weeks before it occurred — that is, in June — she had been forced to
consult a physician, perceiving " her body to be greatly distempered
and her spirits failing, and in that regard doubtful of life." Winthrop, i. *271; *Short Story*, Preface, 12.

The ordeal fairly passed and the worst befallen,
her spirits rose once more.   Indeed she seems to have
now worked herself into a state of exaltation, glory-
ing in her trials and declaring that, next to Christ,
they were the greatest happiness that ever befell her.
At the time of her excommunication the snow still
lay deep upon the ground, though it was our first of
April, nor did the winter break up until some days
later.[1]   The exile could not, therefore, at once be
driven forth ; but until she could be, she was freed
from her semi-imprisonment at Roxbury, and allowed
to remain, though closely within doors, at her own
house in Boston.   At length, some days later, Governor Winthrop sent her a warrant to depart the
jurisdiction, and in obedience thereto, on the $\frac{28\text{th}}{7\text{th}}$ of
$\frac{\text{March}}{\text{April}}$, she left her home, and, going down to the shore,
was conveyed in a boat across the bay to a landing
near her husband's farm at the Mount.[2]   It was the
first stage of her journey.   She was under injunction
to leave the province before the close of the month.
Her original plan was to join Wheelwright's family
at Mt. Wollaston, and go with them by water to Ports-
mouth.   Meanwhile her husband and his companions,
after being refused an abiding - place within their
limits by the Plymouth authorities, found a site for a
plantation to their liking in the island of Aquidneck,
near where Newport now is.   Receiving tidings of
this before she had started for New Hampshire, Mrs.

---

[1] Winthrop, *264.

[2] The precise site of William Hutchinson's house in what is now
Quincy is not known, but his allotment (*supra*, 366, n.) covered the
territory in the immediate neighborhood of the Wollaston Heights
station on the Old Colony railroad, including what is known as Tay-
lor's hill and a part of the large plain north thereof. Lechford's
Note-Book, [177], [214].

Hutchinson changed her plans, and, in the early days
of April, journeyed by land to Providence, and to the
island of Aquidneck in Narragansett Bay.

There she lived for a few troubled years, and there
in March, 1640, she was visited by a formal delegation of the Boston church, whose mission was to
require her companions in exile to explain " their un-
warrantable practice in communicating with excom-
municated persons." There are two accounts of what
took place between those composing this delegation —
one of whom was Major Gibbons — and Mistress
Hutchinson. According to the more reliable of these
accounts, the brief conference was brought to a close
by her remarking that she would not acknowledge the
Boston church to be any church of Christ ; according
to the other and less reliable account, the mere mention of " the church of Christ at Boston " brought on
an expression of temper on her part, in which she
coupled the name of that body with epithets common
enough in Shakespeare's day, but which are now
classed as archaic. That the mission was fruitless
hardly needs to be said.[1]

In 1642 William Hutchinson died ; and, shortly
after, his wife removed to a point on Manhattan Island, it would seem, " neare a place," as Mr. Weld
took care to note down, " called by Seamen, and in the
Map, Hell-gate." While the reason of this removal
is not certainly known, a plan for bringing Rhode Island within the jurisdiction of the Massachusetts colony
was under consideration at the time ; and it has been
surmised that the mere apprehension of such a thing
led to her again going into exile. On the other hand,

[1] Arthur Ellis, *First Church of Boston*, 65; G. E. Ellis, *Puritan
Age*, 351.

her old enemies in Massachusetts very pointedly in-
sinuated that she found herself after a while no longer
appreciated in her place of exile, and so moved away,
" being weary of the Island, or rather the Island
being weary of her." If the least charitable, the last
explanation is, on its face, the more likely of the two.
It was the woman's nature to crave excitement and
notoriety. She could not be happy without it. As
soon, therefore, as she found herself a sensation of
yesterday, she grew restless and felt a call to go elsewhere. If such was, indeed, the true explanation of
her removal to the Dutch settlement at the mouth of
the Hudson, time was not given her to weary of her
new and final place of abode, for she could have been
there but a few months when, in August, 1642, " the
Indians set upon them, and slew her and all her
family, her daughter and her daughter's husband, and
all their children " save one daughter that was carried
into captivity. This child was then eight years old ;
in 1647 she was recovered by the General Court and
brought back to Massachusetts. When the news of
this terrible ending reached Boston, the people there
were deeply moved. They called to mind the defiant
words in which the would-be prophetess had told the
Court that the Lord would surely deliver her from
impending calamity, and would ruin them and their
posterity and their whole State ; and so bade them
take heed how they proceeded against her. And now
the clergy of Massachusetts Bay grimly pointed out
to all their congregations that the Lord God of Israel
— the God of Abraham and Isaac — had indeed and
in his own good way shown himself to his chosen people. He had smote the American Jezebel a dreadful
blow. Thus the Lord heard his servants' groans to

heaven, and freed them from this great and sore affliction ; neither had he shown himself through the devilish delusion of miracles, but in the way of his wonderful providence he had picked out this woful woman,
to make her and those belonging to her an unheard-of
heavy example.

The subsequent fate of John Wheelwright, if less
dramatic than that of Anne Hutchinson, was sufficiently checkered. He had, it will be remembered,
made his way to Exeter during the severe winter of
1637–8. Joined there by his family the following
spring, he once more settled down in the practice of
his ministry. As would naturally have been expected,
he was now pressed by his brother exiles to join them
in Rhode Island. " They sent to him," Cotton says,
" and urged him much to come to them, to a far richer
soil, and richer company than where he lived : yet he
constantly refused " upon the " ground of the corruption of their judgments : ' Professing often, whilst
they pleaded for the Covenant of Grace, they took
away the Grace of the Covenant.' " But Exeter was
not destined to remain his home. Three years later
only, in 1641, the New Hampshire towns voluntarily
put themselves within the jurisdiction of Massachusetts Bay ; and then Wheelwright, being brought again
under the ban of the law, betook himself further east
to Sir Ferdinando Gorges' province of Maine, where
he sat down not far from Cape Porpoise, founding
what is now the town of Wells. He was accompanied
by his mother-in-law, the mother of the Hutchinsons,
who, as she sat in the twilight of those later days,
must often have thought regretfully of her early home
at Alford in the fens of Lincolnshire, — and here, in
dreariest exile, the poor, buffeted old Englishwoman

died. But as Wheelwright calmly meditated in this
last place of refuge over his stormy career, its events
gradually assumed a new character in his eyes, and he
bethought to make his peace with his brethren. Not
improbably he felt the more moved to this course when
tidings of his sister Hutchinson's fate reached him,
leading him to reflect on the real character of the
issues upon which her life had been wrecked. In any
event, a letter of reconciliation from Wheelwright to
Winthrop followed hard upon the destruction of the
Hutchinson family. It was a thoroughly manly effort,
and its terse, pointed admissions gave evidence that
it was the fruit of " an overruling conscience." He
expressed his deep contrition for the part he had
taken in " those sharp and vehement contentions," and
intimated his more mature sense of the inanity of the
points at issue. He confessed that, as he now saw it,
he had then acted sinfully, and he humbly craved forgiveness. In reply a safe-conduct to Boston was sent
him, and he was practically invited to go there and
abase himself before the General Court. This he declined to do, taking the ground that, however willing
he might be to confess himself wrong in respect to
"justification and the evidencing thereof," yet he
could not with a good conscience condemn himself for
such " capital crimes, dangerous revelations and gross
errors " as were charged upon him and had caused his
sufferings. Some further correspondence followed, as
the result of which the General Court in May, 1644,
placed upon its records a vote remitting Wheelwright's sentence of banishment " upon particular,
solemn and serious acknowledgment, and confession
by letter, of his evil carriages and of the Courts justice upon him for them." It is to be hoped that Win-

throp did not draw up this entry as it stands recorded,
for it was couched in a very different spirit from the
letter which invited it. Wheelwright had made no
such confession of guilt and of the justice of his civil
sentence. He could not, nor would he, avail himself
of a pardon, the acceptance of which bound him to so
humiliating a confession.¹

Accordingly, for three years more, the former student at Cambridge and incumbent of Bilsby, now a
man of over fifty, remained buried in the frontier
wilderness of Maine. In 1647 he received a call from
Hampton, near Exeter, and, removing thither, he
there ministered for nearly eight years. At last, in
May, 1654, in answer to some echo of the old Antinomian controversy, — for such echoes still from time to
time came back to New England from the English
press, — the people of Hampton drew up a petition
to the General Court, intended to bring out from that
body some kindly testimonial in Wheelwright's behalf. It was to be a sort of certificate of restored
fellowship and regular standing. Winthrop had now
been dead four years, and Endicott had succeeded
him as governor. Cotton, too, was dead. Weld and

¹ It was at the time this correspondence between Winthrop and
Wheelwright was going on, and the rescinding of the sentence of exile
was under advisement, that Weld's *Short Story*, etc., was printed in
London. As Winthrop was the author of that pamphlet, and knew
better than any one else that the statements contained in it must occasion controversy, he could not but have seen how very desirable it was
to secure the complete confession of Wheelwright in advance. The
pamphlet could hardly have reached America when the vote of May
29th was recorded. This fact may account for the peculiar wording
of that vote. A confession was manufactured in advance by the other
party to the controversy, and put on record. None of the public men
of that time were above such tricks. The best of them seem to have
looked upon low cunning as an admitted feature in statecraft.

Peters, having gone to England years before, were
not destined to return. The old controversial fire, in
that particular form with which Wheelwright had
been concerned, was wholly burned out, and it was
also a period during which the local persecuting spirit
was comparatively quiet, — resting, indeed, prepara-
tory to its next fierce outburst against the Ranters and
Quakers, two years further on.   Accordingly, when
the petition of the people of Hampton reached the
General Court, it presently, in answer thereto, judged
"meete to certifie that Mr. Wheelwright hath long
since given such satisfaction both to the Court and
elders generally as that he is now, and so for many
years hath been, an officer in the church at Hampton
within our jurisdiction, and that without any offence
to any, so far as we know." The words were somewhat negative in their character, but they were the
last in the, so called, Antinomian controversy.

Some two years later than this, towards the close
probably of 1656, Wheelwright left Hampton and
sailed for England. It then lacked a few months only
of being twenty full years since he had first landed
in Boston, a man of forty-four, and there rejoined his
sister Hutchinson. The retrospect could not have
been a pleasant one. He was now sixty-four ; the end
of all his ambitious dreams had been a banishment,
and more than ten years had elapsed since the blood
of Anne Hutchinson was poured upon the ground.
While he had been languishing under the provincial
ban of Massachusetts Bay, his old schoolfellow and
familiar friend had become the Lord Protector of
England.   Nevertheless, the six years he now passed
in England — those which saw the end of the Commonwealth and the beginning of the Restoration —

could hardly have been other than the halcyon years
of his life. During them he was treated with consideration by eminent men; for not only, it would
seem, did he live at Belleau, — the home of Sir Harry
Vane, his old friend and protector, who now " greatly
noticed him," — but he was singled out by Cromwell
for marks of especial regard ; and when he went up to
London for a visit " my Lord Protector was pleased
to send one of his guard " for him, and gave him an
hour's interview.

Pleasure-trips across the Atlantic were not taken
in those days, and the probabilities are that when
Wheelwright returned to England in 1656, he proposed to finish his days there. If such was his in-
tention, the course of political events may well have
induced him to change it. Cromwell died ; and even
before the Restoration, Vane had been committed a
prisoner to his own house. The old Puritan divine
had fallen again upon evil days. On the 4th of June,
1662, Vane was arraigned in the court of King's
Bench, and ten days later he laid his neck on the
block upon Tower Hill. Then Wheelwright seems to
have shaken from his feet the dust of his native land,
though he had passed his seventieth year when, later
in the same summer, he next landed in Boston. His
pulpit at Hampton had long since been filled, but he
now received a call from the neighboring church at
Salisbury, where he was formally installed on the 9th
of December following his return. This was his last
and also his longest settlement, for it continued seventeen years, until his death in 1679. He was then the
oldest minister in New England. He had outlived all
the contentions of his middle life, and every one of
his contemporaries who had taken part in them. He

belonged to a past generation. But priesthoods have long memories. At the time his brethren took no special notice of the patriarch's death, nor does any stone now mark his grave. A portrait, believed on such evidence as is now attainable to be of him,[1] for years hung in the Senate Chamber of Massachusetts, and is now preserved in one of the rooms occupied by the Secretary of State. Painted by an unknown hand in 1677, it represents an aged minister in the sombre Calvinistic garb of the time, — the broad white Geneva bands and black coif, while from under the last straggle thin gray locks. The features, neither large nor harsh, are suggestive of the Shakespeare type of face so common among the English of that time, and in them, though drawn by an unskilled hand and faded now, it yet seems possible to read an expression of sadness and disappointment such as would be not unnatural to a man of eighty-four, so much of whose life had been passed in losing strife and weary exile.

Finally, like most of the Puritan breed, John Wheelwright was far from being a lovable character. His proper place was not the pulpit. He should have been a man of affairs, — a lawyer, a magistrate, possibly a soldier; for he was strong, self-willed, enterprising and courageous. He was ambitious also, naturally craving prominence and taking a grim delight in controversy. Nor did he shrink from conflict with nature, any more than he shrank from it with man. He was not afraid to be alone in a minority, or alone in the woods. A clergyman, he was often engaged in lawsuits; for in matters temporal, as well as in those spiritual, he had the full courage of his convictions and entire faith in himself. That he was an attractive

[1] *250th Anniversary, First Church, Quincy, 12, 151-2.*

man in domestic life does not seem probable; he leaves the impression of one deeply conscientious, but still rigid, overbearing, and hard to please at home, as everywhere else.

None the less, Wheelwright was essentially a man of mark; and a man who, wherever he might have gone, would have left his mark. It may be mere accident, but those familiar with the subsequent history of the Mount have thought they could detect in it indications of the man's power of thus impressing himself on those about him. As will presently be seen, in 1640 that region was incorporated as a town, under the name of Braintree. Again, in 1792, the north precinct of Braintree, which included Mt. Wollaston, was set off as the town of Quincy. It was in what is now the city of Quincy that Wheelwright ministered, and there is no doubt that his parishioners sympathized fully in his views. The first teacher of the church regularly gathered there, two years later, was one of his disciples, whose name was blotted from the famous Boston remonstrance only so late as May, 1640.[1] In subsequent years the north precinct of Braintree, — both as such, and as the town of Quincy, — always showed a marked leaning towards a liberal theology, the more noticeable from the contrast in this respect offered to the rigid orthodoxy which ever characterized the south precinct, still retaining the original name. During the eighteenth century the two precincts more than once, through their pastors, engaged in sharp controversy, never changing their sides,[2] — the original leaven apparently continuing to work, as the pastor influenced the people, and the tendency of the people operated back in the selection of pastors,

[1] *Infra*, 603.   [2] *Infra*, 638, 944.

— until the old order of things passed wholly **away.**
As the twig is bent, the tree inclines; and so it **may**
even be surmised that the seed sown by **Wheelwright,**
in 1637, bore active fruit in the great New England
protest, under the lead of Channing, two centuries
later, deciding the course then pursued by the descendants in the seventh generation of those who at the
Mount had listened to him.

Of the others who shared Mrs. Hutchinson's exile,
William Coddington was the most prominent. He
seems to have been the immediate successor of Thomas
Morton in the ownership of Mt. Wollaston; and, singularly enough, the record of every annual town-
meeting of Quincy, so long as Quincy continued to be
a town, bore recurring evidence to the fact that he
once lived there, and thence went into exile. Since
the year 1640, a portion of the extensive grant made
to him and to Edmund Quincy, jointly, in December,
1635, has been public property, and is spoken of on
the first page of the Braintree records as "The Schoole
Lands." Each year, by a formal vote, — the reason
of which long since passed into a meaningless tradition, — the town of Quincy, as tenant of the land
thus held, appropriated to school purposes a sum of
money as a nominal rent.[1] The name of the school in
which the children of the district including Mt. Wollaston are taught, and the street upon which its building stands, still perpetuate the name of Coddington.

[1] The record of the process through which this land came into the
possession of the original town of Braintree is inexplicably defective;
but some facts connected with it lead to a suspicion that Coddington,
after going into exile, instead of freely giving the land, was judicially
despoiled of it. See communication referred to in the *Proc. Mass.
Hist. Soc.* Series II. vii. 23.

The dominant faction dealt with Coddington in much the same arbitrary spirit with which it had dealt with Wheelwright and Anne Hutchinson. He was neither " convented " nor formally banished; but, though a firm, self-asserting man of a business turn of mind and somewhat grasping disposition, the action of those with whom he had been seven years associated offended him, and, as intense religious bigotry has at no time been conducive to social amenities, the private bearing towards him of many of his old friends doubtless aggravated the difficulties of the situation. Even as early as the autumn of 1637, therefore, Coddington thought of removing with a number of others from the Massachusetts jurisdiction, and obtained leave so to do, a year's time being allowed them for the purpose : but, before their plans were matured, the General Court, at its March session of 1638, — at the very time of the excommunication of Mrs. Hutchinson, — took cognizance of the matter on the strength of a rumor that the emigrants proposed only to withdraw themselves " for a season." Their movements were accordingly expedited by a summons commanding them to appear before the next Court, unless, accompanied by their families, they had previously taken themselves off. The next Court was fixed to be held two weeks later. Deeply indignant, but being, as he himself subsequently expressed it, " not willing to live in the fire of contention," Coddington, together with the others designated in the summons, six in number, made their way to Providence within the designated time. It was in the early days of our April that he left his brick house, on the north side of what is now Liberty Square, said to have been the first brick house ever built in Boston, and he afterwards wrote to Winthrop "what myself and wife and family did endure in that removal, I wish neither you nor yours may ever be put unto." But when, in 1640, — two years later, — he thus expressed himself, his animosities had already passed away; for in yet another letter, written shortly after and likewise to Winthrop, he took occasion to say that he well approved " of a speech of one of note amongst you, that we were in a heate and chafed, and were all of us to blame; in our strife we had forgotten that we were brethren."[1]   Though Wheelwright was eight years his senior, Coddington died first, in 1678.   His name is still venerated in Rhode Island, as that of Winthrop is in Massachusetts; and, while the portrait of the latter looks down from the walls of the Senate chamber of the State-House in Boston, that of the former hangs in the Council-room at Newport. Through several generations his descendants dwelt in the home he had helped to build up and rule over; but in time they also experienced the decay common to families, and the last of them is reported to have died in the almshouse of the place her ancestor founded, lying on a bed which still showed the armorial bearings of her family.

It will be remembered that when Mrs. Hutchinson left the Boston church, after excommunication, Mary Dyer walked at her side.   She was a very proper and comely young woman, the wife of one William Dyer, sometime a citizen of London, and a milliner in the New Exchange; though as Winthrop, to whom we owe these particulars, goes on to say, she and her husband were in Boston "notoriously infected with Mrs. Hutchinson's errors, and very censorious and

[1] IV. *Mass. Hist. Soc. Coll.* vi. 314, 317.

troublesome, she being of a very proud spirit, and much addicted to revelations." They both went with the Hutchinsons to Rhode Island. Mary Dyer would seem to have been one of that class, numerous in those days, whose brains were wholly unsettled by their religion. She remained in Rhode Island, in apparently undisturbed enjoyment of her revelations, for many years, becoming a Quaker in the mean while; but at last, in 1659, hearing of the persecution of that sect in Massachusetts, and loathing her place of refuge "for that there they were not opposed by the civil authority, but with all patience and meekness were suffered to say over their pretended revelations and admonitions," — feeling this call to persecution she came to Boston. What she there did does not appear, but she was speedily arrested and brought before the Court in company with three others. She simply said in her own defence that she came from Rhode Island to visit the Quakers, that she was of their religion, and that the light within her was the rule. They were banished, under pain of death if they returned. Mary Dyer and one other "found freedom to depart;" but within a month they were back again, in company with another woman, who brought some linen for the examination of Governor Endicott, intended to be used as the grave-clothes of that magistrate's victims. They were at once all thrown into prison, and then brought again before the Court, which now sentenced them to death. Mary Dyer's son at this time filled the important office of secretary of the province of Rhode Island, and at his earnest solicitation the death-penalty was remitted in the case of his mother, on condition that she should leave Massachusetts within forty-eight hours. Her companions, William

Robinson and Marmaduke Stephenson, were left for
execution. When the day fixed for their hanging
came, the town had to be put under guard, so great
was the sympathy felt for the condemned. Surrounded by a heavy escort, the three prisoners walked
together from the jail in Cornhill to the gallows,
which had been erected on the Common, Mary Dyer
going between the two others and holding a hand of
each. She must then have been a woman of middle
life, but Edward Nicholson, the marshal, asked her
if she was not "ashamed to walk hand in hand, between two young men?" "It is," she answered, "an
hour of the greatest joy I can enjoy in this world.
No eye can see, no ear can hear, no tongue can
speak, no heart can understand, the sweet incomes
and refreshings of the Spirit of the Lord which now
I enjoy." [1]

When her companions were hanged, she sat beneath
the gallows with the halter about her neck, calmly
looking at the multitude of horrified spectators, whom
a hundred armed men of the train-band kept back
from the scaffolding; for so great was the throng
upon the Common that day, that the draw-bridge over
the canal, which then separated the North End from
the town, broke down under the weight of those
returning home. When her companions were dead
Mary Dyer was taken back to prison, and there she
first learned of the circumstances of her reprieve.
She at once wrote to the governor, repudiating her
son's action, and offering her life as a sacrifice. It
was necessary to use force to get her out of the jurisdiction. She was at last taken back to Newport,
where for a time she seems to have been kept under

---

[1] *Supra,* 408.

restraint; but in the following spring she succeeded in eluding those having her in charge, and, journeying " secretly and speedily," found her way back to Boston. She was again thrown into prison; and again her family piteously interceded for her. She was sentenced once more to be hanged, but at the gallows her life was offered her if she would keep away from Massachusetts. Her reply was: — " In obedience to the will of the Lord I came; and in his will I abide faithful to the death." She now lies buried in some undistinguished part of Boston Common. Assuredly the fate of those two women, who, side by side, walked forth out of the church on that 22d of March, 1638, was sufficiently tragic, — one murdered by savages, the other put to death by her brethren!

To turn from Mary Dyer to John Underhill is like suddenly passing from the solemnity of a funeral to the buffoonery of a pantomime. Captain John Underhill was a Puritan of that Trusty Tompkins type common enough a few years later on in the armies of the Commonwealth, — a curious mixture of fervor, which was apparently genuine, and of licentiousness which was unquestionably so. He seems to have taken religion, as he would have taken any other epidemic which might have chanced to prevail, — and to have felt it sufficiently, not to prevent his scoffing or indulging the flesh, but to make him extremely uncomfortable after he had done so. As a soldier he had seen some service under Prince Maurice of Nassau in the Low Countries; and he came out with Winthrop in a semi-military capacity in 1630. More recently he had served under Endicott in the latter's inglorious Pequot campaign.

Though Underhill belonged to Mrs. Hutchinson's faction, his more earnest efforts seem to have been put forth in Wheelwright's behalf. After the sentence of the latter he sent a strong appeal to Winthrop not to enforce it,[1] and later on he followed Wheelwright to New Hampshire. When called to account for putting his name to the remonstrance he at first retracted in writing, and put the paper in the Governor's hands; but presently he made up his mind to follow the exiled minister, and petitioned the Court for a grant of land which had been promised him. Hereupon he was questioned as to certain heretical opinions alleged to have been uttered by him some time before to the effect, —

" That we were zealous here, as the Scribes and Pharisees were, and as Paul was before his conversion, &c. Which he denying, they were proved to his face by a sober, godly woman, whom he had seduced in the ship, and drawn to his opinions (but she was afterwards freed again). Among other passages he told her how he came to his assurance, and that was thus : — He had lain under a spirit of bondage and a legal way five years, and could get no assurance ; till at length, as he was taking a pipe of tobacco, the Spirit set home an absolute promise of free grace with such assurance and joy, as he never since doubted of his good estate, neither should he though he should fall into sin."

His answers and explanations were not edifying on doctrinal grounds, and so the matter of his signing the remonstrance was brought in question. His retraction was produced by the Governor and read to the Court, but he now said it applied only to the manner, not to the matter of the paper ; in regard to the

[1] iv. *Mass. Hist. Soc. Coll.* vii. 171.

latter he was of the same mind still as he was when
he affixed his name. When asked for a Scripture
"rule by which he might take so much upon him, as
publickly to contradict the sentence of the Court, &c.,
hee alleged the example of Joab his rough speech to
David." The precedent thus adduced having been
disallowed for causes elaborately specified, he then
insisted much "upon the liberty which all States do
allow to Military officers, for free speech, &c., and
that himself had spoken sometimes as freely to Count
Nassau." This argument weighed no more with the
Court than the other; so the captain was committed,
and the next day he was again sent for and banished.

"The Lord's day following he made a speech in the assembly, shewing that, as the Lord was pleased to convert
Paul as he was in persecuting, etc., so he might manifest
himself to him as he was taking the moderate use of the
creature called tobacco. He professed withal, that he knew
not wherein he had deserved the sentence of the Court, and
that he was sure that Christ was his, etc. . . .

"The next Lord's day the same Capt. Underhill, having
been privately dealt with upon suspicion of incontinency
with a neighbor's wife, and not hearkening to it, was publicly questioned, and put under admonition. The matter
was, for that the woman being young, and beautiful, and
withal of a jovial spirit and behaviour, he did daily frequent her house, and was divers times found there alone
with her, the doors being locked on the inside. He confessed it was ill, because it had an appearance of evil in it;
but his excuse was, that the woman was in great trouble of
mind, and sore temptations, and that he resorted to her to
comfort her; and that when the door was found locked
upon them, they were in private prayer together. But this
practice was clearly condemned also by the elders, affirm-
ing, that it had not been of good report for any of them to

have done the like, and that they ought in such case, to have called in some brother or sister, and not to have locked the door, etc."

In September, 1638, after leaving Boston, Underhill went to New Hampshire. The rest of his ludicrous story loses point when told in other than the unconsciously solemn words in which Winthrop first recorded it : —

"The General Court in September gave order to the Governor to write to them of Pascataquack, to signify to them, that we looked at it as an unneighborly part, that they should encourage and advance such as we had cast out from us for their offences, before they had inquired of us the cause, &c. (The occasion of this letter was, that they had aided Mr. Wheelwright to begin a plantation there, and intended to make Capt. Underhill their governor.) Upon this Mr. Burdet returned a scornful answer, and would not give the governor his title &c. and Capt. Underhill wrote a letter to a young gentleman, who sojourned in the house of our governor, wherein he reviled the governor with reproachful terms and imprecations of vengeance upon us all. This letter being shown to the governor and council, the governor by advice wrote to Edward Hilton. He intimated withal how ill it would relish, if they should advance Capt. Underhill, whom we had thrust out for abusing the Court with feigning a retraction both of his seditious practice and also of his corrupt opinions, and after, denying it again ; and for casting reproach upon our churches, &c. : signifying withal, that he was now found to be an unclean person, for he was charged by a godly young woman to have solicited her chastity under pretence of Christian love, and to have confessed to her that he had his will oftentimes of the cooper's wife, and all out of strength of love ; and the church had sent for him, and sent him a license to come and go under the hands of the governor and deputy ; but he refused to come, excusing himself, by letters to the elders, that the license was not sufficient, &c., and, by letters to the Governor, that he had no rule to come and answer to any offence, except his banishment were released.   But, to the matter he was charged with he gave no answer, but sought an evasion.

"The Pascataquack men had chosen Captain Underhill their governor before the letter came to them, and it was intercepted and opened by Mr. Burdet and him.   The captain was much nettled with this letter, and especially because his adulterous life with the cooper's wife at Boston was now discovered, and the church had called him to come and make answer to it.   And upon this he wrote a letter to Mr. Cotton, full of high and threatening words against us ; but he wrote another, at the same time, to the governor in very fair terms, entreating an obliterating of all that was past, and a bearing with human infirmities, &c., disavowing all purpose of revenge.

" But, instead of coming to Boston to make answer to the church, he procured a new church at Pascataquack of some few loose men to write to our church in his commendation, wherein they style him the right worshipful, their honored governor.   All which notwithstanding the church of Boston proceeded with him.   After this, Capt. Underhill's courage was abated, for the chiefest in the river fell from him, and the rest little regarded him, so as he wrote letters of retraction to divers.   And presently [about a year later] being struck with horror and remorse for his offences, both against the church and civil state, he could have no rest till he had obtained a safe conduct to come and give satisfaction ; and accordingly, at a lecture at Boston, (it being the court time,) he made a public confession both of his living in adultery with Faber's wife, and attempting the like with another woman ; and also the injury he had done to our state, &c. ; and acknowledged the justice of the court in their proceedings against him.   Yet all his confessions were mixed with such excuses and extenua-

tions, as did not give satisfaction of the truth of his repentance, so as it seemed to be done rather out of policy, and to
pacify the sting of his conscience, than in sincerity. But,
however, his offences being so foul and scandalous, the
church presently cast him out; which censure he seemed to
submit unto, and, for the time he staid in Boston, (being
four or five days) he was very much dejected, &c.; but, being gone back, he soon recovered his spirits again, or, at
least, gave not that proof of a broken heart, as he gave
hope of at Boston."

At Dover — as the New Hampshire settlement presided over by Underhill and Burdet was now called
— the captain had other troubles to encounter besides
those which his conscience caused him. In fact a
species of civil war, of the smallest conceivable pro-
portions, broke out between that town and the adjoining town of Exeter, as a result of which Underhill
was deposed and one Roberts chosen president in his
place.

Soon after this downfall the ex-governor again went
to Boston, trying once more to make his peace with
the church. Not being satisfied of his repentance,
the church declined to listen to him ; and so, after
a week's waiting, he went back to New Hampshire,
where he seems to have now been in open disgrace.
At last, in the course of the spring and summer of
1640, he came to the last act in this drama of colonial life and manners, — the closing, ludicrous scene
being again in that meeting-house which a little more
than two years before had witnessed the solemn excommunication of Mistress Hutchinson. There is nothing better recorded by Winthrop.

" Captain Underhill being brought, by the blessing of
God on this church's censure of excommunication, to re-

morse for his foul sins, obtained, by means of the elders
and others of the church of Boston, a safe conduct under
the hand of the governor and one of the council to repair
to the church. He came at the time of the court of assist-
ants, and upon the lecture day, after sermon, the pastor
called him forth and declared the occasion, and then gave
him leave to speak. Indeed it was a spectacle which caused
many weeping eyes, though it afforded matter for much
rejoicing to behold the power of the Lord Jesus in his own
ordinances, when they are dispensed in his own way, holding forth the authority of his regal sceptre in the simplicity
of the gospel. He came in his worst clothes (being accustomed to take great pride in his bravery and neatness)
without a band, in a foul linen cap pulled close to his eyes;
and standing upon a form, he did, with many deep sighs
and abundance of tears, lay open his wicked course, his
adultery, his hypocrisy, his persecution of Gods people
here, and especially his pride (as the root of all, which
caused God to give him over to his other sinful courses)
and contempt of the magistrates. He justified God and
the church and the court in all that had been inflicted on
him. Indeed he appeared as a man worn out with sorrow,
and yet he could find no peace. Therefore he was now
come to seek it in this ordinance of God. He spake well,
save that his blubbering &c. interrupted him, and all along
he discovered a broken and melting heart, and gave good
exhortations to take heed of such vanities and beginnings of
evil as had occasioned his fall; and in the end he earnestly
and humbly besought the church to have compassion on
him, and to deliver him out of the hands of Satan.

"So accordingly he was received into the church again;
and after, he came into the court (for the General Court
began soon after) and made confession of his sin against
them, &c. and desired pardon, which the court freely
granted him, so far as concerned their private judgment.
But for his adultery they would not pardon that for ex-

amples sake ; nor would restore him to freedom, though they released his banishment, and declared the former law against adultery to be of no force; so as there was no law now to touch his life, for the new law against adultery was made since his fact committed.

" He confessed also in the congregation, that though he was very familiar with that woman, and had gained her affection, &c., yet she withstood him six months against all his solicitations (which he thought no woman could have resisted) before he could overcome her chastity, but being once overcome she was wholly at his will. And to make his peace the more sound he went to her husband (being a cooper) and fell upon his knees before him in the presence of some of the elders and others, and confessed the wrong he had done him, and besought him to forgive him ; which he did very freely, and in testimony thereof he sent the captain's wife a token." [1]

[1] It is unnecessary in the present work to follow the Captain's career after he thus made his peace with the church of Boston, the magistrates of Massachusetts Bay and Joseph Faber, cooper. He removed to Stamford in Connecticut, and afterward to Flushing, on Long Island. He performed other military duties ; he was a delegate to the Assembly and an under-sheriff, — an altogether respectable and useful man. He was far from being a man of education, and in IV. *Mass. Hist. Soc. Coll.* vii. are a number of letters from him, the spelling of which is remarkable. The following is a specimen taken from a letter to "John Wenthrop esquier, Goferner of the Macetuchets baye," and written from the house of Captain Gibbons, where he apparently tarried during his brief and fruitless visit to Boston in April, 1640 : —

" A mong the rest of my aflickchons, jusli imposed by my sinnfull lif and backsliding prodigalliti in my whole corce, this is on that doth and will agrefate my grefe, thut I am deprife of that chrischan liberti I once had, boght by the preschous blud of the Lord Jesous ; but I hafe made the blod and deth of Christ of non efeckt, therfor I am justli depriued of liberti to visset you, nor dare I aproch youer presenc, tel the Lord mofe you there unto." This queer specimen of one type of Puritan life is supposed to have died at Oyster Bay, L. I., in 1672.

CHAPTER XI.

"AND SHEM AND JAPHETH TOOK A GARMENT AND COVERED THE NAKEDNESS OF THEIR FATHER."

THE course pursued by those in authority in Massachusetts Bay towards Mrs. Hutchinson and her adherents has ever been, and will probably long remain, one of the hotly contested issues in early New England history. So far as external authority is concerned the verdict has been distinct. The action of the General Court of 1637 has been treated as an unjustifiable persecution, which has left a dark stain on the earliest pages of the history of the Puritan Commonwealth.[1] But, on the other hand, the founders have not lacked champions to extenuate, and even to justify their proceedings.[2] By these it has been argued that the colonists came to New England with certain great and laudable objects in view; that to the attainment of these objects unity of opinion and effort was clearly desirable, if, indeed, not absolutely essential. Beset as it was with enemies, and regarded with, at best, unfriendly eyes by those in authority at Whitehall, the continued existence of the enterprise often in those early days hung upon a thread. A mere scandal, a rumor even of internal dissensions, might afford the pretext for a fatal exercise of royal authority. This peril, it cannot be denied, was never absent

[1] Doyle, *The English in America; the Puritan Colonies*, i. 186–8.
[2] Palfrey, i. 488–511.

from the minds of Winthrop and his associates. The whole enterprise, moreover, was a business undertaking, those engaged in which formed a society or partnership by themselves, in which no provision had been made, or was intended to be made, for hostile or antagonistic elements. Massachusetts, within the chartered limits, was to the members of this partnership what his farm or his dwelling is to a freeholder; and they had the same right as the freeholder to expel intruders or dissentients, or persons distasteful to them. Those responsible for the success of the undertaking finally, after careful consideration, were persuaded and fully believed that the expulsion of the more prominent of the so-called Antinomian faction was necessary to peace and prosperity, temporal and spiritual; and, if the whole thing is viewed from the standpoint of the seventeenth century instead of the nineteenth, it will probably be conceded that they were correct in their conclusion.[1] The event certainly vindicated the substantial justice of their course, as a long period of internal tranquillity followed the proceedings of 1638.

This line of argument is plausible, but there are difficulties connected with its acceptance. The analogy of the freeholder may, from a legal point of view, be correct; and yet a freeholder who invited his brethren to come and abide with him and labor on his farm, and who then sternly visited each expression of opinion different from his own with stripes and banishment, would not be regarded as a desirable neighbor or as a judicious man. In its wider scope, also, the same line of argument might equally well be used to palliate the course of those whose persecutions

[1] Lodge, *Short History*, 351.

forced the colonists into exile. In their desire to defend Winthrop, those who reason thus also defend Laud. He, too, as well as his master and Philip II. and Louis XIV., had great public ends in view, the attainment of which was not in his belief consistent with toleration. Even more than Winthrop, Laud might a little later have pointed to terrible civil calamities which had resulted from his inability to carry out a policy of wholesome repression. If, indeed, he had lived only ten years longer he might have cited exultingly the conformity enforced in Massachusetts and the tranquillity resulting therefrom ; and then turned to the dissensions which tore England, and have asserted, truly enough, that he only tried to do in his own country, and failed, what Winthrop had tried to do in Massachusetts, and succeeded. He had striven for the peace of absolute conformity. It is well to consider in the discussion the seventeenth century standpoint; but, in the seventeenth century, good public intentions were not confined to the founders of New England. Others, as well as they, had high considerations of state always in view ; and a concurrence of opinion to a given end was in the seventeenth century eagerly desired by those who ruled elsewhere as well as by those who ruled in Massachusetts.

In the treatment of doubtful historical points, there are few things which need to be more carefully guarded against than patriotism or filial piety. Admirable in their place, these sentiments have less than nothing to do with that impartiality which should be the historian's aim ; and the appeal to them is generally accompanied by some suggestion that the matter in dispute should be viewed, not according to immutable principles, but from the standpoint of the period or the individual. When viewed in this way, there are few historical events which do not admit of some defence. The door is open wide for sophistry as well as charity. True, it is neither safe nor just to apply the standard of one century to the acts of individuals of another century; but, none the less, the fact of being in advance of one's century constitutes greatness, both in the individual and in the people. If, also, the standards of the period are to be exhumed and adopted, they should be applied with rigorous impartiality. Love of country and piety, whether filial or religious, should not be permitted to intervene in one case, and be excluded in another. Judged in the full light of subsequent events, the protestant, civil or religious, of the seventeenth century was better than the seventeenth century inquisitor and persecutor; but when, circumstances being altered, the protestant himself turned inquisitor and persecutor, it is not easy to see on what judicial principal the historian, who has been exciting sympathy by the ancient tale of wrong, can suddenly put in that plea of altered times for the one, which he has systematically disallowed for the others. To do so may be filial, but it is not rational and it is not fair.

In the controversy of 1637–8 Winthrop and his associates seem to have felt the weakness of their position far more than their modern defenders; and they labored hard to hide it. In England the so-called Antinomian persecution was generally and correctly regarded as a religious one. To deny that it was such is impossible now, and was not easy then. In the face of the record of the Synod at Cambridge,

with its endless list of erroneous opinions and "un-
savory speeches," — in the face of the church indictment of Mrs. Hutchinson with its twenty-nine several
counts, — it might almost as well have been contended
that the issue between Luther and Leo X. was not a
religious issue, and that the German reformer was proceeded against simply because his course led directly
to sedition and civil strife, — which it unquestionably
did. But, for obvious reasons, the fathers of the
colony were sensitive on this point. The principles
of religious toleration were much better understood at
that time, by minorities at least, than modern investigators seem disposed to admit. The Long Parliament had not then met, and Laud was in the full
enjoyment of power. The friends of Winthrop and
Weld in England were accordingly, in 1636–8, themselves undergoing persecutions, and those in New
England were loath to supply the prelates with new
examples as well as fresh arguments. Their casuistry
was equal to this, as it was equal to all other occa-
sions. They flatly denied that religious considerations had anything to do with their proceedings.
Whatever they had done, had been done on civil
grounds. They had, it was true, labored and wrestled
with their brethren over matters spiritual, but the
punishments inflicted had been for temporal miscarriages.

Thomas Weld, for instance, in a narrative prepared
especially for use in England, after referring to the
recantation of Cotton, thus stated the case as respected
the others : —

" But for the rest, which (notwithstanding all these meanes
of conviction from heaven and earth, and the example of
their seduced brethrens returne) yet stood obdurate, yea

more hardened (as we had cause to feare) than before ; we convented those of them that were members before the churches, and yet laboured once and againe to convince them, not onely of their errors, but also of sundry exorbitant practices, neglecting to feare the Church, and lying, &c., but after no meanes prevailed, we were driven with sad hearts to give them up to Satan : Yet not simply for their opinions (for which I find we have beene slanderously traduced) but the chiefest cause of their censure was their miscarriages (as have beene said) persisted in with great obstinacy." [1]

So when Coggeshall was arraigned before the Court, he had met the charges preferred against him by saying that they amounted to nothing " but matter of different opinion, and that he knew not one example in Scripture that a man was banished for his judgment." To this Winthrop, in the account of the proceedings he prepared for publication in England, says he replied that if the prisoner " had kept his judgment to himself, so as the public peace had not been troubled or endangered by it, we should have left him to himself, for we do not challenge power over mens consciences, but when seditious speeches and practices discover such a corrupt conscience, it is our duty to use authority to reform both." [2] Cogges-

[1] *Short Story*, xii., xv.

[2] In the letter of the Rev. Thomas Shepard, entitled *New England's Lamentations for Old England's Errors*, the distinction suggested here is very clearly drawn : — " We never banished any for their consciences, but for sinning against conscience, after due means of conviction." This is very like Cotton's argument in his reply to Saltonstall, that a magistrate in compelling a man to religious observances does not compel him to sin, " but the sin is in his will that needs to be compelled." (Hutchinson's *State Papers*, 404.) But the statements made for English effect are ludicrously at variance with Winthrop's emphatic laying down of the law at the Hutchinson trial : — " We see not that any should have authority to set up any other exercises besides what authority hath already set up." (Hutchinson, ii. 486.)

hall's offence, it will be remembered, consisted in his
saying, from his place in the Legislature, that he approved of a paper presented to a previous Legislature,
though his name was not signed to it. It was a case
of constructive sedition ; but constructive sedition resulting in banishment is only in degree a lesser outrage than constructive treason resulting in death.
Whatever their party or country, zealots are all
formed of one material, and Hugh Peters was but
Ignatius Loyola under other conditions ; nor can the
fact that the founders of Massachusetts did the deed
influence the verdict of history. The " conscientiously
contentious " John Wheelwright, silenced for opinion's sake, and expelled from his pulpit at Mount
Wollaston, was a persecuted man no less than the
" conscientiously contentious " John Wheelwright
silenced and expelled for the same cause from his
vicarage at Bilsby.

By investigators of another class it is argued that
these proceedings were reasonable measures of self-
preservation. Those holding this view insist that it
is impossible to arrive at any correct understanding
of the motives which impelled the dominant party in
Massachusetts to their rigorous measures without extending the range of vision so as to take into view the
general condition of European thought and political
and religious movement at that time. They say, and
with truth, that the human mind in many countries
was then in a condition of violent seething ; the old
ligaments which had bound men together were loos-
ened, and the new had not begun to knit. The world
was full of crude abominations. The Anabaptists of
Munster were but a century gone, and the saints of
the Fifth Monarchy were yet to come. The human

mind was sick with *isms* — sick in England and Scotland, sick in France, sick in Germany. For the time
all things seemed to tend towards subversion. The
startling success of Mrs. Hutchinson in her rôle of a
prophetess in Boston, "raised up of God for some
great work now at hand," was significant. It demon-
strates at least how thoroughly the Massachusetts community was impregnated with this uneasy spirit, hov
strongly it sympathized with the morbid tendencies of
the age. In and of herself, Mistress Anne Hutchinson was nothing. At any other time she might have
come to Boston and criticised each Sunday's sermons
to her heart's content, — talking her mystical non-
sense until she stopped from sheer weariness, — and,
while few would have hearkened to her, nobody would
have molested her. She would have passed away as
thousands like her have before and since, and the most
diligent search of the antiquarian would fail to detect
any ripple made by her in the great current of events.
But Mrs. Hutchinson chanced happily. She thirsted
for notoriety, and she struck just the combination of
circumstances which secured it to her. The historian
of to-day, therefore, sees that her success was a symp-
tom, not a cause. It denoted a condition of the body
politic. The clergy were supreme; the people were
restless, and she gave voice to their restlessness. Thus
the great struggle for New England, between the
vague unrest of the time and its conservative forces,
chanced to happen over her body. Had the conflict
resulted otherwise than it did, — had Mrs. Hutchinson sustained herself and had the clergy been vanquished, — she and Wheelwright and the rest would
have been like many others, before and since, who
have inaugurated revolution when they fondly sup-

posed they were guiding reform. She would soon
have been made to realize that the spirit she had invoked far exceeded her powers of control. She would
have disappeared aghast at the excesses and absurdi-
ties of those who had once been her followers. Theo-
retical toleration then meant in practice, what theoreti-
cal liberty meant in practice a century and a half later
in France, — anarchy, pure and simple. The fault
was not in the food : that was as good and strong and
nourishing in 1637 and in 1793 as it is now ; but the
stomach of the body politic was not yet educated up
to the point of assimilating it. Thus the battle over
Mrs. Hutchinson involved the question whether Massachusetts was to be radical and doctrinaire, or conservative and practical, — a man's home or a fool's
paradise. The doctrinaire Vane was wise in principle and wrong in practice ; Winthrop, cool and
prudent, was wrong in principle but right in practice.
Even in his bigotry, he saved Massachusetts.

To this somewhat fanciful and overwrought line of
argument, it may be replied, that it is a doubtful expedient to justify persecution on the ground that, but
for it, a long train of calamities, which never did happen, might have happened. In the early days of
New England the clergy never wearied of reminding
their flocks of the evil deeds of the Anabaptists ; and
they were always predicting a renewal of the horrors
of Munster as a certain result of toleration. That
picture produced much the same effect on the minds
of the timid of those days, as the thought of another
Reign of Terror has produced on the well-to-do of
Europe throughout the present century. There were
alarmists in the seventeenth century just as there are
in the nineteenth ; but the realities of history and the

imaginings of excited men are two very different things. In 1629 the charge made against the first body of emigrants to Salem in Endicott's company was that " they were Separatists, and would be shortly Anabaptists." In 1637 Winthrop doubtless believed in his heart — what he stated at the trial and spread on the Records of the Province and reiterated in his narrative of the proceedings — that the Covenant of Grace, as taught by Mrs. Hutchinson, and social anarchy, or worse, were convertible terms.[1] It is barely possible that at one stage of the controversy there might have been danger of actual strife ; though the presumption — as gathered from the calm, law-abiding tone of the papers which emanated from the minority, and from the submissive way in which they allowed themselves at the close to be disarmed, fined, whipped, disfranchised and banished — is decidedly the other way. There is no evidence of any material in that little community out of which to manufacture revolutions. Certainly Coddington, Coggeshall, Hough, Balston, Hutchinson, Dummer, and even blubbering Captain John Underhill, are strange subjects out of which to conjure up hosts of prophets of Munster, Latter-day Saints, or Fifth Monarchy Men.

But the common-sense view of the controversy of 1637, and its unhappy outcome, would seem to lead the modern investigator to wholly different and more sober-colored conclusions. It was a struggle for civil power and ecclesiastical supremacy in a small village community. As such it naturally — it almost necessarily — resulted in a display of the worst qualities of those engaged in it. It illustrated also with singular force the malign influence apt to be exercised by the

[1] Hutchinson, ii. 514 ; *Records*, i. 211 ; *Short Story*, 40.

priest and the woman as active elements in political life. Stirred by an access of ill-considered popular enthusiasm, the body of the freemen had, at the election of 1636, put a slight upon the time-honored magistrates of the colony, by placing the boyish Vane over their heads, in the office of governor. An ambitious woman, with her head full of Deborahs and the like, and with a genius for making trouble, had then sought to drive from his pulpit, in the chief town, its long-settled pastor, in order to install her own favorite preacher in his place, with her kinsman as that preacher's associate and successor. In her day-dreams she herself probably occupied, in the new order of things she proposed to bring about, the position of a prophetess, — the real guiding spirit of the whole, — with her husband possibly in the judge's seat. Altogether it was an exhilarating vision, — such a vision as self-conscious and usually unappreciated natures have in every time and most places been wont to revel in. But it did so chance that Mrs. Hutchinson fell into just that combination of circumstances which enabled her to succeed up to a certain point. Her success was indeed marvellous ; and it turned her head. Presently she became reckless. She put wanton affronts on the pastor ; and when his brethren rallied to his support, she did not hesitate to assail them also. She made enemies of the whole body of the clergy. Vane sympathized with her ; Winthrop with them. The contest over the possession of the civil offices came first, and resulted in an easy conservative triumph. Vane made the best fight he could ; but the odds were too heavy, and he went helplessly down. Winthrop was reinstated in his old place ; and, practically, the struggle was then over.

This fact both Vane and Winthrop recognized. They were men trained in public affairs and accustomed to their ways. When beaten, the latter, with a sense and dignity which did him infinite credit, accepted the situation as a man should, and patiently bided his time ; the former, when his turn to be defeated came, left the country. The real issue was then decided, and there was no longer anything to quarrel over. Unfortunately there was a woman in the case, and the implacable spirit of theological hate had been aroused. The priesthood demanded a victim ; and the victim met the priesthood at least half-way. It now became a struggle, which would have been ludicrous had it not been so earnest and so painful, between the whole body of the clergy and a female enthusiast, politician and tease. Had Winthrop then been in real control and able to assert a policy, the excitement would speedily have worn itself out, as purely factitious excitements always have worn themselves out when left alone, and always will. In six months from his return to office Mrs. Hutchinson would have been a sensation of yesterday ; while John Wheelwright for the rest of his life would have quietly ministered to his people at the First Church in Braintree. As for real danger to the existence of the colony, there was none. The strength and permanence of the English settlement of Massachusetts rested on too strong a basis to be jeopardized by a change of magistrates, or a noisy quarrel in a vestry. The success of Charles II. and Strafford and Laud in their schemes in England would have placed the colony in much peril ; but in New England its safety lay, not in the fact that Winthrop, or any other man or set of men, held office, but in the oneness, the hard practical sense, and power of political afterthought and self-restraint, of the twelve or fifteen thousand Englishmen who composed it. They were no sheep, to whom Anne Hutchinson was a ravening wolf and for whom John Winthrop was the only shepherd.

The issue was then finally and completely settled at Cambridge on the $\frac{17th}{27th}$ of May, 1637. The whole theory of a continuing danger, to the time when six months later the persecution took place, is without any evidence in its support. The procession of his friends which escorted Vane to the shore, when on the 13th of August he embarked for England, was a final demonstration, — the salvo of musketry which saluted his departing vessel was the volley fired over the grave of a lost cause. The demonstration may under the circumstances have been indiscreet, but it could hardly have excited alarm. The Pequot war had then been brought to a triumphant close ; the conservative party was in undisputed control of every branch of the government; the immigration was large ; the alien law was in operation. The adherents of Mrs. Hutchinson, the so-called Antinomians, were in a majority in a single town only of the whole province, and their party was so completely broken that its leaders were already seeking a place of refuge outside the jurisdiction of Massachusetts. The struggle with them was no longer for power, but for self-preservation. So far from threatening the safety of the community, they were notoriously unable to protect themselves.

Unfortunately Winthrop's course was not now a free one. It was hampered by the presence of those ecclesiastical allies who had borne him back into power. The clergy verifying in their conduct Milton's assertion that "Presbyter was but Priest writ large," — the clergy insisted on the extirpation of an indefinable heresy. They pointed to the compact of January, two years before, wherein "Mr. Winthrop acknowledged that he was convinced that he had failed in overmuch lenity and remissness, and would endeavor to make a more strict course hereafter." They demanded the letter of the bond. Dudley and Endicott also were there, sitting on his either hand at the council-table : Dudley, to whom a faction among the people had adhered because he carried matters with " more severity ; " and Endicott, afterwards the persecutor of the Quakers, and now the mouthpiece of Hugh Peters.[1] The mild-tempered but prudent Win-

[1] That this is the correct explanation of Winthrop's course is, I think, plainly to be inferred from his own language.   In May, 1635, he had failed of a reëlection as governor, and subsequently, in January, 1636, had been informally arraigned before the clergy on the charge of dealing " too remissly in point of justice." He had made the issue that " justice should be administered with more lenity in the infancy of a plantation than in a settled state." The next morning the ministers had " set down a rule in the case " in favor of " strict discipline." Then Winthrop confessed himself, in the language cited in the text, and promised to err no more on the side of lenity. (Winthrop, i. *178.) Sixteen months later, through the direct interposition of the clergy, he had been again chosen governor, and now as the exponent of their policy. Immediately on his return to office he wrote as follows of the Antinomian controversy : — " Few could see where the difference was ; and indeed it seemed so small, as (if men's affections had not been formerly alienated, when the differences were formerly stated as fundamental) they might easily have come to reconciliation." (Ib. *221.) Six months later he records the meeting of the General Court, when its members, " finding upon consultation that two so opposite parties could not contain in the same body, without apparent hazard to the whole, agreed to send away some of the principal." (Ib. *245.) These extracts, with Dudley's and Endicott's interpolations at Mrs. Hutchinson's trial, apparently tell the whole story. Hugh Peters' influence on Endicott, who " as a magistrate did not bear his sword in vain," is set forth in I. Mass. Hist. Soc. Coll. vi. 253–5.

throp remembered his promise, and bent to the storm he could not withstand. What followed was a simple ecclesiastical persecution, of the more moderate kind. " Jezebel " was hunted out. With Winthrop, therefore, all the proceedings subsequent to the May election of 1637 were a political necessity. Like many another public man, he found himself driven by the clamor of those behind him further than he wished, or thought it wise to go. There is reason, also, to believe that his own conscience was thereafter ill at ease in regard to the course he then pursued, and that he feared, because of the sufferings and banishments inflicted, God would visit his wrath and sore displeasure upon the land.[1] The recollection of these things even cast a shadow of remorse over the closing hours of his well-spent life ; for when, twelve years later, the Father of Massachusetts lay dying in his house in Boston, an order for the expulsion of some religious dissentient was brought to him. Turning from Dudley, ever prone to severity, who pressed him to sign it, the dying magistrate refused, saying, — " Of that work I have done too much already." [2] As he uttered those words the memory of murdered Anne Hutchinson, upon whose former home, standing opposite his own, his fading vision may at the moment well have rested, must needs have been uppermost in his thoughts.[3]

The business of the historian is to state facts and conclusions exactly as he sees them. On the one hand it would appear that the Boston movement of 1636–8 — the miscalled Antinomian movement —

[1] IV. *Mass. Hist. Soc. Coll.* vii. 187.
[2] Hutchinson, i. 151.
[3] Ellis, *Puritan Age*, 25.

was a premature agitation, based on a false issue. The power of the clergy could not then have been successfully assailed in Massachusetts; nor was it desirable that it should be. There was need enough for reform; but, to be useful and healthy, reform had to come more slowly and from another direction. Neither did Anne Hutchinson or her following hold forth any promise of better things. Theirs was no protest against existing abuses. On the contrary, in their religious excesses they outdid even the clergy, — they out-heroded Herod. Their overthrow, accordingly, so far as it was peculiar to themselves and did not involve. the overthrow of great principles of religious toleration and political reform, was no matter for regret. Knowingly and intelligently they represented nothing that was religiously good or politically sound. But, unfortunately, their action — as false, premature action is wont to do — brought wiser action and sound principles into disrepute, and seriously retarded progress in Massachusetts. This was conspicuously apparent in the ruthless treatment a subsequent and more deserving reform movement shortly after received at the hands of the party in power; for the fate of Robert Child and his associates in 1646 was a mere political corollary of that of Anne Hutchinson in 1637. At the hands, therefore, of an historian whose intelligence is not mastered by his sympathies, she and her friends, including Governor Vane, are entitled to no consideration. They went on a fool's errand, and they brought great principles into lasting odium.

On the other hand, the way in which the adherents of Vane and Mrs. Hutchinson were suppressed cannot be defended, without including in the defence the

whole system of religious and political intolerance of
that time. But why should it be defended? It is
impossible to ignore the fact, and worse than useless
to deny it, that the New England Puritans were essentially a persecuting race. They could not be otherwise. They believed that they were God's chosen
people. As such, they were right; all others were
wrong. If, therefore, they failed to bring up their
children in the strait and narrow way, and to protect
them and all the people from the wiles of the Evil
One, God would not hold them guiltless. The Israelites were their models in all things, and the precedents which guided their action were precedents
drawn from the books of the Old Testament. "So,
by the example of Lot in Abraham's family, and
after Hagar and Ishmael, he saw they must be sent
away." The Israelites were not an attractive or an
amiable or a philosophical race; they were narrow,
devout and clannish. No one ever presumed to so-
phisticate away their cruelties or their persecutions.
Yet withal they were a strong and an aggressive people, believing certain things implicitly; and, accordingly, they impressed themselves and their beliefs on
the human mind. Their very imperfections were essential elements of their strength. They believed to
fanaticism; and it was the strength of their fanaticism which caused their belief to dominate. It was
the same with the Puritans of New England. They
persecuted as a part of their faith.

It is true that in so doing the Puritan exiles to New
England showed that they were not in advance of
their times. That they were not, was again an element of their strength; for they were essentially
practical men, and not idealists. As such, being of

the seventeenth century, they objected to persecution chiefly as applied to themselves. It was enough for them that their charter and the fundamental principles of their community gave them the right to prescribe who might settle among them, and to expel dissentients and intruders. They exercised that right.

But is there any good reason to suppose that the crushing-out process of 1637 resulted more favorably in Massachusetts than elsewhere? The historians of the New England school have insisted that it did, — that in this case at least, whether harshly and oppressively used or not, persecution was justified by the result.[1] They point to the fact that peace, quiet and safety were by means of it restored, and that a long period of internal tranquillity followed the year 1637. The exiles even, in many cases, made their submission and returned. All this is true. Exiles have usually, in all ages and in all countries, looked fondly back on their old homes, and returned to them as soon as they were permitted so to do. As respects the long period of peace and tranquillity, there can be no question that such a period followed the violent measures of 1637–8. This was well expressed in a tract published in London in 1643, in which the boast was made that, since the banishment of the friends of Mrs. Hutchinson, " not any unsound, unsavourie and giddie fancie have dared to lift up his head, or abide the light amongst us." [2] But, though there can be no question that a period of peace and tranquillity did then settle down on Massachusetts, or that it lasted through the lives of six generations of those born on the soil, there may well be great question whether this peace and tran-

[1] Palfrey, i. 509 ; Lodge, 351.
[2] i. *Mass. Hist. Soc. Coll.* i. 247.

quillity were good things, — whether, indeed, those
blessings were not purchased for Massachusetts, as
they have been for other countries, at a heavy price.
When Vane, in the December council of 1636, was
cowering under the fierce diatribe of Hugh Peters, he
showed true insight in exclaiming, "the light of the
Gospel brings a sword." [1] These few words, like a
sudden electric flash, revealed the whole situation,
laying bare the errors of those with whom he was
contending. Then and afterwards, it was in New
England as it has been and still is elsewhere: " the
spiritual growth of Massachusetts withered under the
shadow of dominant orthodoxy; the colony was only
saved from atrophy by its vigorous political life," and
the rule of its established church, "so long as it en-
dured, was a rule of terror, not of love; her ways were
never ways of pleasantness, her paths were never
peace." [2]

Yet it has more than once been assumed by the
Massachusetts historians, in a sort of matter-of-course
way, that the sterile conformity, which for more than
a century after the suppressions of 1637–8 prevailed
in the Puritan Commonwealth, was desirable, — that
magistrates like Stoughton and divines like Mather,
and a literature of forgotten theology and unreadable
homilies, were fruits indicating a good tree. That
what happened then did happen is true; that it
naturally resulted from what went before is equally
true; but that better things could not have happened
is taken for granted. That in time the intellect of
Massachusetts — schooled by self-government through
a long struggle with nature and against foreign en-

[1] *Supra*, 424.
[2] Doyle, *Eng. in Am. ; the Puritan Colonies*, i. 187–8.

croachments — did work itself out from under the
incubus of superstition, prejudice and narrow conformity imposed upon it by the first generation of
magistrates and ministers, cannot be denied; but it
is certainly going far to infer therefrom that, in this
especial case, superstition, prejudice and narrow conformity were helps instead of obstacles. It is not
easy indeed to see how the *post ergo propter* fallacy
could be carried further. It is much like arguing,
because a child of robust frame and active mind survives stripes and starvation in infancy, and bad instruction and worse discipline in youth, — struggling
through to better things in manhood, — that therefore
the stripes and starvation, and bad instruction and
worse discipline, in his case at least worked well, and
were the cause of his subsequent excellence. It is
barely possible that New England, contrary to all
principle and precedent, may have profited by the
harshness and bigotry which for a time suppressed all
freedom of thought in Massachusetts; but it is far
more likely that the slow results afterwards there
achieved came notwithstanding that drawback, rather
than in consequence of the discipline it afforded.
Certainly the historians who with such confidence set
aside all the lessons of human experience — in order
to assert that, in the case of their ancestors, whatever
was, was right, as well as best — would be slow to
apply the same rules or draw similar conclusions in the
case of such as persecuted, banished or suppressed
those who thought like their ancestors.

974.4   Adla   322-77

Adams
THE ANTINOMIAN CONTROVERSY

DATE DUE

FEB 13'79			